W9-CID-740

THE
BRANDON
MEN

THE BRANDON MEN

IN THE SHADOW OF KINGS

SARAH BRYSON

AMBERLEY

For Ellie

First published 2021

Amberley Publishing
The Hill, Stroud
Gloucestershire, GL5 4EP

www.amberley-books.com

Copyright © Sarah Bryson, 2021

The right of Sarah Bryson to be identified as the Author of this work has been asserted in accordance with the Copyright, Designs and Patents Act 1988.

All rights reserved. No part of this book may be reprinted or reproduced or utilised in any form or by any electronic, mechanical or other means, now known or hereafter invented, including photocopying and recording, or in any information storage or retrieval system, without the permission in writing from the Publishers.

British Library Cataloguing in Publication Data.
A catalogue record for this book is available from the British Library.

ISBN 978 1 4456 8627 1 (hardback)
ISBN 978 1 4456 8628 8 (ebook)

1 2 3 4 5 6 7 8 9 10

Typesetting by Aura Technology and Software Services, India
Printed in the UK.

Contents

SCOTLAND

WALES

BATTLE OF
TOWTON

LINCOLN

TATTERSHALL
CASTLE

BATTLE OF
STOKE FIELD

CAISTER
CASTLE

GRIMSTHORPE
CASTLE

BATTLE OF
BOSWORTH

HENHAM
PARK

BUCKDEN
TOWERS

WESTHORPE
HALL

CHURCH OF
ST PETER &
ST PAUL,
WANGFORD

BATTLE OF
TEWKESBURY

BATTLE OF
BARNET

WINDSOR
CASTLE

LONDON

BATTLE OF
BLACKHEATH

GUIULDFORD

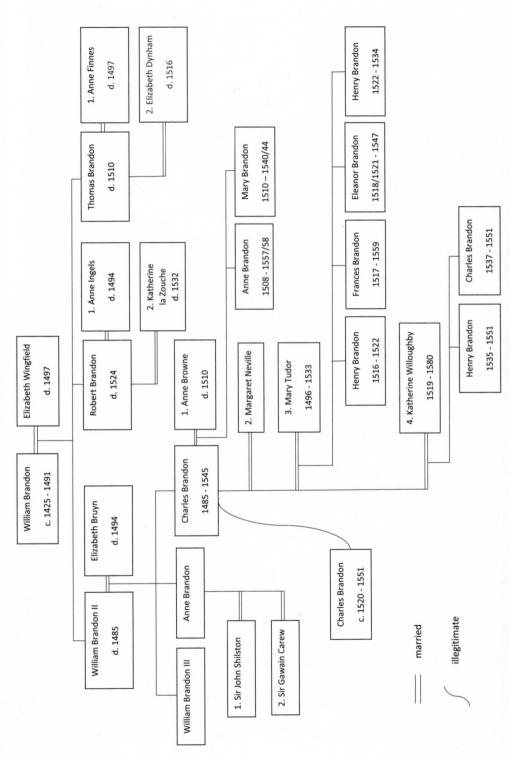

Brandon Family – Male Line

William Brandon
c. 1425 - 1491

Elizabeth Wingfield
d. 1497

Thomas Brandon
d. 1510

1. Anne Finnes
d. 1497

2. Elizabeth Dynham
d. 1516

Robert Brandon
d. 1524

1. Anne Ingels
d. 1494

2. Katherine
la Zouche
d. 1532

William Brandon II
d. 1485

Elizabeth Bruyn
d. 1494

Charles Brandon
1485 - 1545

1. Anne Browne
d. 1510

2. Margaret Neville

3. Mary Tudor
1496 - 1533

4. Katherine Willoughby
1519 - 1580

Anne Brandon

William Brandon III

1. Sir John Shilston

2. Sir Gawain Carew

Charles Brandon
c. 1520 - 1551

Anne Brandon
1508 - 1557/58

Mary Brandon
1510 – 1540/44

Henry Brandon
1516 - 1522

Frances Brandon
1517 - 1559

Eleanor Brandon
1518/1521 - 1547

Henry Brandon
1522 - 1534

Henry Brandon
1535 - 1551

Charles Brandon
1537 - 1551

married

illegitimate

Brandon Family – Female Line

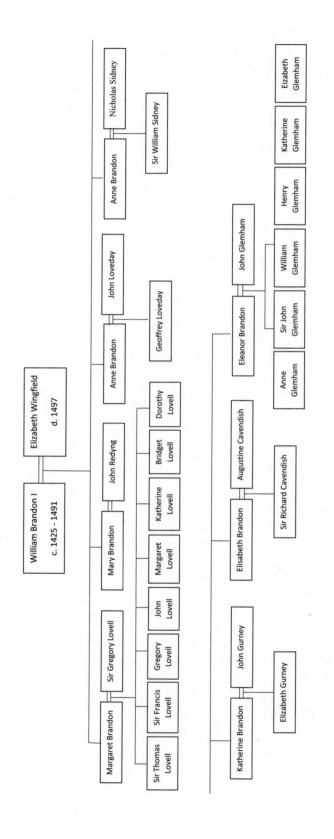

married

● Order of births unknown

Introduction

I have long been fascinated with the periods of history commonly known as the Wars of the Roses and the Tudor age. The more I read about this time, the more I wanted to know. As I read, I came across a fascinating man who went by the name of Charles Brandon.

Who was this man who became a duke and most 'beloved friend' and brother-in-law to King Henry VIII? I wanted to know more; I wanted to get to the very heart of this man to find out who he was, where he came from, how he came to occupy such a prominent position and why he did what he did.

The more I began to investigate Charles Brandon's life, the more I became absorbed in his family history. It is a common misconception that Brandon rose to prominence from utter obscurity. As I researched, I became very much aware that this was not the case. Charles Brandon, who was Duke of Suffolk, came from a line of men who were close to royalty, who worked hard, weathered turbulent times throughout English history and did very well for themselves.

Books on the Wars of the Roses and the Tudor age rarely mention these men; they are typically only concerned with Charles, Duke of Suffolk. Yet the Brandon men boasted a long, close relationship with England's kings. They were wealthy, powerful men in their own right who rose to grand heights and amassed great wealth.

Of the four generations of Brandon men considered in this work, it is Charles, Duke of Suffolk, about whom we have the most documented information. He rose to prominence during the reign of Henry VIII, and even though his uncles were present at court at the time, it was Charles himself who had the greatest influence upon the actions of the second Tudor king. It is therefore the life of Charles, Duke of Suffolk that takes up the most substantial part of this book. That is not to say that the lives of his father, uncles, grandfather or sons were not equally as interesting or remarkable – simply that we have a wealth of information on him through court documents, rolls and correspondence, some of it originating with Charles himself.

It is my aim to give new life to the men of the Brandon family by detailing each man's life and pulling back the layers to explore just who these men were. Wherever possible I have used primary sources such as contemporary correspondence, parliamentary records, court documents and wills to gain a true understanding of them and their actions, and to explore their relationships with the monarchs they served – Henry VI, Edward IV, Richard III, Henry VII, Henry VIII and Edward VI. Moreover, by exploring the political and social events surrounding them, I intend to present a rounded portrait of what life was like during this period, spanning more than a hundred and thirty years and covering four generations of Brandon men.

Why the men and not the women? Quite simply, it was rare for the deeds and accomplishments of women to be recorded during the fourteenth and fifteenth centuries. During this time a woman's primary role was to manage the home and to produce children. Unfortunately, very little has been documented about the lives of the early women of the Brandon family. However, this is not to say that there are no records, and the few glimpses of the early Brandon women that have been recorded are examined within these pages. In addition, there is an overview of Charles, Duke of Suffolk's daughters and granddaughters.

I hope that this book will banish lingering myths about the Brandon men. More than that, I hope it will finally show what fascinating and talented men they were, and tell the story of how they managed to prosper and grow in the courts of the Yorkist, Lancastrian and Tudor kings.

1

Setting the Scene

From the surviving records, we can trace four generations of the Brandon family. The first, Sir William Brandon, was born *c.* 1425 and went on to have three sons: William (14??–1485), Robert (14??–1524) and Thomas (14??–1511). Of these three, only William had children who survived to adulthood. He had two sons: William (dates unknown), who did not reach adulthood, and Charles (1485–1545).

Charles had four sons: Henry (1516–1522), Henry (1522–1534), Henry (1535–1551) and Charles (1537–1551). He also had an illegitimate son who was born around 1521 and named after his father. Of Charles Brandon's legitimate sons none survived to have their own sons, the oldest dying when he was sixteen years of age. His illegitimate son grew to adulthood but, as far as we know, did not have children of his own. With the death of Charles Brandon in 1551, the male line of the Brandon family ended.

To place the Brandon men and the kings they served in a historical context we must look briefly at events in Europe between the years 1337 and 1453, when much of Europe was convulsed in what came to be known as the Hundred Years War. This period of history completely altered the fortunes (and destiny) of England, which began it with extensive holdings in France (although a fraction of the territory it had once held). The English fought brilliantly successful military campaigns, only to eventually lose all but a tiny foothold on continental Europe. Both France and England had their populations decimated by the arrival of bubonic plague in 1348 and its frequent re-occurrence. (This effectively ended the feudal system in England as labour was scarce and wages rose; in France it caused peasant rebellions that were savagely put down by the nobility.)

Although the two kingdoms had clashed periodically since the twelfth century, a serious conflict started in 1337 when King Philip IV of France declared that all 'English' land south of the River Loire was forfeit. In response, King Edward III invaded France and established an English holding in Flanders through which he could attack and lay claim to northern and north-eastern France.[1] From that time England's kings sought to reclaim not only the land they believed was theirs but also the French crown, which they claimed by right of marriage. Early English military success never quite achieved a re-conquest, however, and on Edward III's death in 1377 his successor, Richard II, was only ten years old. By the time Richard was deposed by Henry Bolingbroke, the Earl of Derby who became Henry IV, English forces were on the verge of being expelled from France. Henry, buoyed by popular support in England for renewing hostilities (and an appetite for plunder and commercial opportunities), reversed this process when he and his successor Henry V achieved astonishing military successes against a divided and weakened France. However, they never did regain the lands lost by King John in 1214, and with the death of Henry V in 1422 the English were never again to be in the ascendant in France.

Henry V was a strong king who brought stability to England. He was also an excellent military leader and united England in the great cause of defeating the French armies. Upon his death, he left a nine-month-old son (also named Henry) as his heir, which necessitated a governing council. This was not a promising start to the new reign. Henry's will stated that his brother John, Duke of Bedford, should be the Governor of Normandy and Regent of France while his other brother, Humphrey, Duke of Gloucester, should be appointed Protector of England and guardian of the infant king. However, Gloucester was only in charge while Bedford was out of the kingdom and when Bedford returned Gloucester had to defer to him. There were a further twenty lords and bishops to make the major decisions and maintain the day-to-day business of kingship.[2]

By 1425, Cardinal Henry Beaufort, young Henry VI's great-uncle and one of the richest and most influential men in England, had fallen out with the Duke of Gloucester. Gloucester had attempted to claim the French county of Hainaut by right of his wife, Jacqueline of Hainaut. This greatly angered another claimant, the Duke of Burgundy, who was an ally of England against France. Beaufort had spent a great deal of time, money and effort in getting Burgundy on England's side, and Gloucester's actions had set this back. Compounding matters, Gloucester's campaign was a failure. Tensions were rising between Beaufort and Gloucester, and Beaufort ended up writing to John, Duke of Bedford, Gloucester's brother, asking him to return from France. Bedford returned and helped to calm tensions – for a time.[3]

Between May and June 1429, England lost the stronghold of Orleans thanks to the astonishing efforts of Joan of Arc in rallying the French troops. England's foothold in France began to crumble. Worse news was to come on 16 July. On this day, a French king was crowned at Reims – and it was not Henry VI, as the Treaty of Troyes had stated it should be.[4] Instead, the new king was Charles VII, son of Charles VI. Under the Treaty of Troyes, sealed on 21 May 1420, Henry V was to marry Charles VI's daughter Catherine of Valois and inherit the French crown on the death of Charles VI. At the time of its signature, the French king (also known as Charles the Mad) had disinherited his son – but here he was being crowned king.[5]

Despite these problems, England during the 1420s and 1430s was a stable country ruled by an efficient council. On 12 November 1437, however, King Henry VI's minority came to an end and he took full control of his kingship and England.[6] At this point, the country began to collapse. Henry VI was not a capable leader. His father had set the standard and ruled efficiently, and Henry VI simply could not live up to his example.

The Rise of the Brandon Family

The early history of the Brandon family is murky at best. It may be possible that the family originated from Brântome in France. The town of Brandon in Suffolk is mentioned in the *Little Domesday Book*, compiled in 1086 as a summary of the townships within

East Anglia.[7] It is possible that a man from Brântome came over in the service of William, Duke of Normandy, who defeated Harold Godwinson at the Battle of Hastings in 1066, and that this man was granted land in East Anglia as a reward. Then, during the writing of the *Little Domesday Book*, with the information recorded by six different scribes, it is possible the name was anglicised to 'Brandon'. The name Brandon can be traced through English records as far back as the twelfth century.[8] 'De' is French for 'of', and it may be that those mentioned within these records picked up the name 'de Brandon' to refer to themselves as being from the township of Brandon. It may well be the case that when the Hundred Years War commenced, the 'de' was dropped to remove any association with France. Unfortunately, records from that time are lacking, and this is simply speculation.

In early 1410 there is a mention of a Robert Brandon 'of Lynn, Norfolk'. In 1420, and again in 1426, Robert Brandon was provided securities in the Exchequer for the keeping of 'La Lovecon' in Lynn. He became a member of the Guild of the Holy Trinity before 1422 and in 1433 served as the guild's treasurer. By July 1425 he was recorded as being an esquire,[9] a title just below the rank of knight. This indicated that Robert possessed at least some property and wealth to maintain himself and his family. In the same year, he was appointed as the collector of customs in Lynn and Yarmouth; he would hold this position for almost twenty years.

In May 1434, Robert Brandon was among a large number of men in the country of Norfolk who were ordered to swear an oath that they would keep the king's peace.[10] Two years later, on 5 March 1436, Robert Brandon was dispatched to Lynn with three other men to seize all ships and vessels weighing sixteen tonnes or more, and to have them sent with their crews to the port of Winchelsea by 1 April for the use of Richard, Duke of York and his men, who were shortly to go to France upon the king's business.[11]

While we have no documentary evidence, there is a strong possibility that Robert was the father of William Brandon (*c.* 1425–1491). William's Brandons were from Norfolk, as was this Robert. Later, William Brandon's son, also called Robert, would be associated with the port of Lynn as the collector of customs[12] and it is highly probable that this position came through family connections.

Very little is known of William Brandon's early life. Not even the date of his birth has been recorded, although it is believed that he was born around 1425.[13] Details of his life only begin to emerge in the 1460s, when he became a retainer of John Mowbray, Duke of Norfolk, and began to build up his land and power base.

By the late 1430s, Henry VI's personal preferences as to how he wished to live his life were becoming apparent. He was a profoundly religious man who spoke simply and was much more interested in matters of Church than government. Pious, kind and generous, he rarely lost his temper and was easily manipulated. He encouraged morality and piety, yet some within his court frequently abused his patronage and talked him into spending money unnecessarily. The royal household was regularly in debt, and by 1450 these debts amounted to £372,000 and were increasing yearly. Henry had a habit of giving large and lavish gifts to his courtiers, including estates and land that belonged to the royal treasury, thus depriving the Crown of a vital source of income.

In addition, Henry was opposed to anything even slightly immoral and disliked anything to do with war. As king, one of Henry's most important duties was of course to protect and defend the kingdom. Yet he was averse to war, often refusing to take up arms against his enemies. Philippe de Commines, a writer and diplomat in the Burgundian and French courts, described Henry VI as 'a very ignorant prince and almost an idiot'.[14] The Abbot of St Albans, John Whethamstead, described Henry as a simple and upright man. Even John Hardyng, an English chronicler writing in the time of Henry VI, described the king as of 'small intelligence'.[15] In short, the king was the total opposite of his father. Rather than a leader of men, capable of the tough decisions and able to lead troops into battle, Henry was easily manipulated and often deferred to the whims of his closest councillor at the time.

One of those men to step up and become a member of the council was William de la Pole, 1st Duke of Suffolk. Appointed in 1431, he worked well with both the Duke of Gloucester and Cardinal Beaufort, two men who opposed one another greatly. Suffolk worked hard, gained a reliable reputation and soon became invaluable.[16]

Meanwhile, England's position within France was deteriorating, and Henry VI sought peace. With the Crown's coffers depleted due to the long years of war and the king's lavish gifts, there was barely a stronghold within France that could be held against the French. Suffolk agreed that peace was the best option for England and was a major player in negotiating terms. A treaty was negotiated that weighed heavily in France's favour.

Henry VI would marry fourteen-year-old Margaret of Anjou, the daughter of René, Duke of Anjou. Despite possessing an impressive title, René was poor and only provided a scant dowry for his daughter. However, as the niece of the French king, she was still a worthy bride for a king of England. Henry VI and Margaret of Anjou married on 23 April 1445.[17]

Now with the upper hand, France demanded that England return the county of Maine to the Duke of Anjou in return for a two-year truce. The terms were humiliating for England, and yet Henry VI agreed. Much of the land that had been so fiercely contested during the Hundred Years War had now been given back to France in return for nothing more than a short-term peace and the promise of further negotiations.

Although his power within the council was fast dwindling, Humphrey, Duke of Gloucester was staunchly opposed to the agreement. Knowing this, Suffolk sought to put an end to Gloucester before he could make a stand against him. In February 1447, Gloucester was called upon to appear before Parliament at Bury St Edmunds. The suspicious duke arrived ten days late, and on his arrival on 18 February was arrested. However, there was to be no trial. Gloucester died on 23 February, most probably of a stroke.[18]

In 1447, Richard, Duke of York was removed from his post as Lieutenant of France and sent to act as Lieutenant of Ireland. The Duke of Somerset was sent to France in his stead but did not take up his position until 1448, whereupon he ordered an attack on the town of Fougères in Brittany, robbing the wealthy and ransacking the city. The Duke of Brittany was greatly offended by the attack and appealed to King Charles VII. Feeling that England had breached the peace treaty, Charles VII declared war on 31 July. His troops attacked Rouen, and the city fell on 29 October 1449. English forces were forced into a prolonged retreat, swiftly losing the towns of Harfleur, Honfleur, Fresnoy and Caen. Soon the English had lost control of the whole of Normandy.[19]

By the end of the 1440s, the Hundred Years War was coming to an end. England had nothing to show for decades of fighting. The English claim to the French throne was meaningless, and the only apparent gain for the country was a queen who had brought with her a derisory dowry. It was evident that Henry VI was incapable of strong leadership. In addition to the problem of an ineffectual king, the public coffers were nearly empty, Crown expenditure being far higher than income.

Suffolk was blamed for the grievous losses in France, the state of the Crown finances and the broken treaty with France. On 7 February 1450, he was charged with high treason. The accusations against him included giving away the county of Maine and its capital city of Le Mans, passing secrets to the French, stealing money from the Crown, tricking the king into granting him lands and titles, and supporting the French king against England.

Suffolk pleaded with Henry VI. In turn, the king ruled that Suffolk was not guilty of treason but that he was guilty of several other, more minor crimes. Instead of having him executed, the king exiled Suffolk from England for five years. On 30 April, Suffolk left England but his boat was intercepted by another, the *Nicholas*. Its crew hauled him aboard and gave him a mock trial before removing him to a smaller boat, where he was beheaded. His decapitated head, stuck on a pole, was found next to his body two days later on a Dover beach.[20]

Meanwhile, William Brandon had fallen out with John Mowbray, Duke of Norfolk. Between December 1447 and January 1448, William Brandon, Robert Wingfield and his son were indicted at the King's Bench for several offences including theft, assault and threatening behaviour. The primary accusation against them was that they had challenged the Duke of Norfolk's authority. It was claimed that on 6 December 1447, Robert Wingfield and his son had made threats against the duke's chaplain, Richard Hadilsay. Norfolk stepped in and ordered the younger Wingfield to bind himself to keep the peace. Wingfield refused and was taken to Melton jail. Robert Wingfield then instructed William Brandon to rescue his son from jail, which William did three hours later. Furious, Norfolk issued letters stating that William Brandon and the younger Wingfield were not to come within seven miles of his person. However, both men defied this order and spent Christmas at Letheringham, which was within the forbidden seven-mile radius.

Wingfield junior continued to cause trouble for Norfolk. He hunted in Hadilsay's park as well as breaking into his chambers. On 23 January 1448, Wingfield was brought up before the King's Bench to explain why he should not forfeit the bond against him. Much to everyone's surprise, Wingfield produced a royal pardon.[21]

More trouble unfolded between the Duke of Norfolk, the Wingfields and William Brandon during 1448. On 1 September, a commission of oyer and terminer (which literally means 'to hear and determine') was set up to hear a complaint by Richard Wingfield that in August 1443, John Mowbray, Duke of Norfolk, Edmund Fitz William, John Leventhorpe, Gilbert Debenham, George Sampson, Richard Southwell and Edmund Stapilton had brought carts carrying cannons to Richard Wingfield's home at Letheringham. The nub of the issue was that Wingfield's home had been granted to him for life by the Duke of Norfolk's father, and Norfolk wanted it back. The mob attacked Richard's home, throwing stones and breaking the walls, towers and chimneys. They then set the house on fire, as well as the cornfield nearby. After this they hunted in Richard Wingfield's park, killing and taking away his deer. Richard claimed that they stole £5,000 worth of goods. As part of the complaint, William Brandon Esq. stated that 350 marks of his goods and 100 marks in coin had also been stolen.[22]

On 26 November, Norfolk was bound to pay £2,000 to keep the peace and the case was adjourned to the following year. In May, Norfolk was granted Wingfield's home; however, in return, the duke was required to hand over the manor of Weston by Baldock in Hertfordshire. He also had to confirm Wingfield's position as chief steward of the Mowbray lands for life and pay Wingfield 3,500 marks in damages. There is no mention of any settlement for Brandon's claim for loss of goods.

By 1448, William Brandon was being referred to in the Patent Rolls as an esquire. The title of esquire was commonly given to men who were part of the landed gentry, those who could afford to live off the rents from the land they owned but were below the rank of knight. William Brandon had amassed enough of an estate to be able to live off of the rents of people working his land.

At Easter 1449, William Brandon took Thomas Caundysh to court claiming that

> on 10 September 1445, in the parish of St Faith, London, he demised at farm to Thomas Caundysh a third part of the manor of Grymston (Grimston Hall), Suffolk, with appurtenances, to hold for two years, at an annual rent of £6, payable at Easter and Michaelmas. TC held this property for these two years, but has not paid the £12 due for this rent. Also, as there had been various disagreements between them regarding this property and other matters.[23]

For his part, Thomas Caundysh stated that 'regarding the £12 arrears, Brandon never demised this property to him in the form stated'.[24] Unfortunately, the outcome of the case is not provided, and it is unknown if Brandon ever received the rents due to him.

William Brandon's trials continued, and the following year at Michaelmas 1450 he was taken to court by Thomas Salle and his wife Isabelle, widow of John Standon. They claimed that 'on 20 June 1442 William Brandon made bond with JS in £5 3s 6d, payable at St Peter ad Vincula then next. However, he did not pay JS, and has not paid Isabel, either before or after her marriage to TS, to their damage of £20.' They then went on to show the bond and the letters patent of Alexander Prowet, commissary general of Robert, Bishop of London, appointing Isabel as the administrator of the goods of John Standon. Brandon knew that he was in the wrong and owed the money, and he asked to settle the matter out of court.[25] The outcome is unknown, but it seems likely that Brandon made some kind of agreement and paid the money owed.

Meanwhile, the political situation in England was becoming serious. The country was heading for civil war. Famously known as 'the Wars of the Roses', the ensuing conflict continued intermittently from 1455 to 1485, but the seeds were sown in 1450 when Richard, Duke of York returned to England from Ireland and, having arrived in London on 27 September, offered to take over the position on the council left vacant by the death of the Duke of Suffolk. Descended from Edmund of Langley, 1st Duke of York and fourth surviving son of King Edward III, the Duke of York felt he had rights to the position. However, this was not to be. Instead, up stepped Edmund Beaufort, 2nd Duke of Somerset.

Somerset and York had already clashed when Somerset was sent to take over York's position as Lieutenant in France and disastrously ordered the attack upon Fougères, which had provoked Charles VII to break the treaty and attack England. Somerset soon became a close adviser and friend to Queen Margaret of Anjou.

Parliament was recalled on 6 November, and both Somerset and York were required to attend. York arrived on 23 November, and John Mowbray, Duke of Norfolk, arrived the following day. Norfolk was a close ally and supporter of York and had brought an armed retinue. Tensions were high within the city, with Somerset and York set fiercely against one another. When Parliament was finally prorogued in December, London began to settle. However, York had won no support.[26]

In March 1452, York and his army met the dukes of Buckingham, Exeter and Norfolk outside Dartford. York enumerated his grievances, blaming Somerset for breaking the truce with France and losing Normandy. Furthermore, he claimed that Somerset was planning on selling Calais to the Duke of Burgundy, and was embezzling money from the Crown. York wished to bring this information before the king.

York believed he would be allowed to present his grievances to the king in private. However, when he arrived for the meeting he found that Somerset was present. York was then taken to London and forced to swear allegiance to the king at St Paul's Cathedral. The Duke of Somerset had won this round.[27]

In August 1453, Henry VI fell into a stupor while at his hunting lodge at Clarendon, near Salisbury. England had lost the Battle of Castillon the previous month and with that defeat came the loss of Bordeaux and all French territory previously held by England except for Calais and the surrounding lands. In effect, all the gains made by Henry V had been lost.[28] It was believed that this news had such a traumatic impact upon the king that he fell into a catatonic state. Although Henry was alive, he seemed to be completely unaware of his surroundings. He could not talk or feed himself and had to be looked after by those around him.

Two months later, on 13 October, the feast day of Edward the Confessor, Margaret of Anjou gave birth to a healthy baby boy named Edward. Henry VI failed to recognise or even react to his infant son when he was brought before him. Something had to be done, and soon a council was being formed to rule in the king's name.

York was excluded from this council at first, but soon he was being summoned in the hopes that his quarrels with Somerset could be settled to ensure peace in England. York would have none of this, and when he arrived at Westminster on 12 November he set out to bring about Somerset's downfall. He had his ally the Duke of Norfolk attack Somerset verbally in front of the council, accusing him of treason; the claim was that Somerset had deliberately provoked the French king to war, resulting in the loss of the French territories. Norfolk demanded that Somerset be arrested, and shortly afterwards Somerset was sent to the Tower of London. The Duke of York became the leader of the council.

Margaret of Anjou immediately challenged York on behalf of her son, but since she was a woman, her protests fell on deaf ears.[29] For now, Richard, Duke of York held the upper hand.

2

The Wars of the Roses

Although not named as such during the fifteenth century, the Wars of the Roses were a brutal period in English history, when the country's nobles split into two factions: the Lancastrian side, fronted by the Duke of Somerset in the name of Henry VI, and the Yorkist side under the Duke of York. It was a period in which political quarrels turned into blood feuds and men were drawn into battles for their very lives.

Yet despite the periodic bloodshed, slaughter and upheaval, there were spells of stability when, although there was tension, life went on as usual. Men and women woke in the morning, said their prayers and went about their daily work. Children were born, marriages celebrated, saints' days honoured, and goods were bought and sold. Despite the changes of king on the throne and the battles that saw the deaths of many men, there were long periods of peace in England. Philippe de Commines stated, 'Out of all the countries which I have personally known, England is the one where public affairs are best conducted and regulated with least violence to the people. There neither the countryside not the public are destroyed, nor are buildings burnt or demolished. Disaster and misfortune fall only those who make war, the soldiers and the nobles.'[1]

This was a war of the nobility, with Yorkists and Lancastrians fighting both in parliament and on the field of battle. In turn it affected the gentry, and men who served their lords faithfully had to choose sides, for if their lord were to die in battle – or, worse, be attainted and stripped of his lands and title – the trickle-down effect would damage those who served him. The Brandons were part of this: William Brandon served John Mowbray, Duke of Norfolk, who was, for the time being, still loyal to Henry VI.

On 25 December 1454, Henry VI woke from his stupor. He had no recollection of anything that had happened to him and was delighted to meet his son for the first time. With the king returned to health, York's protectorship ended. Somerset was released from the Tower and returned to the council, all charges against him dropped. York quickly retreated to his lands in the north and began to gather men around him.[2]

Soon a great council was set to meet at Leicester. However, York would not have a repeat of Dartford where he was tricked and taken to London to swear continued allegiance to the king. Instead, he and Richard Neville, Earl of Warwick, gathered an army and headed south. Meanwhile, Henry VI and his men headed north. Letters were sent to York and Warwick ordering them to disband their armies and meet the king at St Albans, accompanied by only 200 and 160 men respectively. Both objected, claiming they were merely trying to defend their king against the treasonous acts of Somerset.

York and his army arrived at St Albans at 7 a.m. on 22 May 1455, a couple hours before the king and his army. The king and his men took up a position within the town, and talks began between York and Henry VI, with the Duke of Buckingham and Somerset acting as mediators. York argued for the removal of Somerset. Although these talks ostensibly took place between York and the king, it is highly doubtful that Henry VI himself took part.

With talks proving fruitless, the Earl of Warwick attacked the town at around 10 a.m. Soon the town was overrun, and Henry VI was injured during the fighting, an arrow cutting his neck. He was bundled up and hidden in a tanner's cottage. Somerset was slain. Afterwards, York found the king and pledged his loyalty. Having no choice, Henry VI accepted York's words. With Somerset's death, Richard, Duke of York now became the leading power on the King's Council, resuming the title of Protector.[3]

Soon Parliament demanded that all lands gifted by the Crown were returned in order to boost the royal treasury. York tried to enforce the wishes of Parliament, but understandably there was little enthusiasm among the nobles to give up their land and revenues. In the end, the idea was rejected, and York had little choice but to resign as Protector on 25 February 1456. Meanwhile, Margret of Anjou was building up her power base.

Earlier, on 18 July 1454, a commission had been set up to look into the complaint by Thomas Clement and William Brandon that one Robert Rokkeley and his associates stole their ship the *Karvile*, which had been loaded with provisions and supplies to serve King Henry VI. It is most likely that the *Karvile* was one of several ships sent to patrol the English Channel on the alert for enemy ships. Thomas and William sought the return of their ship and all the supplies on board.[4] Once more, the result of this commission is not recorded, and it is unknown if Brandon and Clement saw the return of their ship. What it does show is that in 1454 William Brandon was wealthy enough to have invested in part ownership of a merchant's vessel.

By 1455, William Brandon was escheator in Norfolk.[5] An escheator was responsible for the taking of estates from a deceased person with no heir or claimant and returning those estates to the Crown. Despite falling out with the Duke of Norfolk in 1448, it appears that by 1455 Brandon was back in favour. In July of that year, in recognition of his faithful service, the duke granted Brandon the custody and marriage of the heir of John Clippesby.[6]

On 19 November 1457, William Brandon was pardoned 'for all felonies, offences, concealments, deceptions, escapes of felons, fines, issues forfeit, and amercements before 12 November last and any consequent outlawries'.[7] In the same year, he was appointed Marshal of the Marshalsea Prison in Southwark. It seems likely that his position at the prison followed his formal pardon, which was probably given in order for him to receive an official post. The prison was run for profit, and those within its walls would have to pay the marshal for certain rights, such as access to better conditions, soap, water, food etc. As marshal, Brandon could demand whatever payment he chose for each item and make a hefty profit.

The following year, on 10 May 1458, William Brandon and John Neville were bound to Queen Margaret for a sum of 100 pounds, the amount to be paid by the feast of Saint Martin, 11 November. The sum was later cancelled upon the queen's request.[8] The reason behind the bond is not stated.

By the end of 1458, William Brandon was being tasked with more and more responsibilities. On 30 December, William and four other men were tasked with arresting twenty-eight men who were suspected of 'lying in wait, ill-treating and spoiling within the king's realm' and had to bring them before the Court of Chancery.[9] Two months later, on 24 February 1459, William and five other men were commissioned to seek out and arrest over fifty men on the same charge and bring them before the same court.[10]

On 30 June, William Brandon and five other men were ordered to arrest a soldier called Ralph Legh and bring him before the king in Chancery to answer certain charges.[11] The charges are unknown today, but such orders throughout the period from December 1458 to June 1459 show that William was held in enough esteem that he was considered capable of seeking out those who committed crimes, bringing them before the Court of Chancery and keeping the king's peace.

Meanwhile, tensions were simmering at court. On one side were Richard, Duke of York, Richard Neville, 5th Earl of Salisbury, and his son Richard Neville, 16th Earl of Warwick; on the other stood the king, Queen Margaret and the council. Both sides could not rule England. Something had to give.

The first move was made by the Earl of Salisbury when he and his men marched to Ludlow Castle to meet up with the Duke of York. On the way there, the Earl of Salisbury's army met with the queen's army, led by Lord Audley. Although outnumbered almost two to one, the Yorkist army was victorious, and Lord Audley was killed. The Yorkists had stuck the first blow, but Margaret of Anjou was not ready to give up just yet.

Upon his arrival at Ludlow, the Earl of Salisbury joined forces with the Duke of York and the Earl of Warwick, who had brought his men over from Calais where he was head of the garrison. Soon a mighty army led by the king himself was marching up to Ludlow to face the Duke of York. The Yorkists had a choice to make: settle in at Ludlow and hope to plead their case, or flee.

On the night of 12 October 1459, the royal army appeared outside Ludlow. They made camp, and the king sent Richard Beauchamp, Bishop of Salisbury, to speak with York, Salisbury and Warwick, to give them terms for their surrender. Henry VI would pardon everyone except for Salisbury, York and Warwick.

In response, the trio claimed that the queen was set against them and that they were defending themselves.

Andrew Trollope, who had been loyal to the Earl of Warwick, took the men who had come from the Calais garrison and defected to the king's side. Knowing that they were outnumbered, and no mercy would be shown to them, York, Warwick and Salisbury fled. York and his second son, Edmund, Earl of Rutland, rode west and took a ship to Ireland. Salisbury and Warwick, meanwhile, fled to Calais with York's eldest son, Edward, Earl of March.[12]

An English Chronicle, written before 1471, records:

> In this same tyme, the reame of Englonde was oute of alle good gouernaunce, as it had be meny days before, for the king was simple and lad by couetous counseylle, and owed more then he was worthe. His dettes increased dayly, but payment was there none; alle the possessyons and lodeshyppes that perteyned to the croune the king and yeue awey, some to lords and some to other simple persones, so that he had almost noughte to lefe onne. And suche ymposiciones as were put to the peple, as tazes, tallages, and quynymes, alle that came from theym was spended on vayne, for he helde no householde ne meyntened no warres. For these mysgouernaunces, and for many other, the hertes of the peple were turned away from thayme that had the londe in gouernance, and there blyssyng was turnyd in to cursing.[13]

In essence, the king had exhausted all available financial resources, and the people believed he was merely a puppet of his councillors and that England was not being ruled by someone who was God's emissary on earth. To cope with the lack of funds in the royal treasury, the people were taxed heavily, leading to the people turning away from their king and, instead of praising him, cursing his rule.

While York, Salisbury and Warwick had been in self-imposed exile, they had not been idle. They gathered men and on 26 June 1460 the Earl of Warwick landed at Sandwich with a force of approximately 2,000 men, including the Earl of Salisbury and

Edward, Earl of March. As the men marched north through Kent, men quickly joined their forces, bolstering their numbers. The king had to act.

The Battle of Northampton took place on 10 July 1460. The size of each army is difficult to ascertain; however, it can be established that the Yorkist forces, led by the Earl of Warwick, greatly outnumbered those of the king. During the battle, Lord Grey, in command of a wing of the king's army, defected and joined with the Earl of Warwick. As a result, Warwick crushed the king's army. Humphrey Stafford, 1st Duke of Buckingham, was killed, and King Henry VI was captured. The king was now under Yorkist control. Warwick returned to London with the king as his prisoner and quickly set himself up to rule in the name of the king. Margaret of Anjou and her son Edward fled to Wales.[14]

Two months later, Richard, Duke of York returned to England, proclaiming that he wished only for his title and lands to be returned to him. However, when he arrived in London, he made it known that he was making a claim to the English throne. Parliament was shocked. Henry VI was God's anointed king, and even though the Duke of York had a strong claim, it was unheard of to cast one king aside and put another in his place. Finally, a compromise was reached. Henry VI would remain on the throne as long as he lived, and upon his death Richard would become king, and his heirs after him.

When Queen Margaret of Anjou heard about the decision to disinherit her son, she refused to lay down her arms. Despite false rumours that her son was not the legitimate child of Henry VI, Margaret resolved to fight for her son's rights.[15]

Margaret sent the Earl of Angus and an army of Scottish soldiers south while York, Salisbury and Edmund headed north. Realising that his forces were outnumbered, York entrenched himself at his castle of Sandal near Wakefield, Yorkshire. While he was waiting for reinforcements, on 30 December 1460, he was drawn out of the safety of the castle along with Salisbury and Rutland. It was here that Margaret struck a decisive blow.

The battle of Wakefield is one of the most confusing battles to take place during the Wars of the Roses. It is unclear just why the Duke of York left the safety and protection of his castle and marched with only a minimal force against the Lancastrian army. Several theories have been proposed, including that the duke and his men were attacked while foraging for food; that they were taunted and lured out; that they vastly underestimated the number of the Lancastrian army; or that there was a Christmas truce and the Lancastrian forces broke it. Whatever the reason for his decision, the Duke of York, his son Edmund, Earl of Rutland and the Earl of Salisbury were slaughtered. They were beheaded, and their heads placed upon Micklegate Bar at York, a paper crown mockingly placed upon York's head.[16]

Upon hearing of the death of his father and brother, Edward, now Duke of York, sought revenge. He led an army east to meet with the Earl of Warwick, whose father had also been killed at Wakefield. Before he could meet up with Warwick and his men, Edward heard the Lancastrian forces were close by and went to meet them. The ensuing battle of Mortimer's Cross took place on 2 February 1461. The battle was decisive, with the Lancastrian forces slaughtered.

Fifteen days later, on 17 February, the Earl of Warwick and his army met with an army assembled by Queen Margaret at St Albans in a battle that would become known as the Second Battle of St Albans. This time the Lancastrian forces were victorious. A reported 2,500 men were killed, and the Earl of Warwick and his men fled, leaving a bewildered King Henry VI sitting under a tree.

The queen soon met up with her husband, and Henry VI knighted his son before they returned to London. However, the gates of London did not open, and the Londoners would not accept the king, so he and his army were forced to return north.[17]

London did open its gates to Edward, Duke of York and the Earl of Warwick. There, on 4 March, Edward attended Mass at St Paul's Cathedral where he was publicly proclaimed King of England. However, he would not be crowned until the situation with Henry VI had been sorted.

The Duke of York, the Earl of Warwick and a large army marched towards York to meet the forces of Henry VI. The two armies would meet on 29 March 1461 in one of the bloodiest battles in English history. The battle of Towton also has the dubious distinction of being the largest battle ever fought upon

English soil: there were approximately 60,000 men on the field. On Palm Sunday, the Lancastrian army met the Yorkist army. It was a cold and snowy day. The wind was blowing hard and the harsh conditions limited the soldiers' vision. The Yorkist army was positioned with the wind behind them so that when the archers fired their arrows they were carried into the Lancastrian lines. In contrast, fired into the wind, the Lancastrian arrows fell short and were quickly gathered up by the Yorkist men.

Soon the Duke of Somerset, leading the Lancastrian forces, spurred his army forward and they clashed with the Yorkist army. It has been reported that the fighting lasted for ten hours, men hacking and slashing at each other, cries of agony filling the air as both sides battled for dominance. Neither side was able to claim victory until the sudden appearance of John Mowbray, Duke of Norfolk and his men on the side of the Duke of York. It is possible that as a healthy man in his thirties and as a retainer of the duke, William Brandon would have been part of Norfolk's force. If so, then he was able to say that he had survived one of the most horrific battles in English history.

With the addition of fresh reinforcements, the Yorkist army soon gained the upper hand, and the Lancastrian army was defeated. Of the estimated 60,000 men upon the field, it was believed that around 29,000 were killed and thousands more injured. Mass graves were dug out of the frozen earth to bury the dead.[18] Henry VI, Margaret of Anjou, their son Edward, the Duke of Somerset and whoever remained alive of the Lancastrian forces fled to Scotland. Shortly after, Edward, Duke of York returned to London. He was crowned King of England at Westminster Abbey on 29 June 1461.[19]

Under the rule of Edward IV, Brandon's prospects continued to rise. Even before his accession, on 20 October 1460 John Curde of Fransham in Norfolk was reported as owing William Brandon and John Wingfield the sum of £100[20] (the equivalent of £64,300 today).[21] It remains unclear why Curde owed the pair such a huge sum, but it shows us that William Brandon had a lot of money spare to lend.

The following year, on 6 November 1461, John Mowbray, 3rd Duke of Norfolk, died. The dukedom and wealth was inherited by his seventeen-year-old son, also called John.[22] William Brandon had had an interesting relationship with the duke, serving him faithfully, but only as long as it served his purposes. In 1448, Brandon had turned upon the duke and aligned himself with his own wife's brother, William Wingfield. However, by 1455 Brandon was back serving Norfolk. Seeking to realign himself with Norfolk would have provided Brandon with security and protection that he would not have had if venturing out on his own. If he were to face any trouble or difficulties, as a retainer of the duke, he could always seek Norfolk's support in acquiring security, land and positions. From the surviving letters of the Paston family, it seems that the late duke had been easily manipulated and that Brandon had the duke's ear. This was the same for the duke's seventeen-year-old successor. In June 1469, John Paston wrote:

> Thomas Wygfeld told me, and swore on to me, that when Brandon meuvyd [moved] the Kyng, and besowght hym to shew my Lord favour in hys maters ayenst yow, that the Kyng seyd on to hym ayen, 'Brandon, thow thou can begyll the Dwk of Norffolk, and bring hym abow the thombe as thows lyst, I let the wet thow shalt not do me so; for I undyrstand thy fals delying well inow.' And he seyd on to hym, more over, that if my Lord of Norffolk left not of hys hold of that mater, that Brandon shold repent itt, every vayn in hys hert, for he told hym, that he knew well inow that he might reauyll [rule] my Lord of Norffolk as he wold; and if my Lord dyd eny thing that were contrary to hys lawys, the King told hymhe knew well inow that it was by no bodys menys but by hys; and thus he depertyd fro the Kyng.[23]

Even Edward IV knew that William Brandon could exploit and hold sway over both the 3rd Duke of Norfolk and his son. There seems to be no malice in this hold, and it is clear that Brandon used subtle persuasion to influence both dukes into taking actions and making decisions that he thought best. This was a man, a mere esquire, who used his strong personality to dominate and influence senior members of the aristocracy.

On 3 January 1462, William Brandon was granted the manors of Shire and Vachery, Surrey, with an annual income of 36 pounds, for life. These manors had formerly belonged to James Butler, 5th Earl of Ormond. Butler had been a staunch Lancastrian supporter and had been beheaded on 1 May 1461 after the Yorkist victory at Towton. Brandon is described as the king's servitor and an esquire in the grant, which clearly shows that William Brandon supported and attended King Edward IV.[24]

At Easter the following year William Brandon was once more back in the law courts. This time a John Derby claimed that

... on 1 April 1460, in Southwark, William Brandon bought from him certain parcels of woollen cloth for £6 8s 6d, payable on request, namely 7½ yards of murrey, 10½ yards of green, 6 yards of blue, 6 yards of black of Lyre, 10 yards of black lining, 1 yard of white kersey, 1 yard of tawny, 2 yards of red and 1½ yards of motley. However, WB has not paid, to his [John Derby's] damage of 40s.[25]

Brandon admitted that he did purchase these items from Derby and said he would pay him the money owed.

It is unclear when William Brandon married, although it is thought to have happened before January 1462. He was married to Elizabeth Wingfield, daughter of Sir Robert Wingfield. This was quite a match for William, as his new father-in-law was not only a knight of the realm but also a landowner, administrator and a Member of Parliament for the county of Suffolk. The marriage produced three sons, William, Robert and Thomas, and seven daughters, Margaret, Anne, Mary, another Anne, Katherine, Elizabeth and Eleanor.[26]

William Brandon would see his daughters married well. Margaret married Sir Gregory Lovell and became Dame Lovell. They had a son named Thomas, who by 1518 had been knighted and become a member of the court, and a daughter named Eleanor.[27] Anne married John Loveday; Mary married John Redyng; the second Anne married Nicholas Sidney, and their son William Sidney, who grew up in his uncle Thomas' house, would become a close associate of Charles Brandon, Anne's nephew.[28] Katherine married John Gurney, Elizabeth married Augustine Cavendish, and Eleanor married John Glemham.[29] These marriages brought the Brandons close alliances with several families, allowing them to network, gain favours, influence people of importance and, as always, advance their own position.

In 1465, William Brandon was again in court. This time John Shukburgh claimed that on '26 May 1459, at Westminster, William Brandon bought from him one hood ("penulam") of miniver, one hood of grey belly fur and a half hood of miniver for 40s, payable on request. However, WB has not paid, to his damage of 100s.' William Brandon agreed to pay the money owed by the fourteenth day after Michaelmas.[30] Brandon was also taken to court by Bartholomew Sciatis, who claimed that 'on 16 June 1462, in London, William Brandon made a bond with him in £10 15s, payable at the feast of the Purification then next. However, WB has not paid this sum, to his damage of 10m.'[31] He then showed the bond to the court. In reply, William Brandon stated

> ... that this bond is not of his making. Parties on country, jury here at quindene of Easter. WB then presents in court the king's letters close, dated 22 January 1465, directed to the justices [recited in full], citing the privileges of members of parliament and their servants and their immunity from arrest by the courts during sittings of parliament. It states that WB was one of the burgesses for Southwark during the present parliament, and despite this immunity he was nevertheless arrested to answer BS on this charge. It therefore orders the court to have regard for this, cease process against WB and release him from arrest.

Upon hearing this, the court immediately released Brandon without his having to pay the bond!

On 10 September 1467, William Brandon Esq. was granted one-twentieth of 'the manors of Newsom, Thresk, Kyrkeby Malesart, Hovyngham and Burton in Londesdale (Yorks.), Eppeworth (Lincs.), Melton Moubray (Leics.), Caloughdon and Kyngton (Warws.), Chacombe (Northants.), Weston and Alcombury (Hunts.) and Hinton'.[32] Other recipients mentioned in this grant were John Mowbray, Duke of Norfolk and Richard Neville, Earl of Warwick. William Brandon was now being associated with high-profile men at court, including the very man who had helped to put Edward IV on the throne. A year later, on 10 September 1468, William Brandon was among ten men selected to be commissioners of the peace for the jail of Ipswich.[33]

By 9 May 1468, William Brandon was again pardoned for any offences that he committed before 4 April as Marshal of the Marshalsea Prison in Southwark.[34] Eight years later, on February 8 1476, William Brandon is again recorded as being Marshal of the Marshalsea.[35] It is unclear if William held the title for the entire period between 1457 and 1476, although it is highly likely.

As early as 14 November 1462, William Brandon was being referred to as Brandon 'of Suthwerk'.[36] Suffolk Place was built close to the prison. This would suggest that construction had begun either in the late 1450s or early 1460s and that by 1462 Brandon was living permanently at his new residence. Suffolk Place would become the Brandon family's main dwelling within the area of London. Dominic Mancini, an Italian scholar, described Southwark as 'a suburb remarkable for its streets and buildings, which, if it were surrounded by walls, might be called a second city'.[37] Southwark had a population of approximately 8,000 people, many of them foreigners as they were forbidden to live within the walls of the City. It was also a place well known for its brothels as it was an area outside of the rules of the City of London. In 1502 Brandon's youngest son, Thomas, added to Suffolk Place by leasing 48 acres of meadow surrounding the property. He turned this meadow into a park, which included a fishpond stocked with fish to eat.[38]

In December 1466, William Brandon and his brothers-in-law John and Robert Wingfield were held for two bonds each of 200 marks, payable to Sir William Hampton, Alderman of London, by All Saints Day 1472 and 1473.[39]

On 13 November 1469, William was appointed as 'controller of the great and petty custom, the subsidy of wools, hides, and wool-fells and the subsidy of the 3s in the tun and the 12d in the pound in the port of [Ipswich]'.[40] With wool being one of the major exports in England, the position was important as William was in charge of ensuring that all customs and fees were paid. Such a post meant that William handled a great deal of the king's money, so it was one that required trust.

Sometime before September 1464, King Edward shocked his council and country by secretly marrying Lady Elizabeth Woodville. The Earl of Warwick had been negotiating a marriage between Edward and Bona of Savoy, sister-in-law to the French king,

Louis XI. Elizabeth was no princess, and although her mother was Jacquetta of Luxembourg, daughter of the Count of Saint-Pol, Dowager Duchess of Bedford and Countess Rivers, Elizabeth was merely a widow of a knight with two young sons.

This marriage began the rumblings of discord between the king and his long-time friend and confidant, the Earl of Warwick. Not only had Warwick been made to look like a fool, having been negotiating a marriage which would never happen, but he had not been privy to the king's secret business. In addition to this, they had begun to fall out over which country England should become allied to; Edward preferring Burgundy, and Warwick France. Slowly, Warwick was being pushed out, his grip upon Edward loosening until he held little power or control over the man he had helped put on the throne.

In 1466, Henry VI was captured and brought back to London. With the old king once more under his control, King Edward no longer had to worry about rival factions appearing to jeopardise his rule. However, between May and July 1496, things began to collapse. An uprising started in the north, and Edward gathered an army and marched to meet the rebels. It was discovered that the rebels numbered around 20,000 and the king and his men were vastly outnumbered. He called upon reinforcements, yet none came. Soon the rebels were marching south, and the two sides met at the battle of Edgecote Moor on 26 July 1469.

Previously, on 11 July 1469, Warwick had organised the marriage of his eldest daughter, Isabelle, to Edward's younger brother George, Duke of Clarence. The earl soon had Clarence under his influence, and Clarence became unhappy with the king. Warwick had gone to Calais and returned with his garrison to support not the king, but the rebels. The Yorkist army was defeated at the battle of Edgecote Moor and Edward was taken prisoner. Edward was taken to Warwick Castle by the Earl of Warwick and George, Duke of Clarence. The Earl of Warwick attempted to rule in the king's name but was unable to rally the support he needed.

Soon the trio rode back to London, and Edward forgave the Earl of Warwick and his brother for their traitorous actions. In March 1470 there was another uprising, called the Welles uprising, instigated by a prominent Lincolnshire nobleman of that name, probably in support of Warwick and Clarence. Edward IV and his army attacked the rebels at Empingham on 12 March and routed them. The losing side fled for their lives, casting off their coats so they could run faster, and the battle became known as the battle of Losecoat Field. Edward IV was back in charge, and the Earl of Warwick and George, Duke of Clarence fled to France to ally with Margaret of Anjou and her son, Prince Edward.[41]

3

My Greatest Enemies

In 1469, the elder William Brandon was part of an army of 3,000 men that was sent by the Duke of Norfolk to besiege Caister Castle.[1] The castle had belonged to one Sir John Fastolf, and when he died in 1459 he had left the property to his lawyer, Sir John Paston.

Caister Castle was a magnificent fortification situated near the town of Great Yarmouth in Norfolk. It consisted of two rectangular courtyards, named the Inner Court and Outer Court. A moat surrounded these and the Outer Court was only accessible via a drawbridge on the north side. The Inner Court contained the state apartments and living areas as well as the Great Tower and chapel. The Great Tower, which still stands today, consists of five storeys and is more than 27 metres high and over 7 metres in diameter. The castle is thought to have contained some forty chambers, the majority in the Inner Court. There were the state rooms, a wardrobe, the chapel, two halls, a kitchen, a cellar, a buttery, a pantry, an armoury, a brewery, a bakery and stables. In addition, there was a cloister which provided access to the chapel and above the cloister was a gallery. There were also many garderobes (toilets) and fireplaces.[2] The total cost for the build was estimated to be £6,000. Constructed to provide both military defence as well as domestic comforts for its occupants, Caister Castle was a prize possession, and the Duke of Norfolk coveted it and aimed to add it to his already extensive estates.

Norfolk challenged Fastolf's will, suggesting that Paston had tricked Fastolf into giving him the castle and even going so far as to suggest that Paston had edited Fastolf's will after it had been made. A legal case ensued with both Paston and Norfolk claiming rights to the castle. In August 1469, Norfolk's retainers, including William Brandon, attacked the castle. Lady Margaret Paston was in residence with roughly thirty other people. She wrote to her son regarding the situation:

> I greet you well, letting you wit that your brother and his fellowship stand in great jeopardy at Caister, and lack victual; and Duabeney and Berney be dead, and divers other greatly hurt, and they lack gunpowder and arrows, and the place sore broken.; so that, but they have hasty help, they be like to lose both their lives and the place, to the greatest rebuke to you that ever came to any gentleman, for every man in this country marvelleth greatly that ye suffer them to be so long in so great jeopardy without help or other remedy.[3]

Sir John's son (also John) tried to get a writ of ownership from King Edward IV, even going so far as to seek the assistance of Queen Elizabeth's brother, Anthony Woodville, 2nd Earl Rivers, hoping he would intercede on his behalf with the king, but he was unsuccessful.[4]

In another letter, Margaret Paston states that 'we were in sore lack of victuals and gunpowder: men's hearts, lack of surety of rescue, were driven thereto take appointment [surrender]'.[5]

Unfortunately, there are no surviving accounts of the actual siege of Caister Castle. It started on Monday 21 August and lasted until September.[6] Two men, Duabney and Berney, were killed and several others injured. Margaret Paston wrote that gunpowder and arrows were used. However, it would not have been in Norfolk's interest to destroy the fabric of the castle during the siege, and it is most likely a lack of supplies and men within the castle walls that saw Lady Paston and her fellow inhabitants yield to their attackers.

Six years after losing Caister Castle, John Paston was still seeking the castle's return. On 23 October 1475, he wrote to his brother:

> AFTER all duties of recommendation please it you to understand that I have spoken with my lady since I wrote to you last and she told me that the king had no such words to my lord for Caister

as ye told me but she saith that the king asked my lord at his departing from Calais how he would deal with Caister and my lord answered never a word. Sir W Brandon stood by and the king asked him what my lord would do in that matter saying that he had commanded him before time to move my lord with that matter and Sir W Brandon gave the king to answer that he had done so. Then the king asked Sir WB what my lord's answer was to him and Sir WB told the king that my lord's answer was that the king should as soon have his life as that place and then the king asked my lord whether he said so or not and my lord said yea And the king said not one word again but turned his back and went his way, but my lady told me and if the king had spoken any word in the world after that to my lord, my lord would not have said him nay.[7]

Paston's letter provides another instance where William Brandon was closely involved with the Duke of Norfolk as well as King Edward IV. When the duke would not answer the king's question, Edward turned to Brandon, who stated Norfolk would rather give up his life than Caister. Certainly, this type of interaction would not have pleased the Pastons.

In addition to this, John Paston had been told that Edward IV believed that not only was William Brandon a retainer of Norfolk, speaking on his behalf, but that he was also controlling the pliable duke. In 1469 John Paston wrote:

Thomas Wingfield told me and swore unto me that when Brandon moved the king and besought him to show my lord favour in his matters against you that the king said unto him again Brandon though thou canst beguile the Duke of Norfolk and bring him about the thumb as thou list I let thee weet thou shalt not do me so for I understand thy false dealing well enough And said unto him moreover that if my Lord of Norfolk left not of his hold of that matter that Brandon should repent it every vein in heart for he told him that he knew well enough that he might rule my Lord of Norfolk as he would and if my lord did anything that were contrary to his laws the king told him he knew well enough that it was by nobody's means but by his and thus he departed from the king.[8]

This is a harsh letter, but one which shows the status and power that William Brandon held. The Duke of Norfolk might have been one of the most powerful men in East Anglia, but he was ultimately vulnerable to William Brandon. Starting as a young man eager for advancement, Brandon had worked his way up the ranks to the point that even the king was aware that Brandon could whisper in the duke's ear and affect his decisions. It is interesting to consider just how much control Brandon had at this time, when power and status meant everything.

Finally, Edward IV stepped in, and when the Duke of Norfolk's son, also John, died in 1476, Sir John Paston appealed once more to the king. This time Edward IV supported his claim in return for a payment of 100 marks. Paston paid this and Caister Castle was finally back in the ownership of the Paston family.[9]

On 17 July 1471, John Paston wrote to his mother:

Also and Sir Thomas Wingfield come to Norwich, that he may have as good cheer as it please you to make unto that man, that I am most beholden to for his great kindness and good-will; for he taketh full my part against my greatest enemies, [the] Brandons, and his brother William; for at my first coming to Sir Thomas Wingfield, both William Wingfield and William Brandon the younger were with Sir Thomas, and had great words to mine own mouth, and in chief William Wingfield; and wheresoever he may meet me on even ground, he will do much, but and we meet evenly, no fears, so I have your blessing.[10]

So the Brandons are John Paston's 'greatest enemies', along with William Wingfield. The Wingfield brothers – Thomas, the elder, and William – had fallen out, and William Brandon II, whose mother was Elizabeth Wingfield, sister of both Thomas and William, had sided with the younger brother against the Pastons.

In 1478, Sir John Paston wrote that

... yonge William Brandon is in warde and arestyd ffor thatt he scholde have fforce ravysshyd and swyvyd an olde jentylwoman, and yitt was nott therwith easysd, butt swyvyd hyr oldest dowtr, and than wolde have swyvyd the other sustr bothe; wherforr men sey ffowle off hym, and that he wolde ete the henne and alle hyr chekynnys; and som seye that the Kynge ententdyth to sitte upon hym, and men seye he is lyke to be hangyd, ffor he hathe weddyd a wedowe.[11]

John Paston's letter suggests that sometime during or before 1478, William Brandon II forced himself upon an older woman and tried to have some form of relationship with the woman's daughters. In addition to this great offence, the letter claimed that Edward IV was not pleased by this news and that the punishment for such horrible crimes was to be hanged. This was a damning allegation, one which could prove fatal, yet it is interesting to note that there is no record of William Brandon serving time in prison, or indeed receiving any punishment. It could be that this was all just gossip, or that those alleging these crimes did not have enough power behind them to see Brandon formally charged. Whatever the truth of the matter, William Brandon paid no penalty; but the Pastons were grasping at any opportunity to bring the Brandon family to ruin.

The conflict between the Paston and Brandon families could have originated in 1469 with the siege of Caister Castle, but the Pastons showed such hatred towards the Brandons one can only wonder if their differences dated back further. Unfortunately, we have no surviving letters to reveal the personal thoughts of the Brandon men. However, it would not be a stretch to think that the feelings were reciprocated. These two East Anglian families were vying for power and dominance, each seeking to further their interests, enlarge their land base and improve their standing within the ever-fluctuating English court.

In the meantime, in France, King Louis was promoting reconciliation between the Earl of Warwick and Margaret of Anjou. Warwick's youngest daughter, Anne, was married to Margaret and Henry VI's son, Edward, in 1470. It was planned that Warwick would return to England to fight for the Lancastrian cause, with Prince Edward returned to the succession upon their victory.

Upon hearing this news, Edward IV headed north with an army, only to find that Warwick was planning to land on the south coast with sixty French ships and approximately 5,000 soldiers. Meanwhile, Warwick's brother John Neville, 1st Marquess of Montagu, was marching down from the north with an army. Edward turned and attempted to march back to London but soon realised that he had been outwitted: he was now caught between Warwick and Montagu. He hastily disbanded his army and fled to the safety of Burgundy.[12]

In London, Henry VI was taken from the Tower of London and restored to the throne. We have no knowledge of any of the four Brandon men's thoughts upon this sudden turn of events. A king had been replaced by his precedessor. It must have been a worrying time, with concerns arising as to whether they would still receive payments and grants with Henry VI back on the throne.

In early March 1471, Edward IV returned to England, landing at Ravenspur in the East Riding of Yorkshire (a town now lost to coastal erosion). Initially, Edward claimed that he did not seek the throne, only to be restored to his rightful title of Duke of York, previously held by his father. Marching south, Edward gained supporters and was reunited with his brother George, Duke of Clarence. It is likely that Clarence perceived the situation: with Henry VI restored to the throne and his son and heir Prince Edward next in line, he had no hope of ever becoming king. Warwick could do nothing for him. His brother Edward, however, could. With the brothers reunited, Edward continued south and entered London on 12 April. Henry VI was quickly returned to the Tower.

Soon Warwick's army arrived at St Albans, and Edward left London to settle matters with his adversary once and for all. The battle took place at Barnet, outside St Albans, and became known as the battle of Barnet. It is estimated that Edward IV had 9,000 men and Warwick 12,000. *The Arrival* tells us that Warwick fired his guns at Edward IV's army during the night but misjudged their position. By ordering his men to stay quiet, Edward saved his army from being raked by the cannon fire.

The battle took place on 14 April 1471. In the morning there was a heavy mist, and fighting began between 4 and 5 a.m. Due to the lack of visibility, the two armies were not conventionally aligned: Edward's right guard flanked Warwick's left, and the Earl of Oxford, leading Warwick's right wing, flanked Edward's left. This caused the battle to be turned around, and soon Oxford's men had smashed through Edward's left flank. Thinking they had won the battle, they seized the opportunity to begin pillaging. However, the fighting continued, and when Oxford's men returned bearing their insignia of a star with rays, it was mistaken for Edward IV's sun with streams, and Warwick's men cried treason. Soon Warwick's men were defeated, and Warwick killed.[13]

There is no mention of William Brandon, retainer of John Mowbray, 4th Duke of Norfolk, participating in the battle of Barnet. However, it is known that William Brandon did fight in the battle of Tewkesbury just two weeks later. Many of the men who fought for Edward at Barnet also participated at Tewkesbury, so it is highly probable that Brandon was one of the men who fought two hard battles in less than a month.

It is also interesting to note that both John Paston II and John Paston III fought at the battle of Barnet, but on the Earl of Warwick's side.[14] The Paston and the Brandon families had been adversaries for many years, their rivalry famously exploding at the siege of Caister Castle. Assuming William Brandon was at Barnet, one cannot help but wonder whether, though the thick mist and heavy fighting, he saw the Paston brothers, his rivals and enemies. As he turned, sword brandished, could he have spotted the Paston coat of arms and moved to end their family's bitter rivalry once and for all? Of course, it is all simply speculation.

By now Margaret of Anjou and her son were in England seeking to regain the throne. Marching north from Exeter, Margaret and her troops sought to outmanoeuvre Edward IV and his army, who were coming up from the south. Finally, the two armies met on a field outside Tewkesbury.

The Battle of Tewkesbury took place on the morning of Saturday 4 May 1471. Edward's army had marched approximately 36 miles in blistering heat before they arrived at the battle site. The army then camped, getting what rest they could before the battle the following day. Edward IV set up his army in the traditional three lines, with the vanguard commanded by his brother Richard, Duke of Gloucester. It is not recorded under what commander William Brandon fought. It has been suggested that the Wingfields were associated with Richard, Duke of Gloucester and therefore fought in the vanguard. William Brandon was a close associate of the Wingfields, so it is possible that he too fought in the vanguard. If so, then Brandon would have been in the very thick of the battle.

The Lancastrian army had the Duke of Somerset and Sir Edmund Beaufort leading the right flank, Lord Wenlock holding the middle and the Earl of Devon leading the left. Edward had ordered two hundred horsemen to stay back close to a nearby wood so they could keep watch and ensure the Yorkist army could not be outflanked.

The gunners fired first, followed by the archers. While the Yorkist arrows reached their mark, the Lancastrians fell short in their attempts. Somerset knew he had to attack. He secretly manoeuvred his men through bracken and wooded terrain, so they were coming down a slope to attack the flank of the Yorkist army. Edward IV's men turned and attacked. Richard of Gloucester turned his men to help his brother. The combined strength of Edward and Richard's men helped to push the Lancastrians back. The two hundred men Edward IV had set aside to watch from the wood attacked, and these combined forces hit the Lancastrians hard. Men scattered. Many Lancastrian soldiers were slaughtered, and the field into which they fled was known thereafter as the Bloody Meadow.

With this done, Edward IV turned his attention to the second Lancastrian battle formation, commanded by Lord Wenlock. When Somerset attacked, and Edward IV and Richard's men counterattacked, it is unclear why Lord Wenlock, who was leading the centre forces of the Lancastrian army, did not immediately attack but paused at this critical juncture so that the Lancastrian forces lost momentum. The Yorkist army drove forward, and the Lancastrian forces were resoundingly defeated. During this final phase of the battle, Prince Edward, Henry VI's son and heir, was killed.[15] With Prince Edward's death, the Lancastrian cause was lost.

William Brandon was knighted by the triumphant King Edward IV on the field of Gaston, next to the site of the battle, so we may assume his contribution in the battle was significant. Thus he continued in his rapid advancement.[16]

A victorious Edward returned to the capital, and on the night of 21/22 May 1471, Henry VI was found dead in his room in the Tower of London.[17] *The Arrival* reported that the Lancastrian king died from 'pure displeasure and melancholy' due to the death of his son and the loss of the Lancastrian cause.[18] However, it is generally believed that he was murdered. In 1910, Henry VI's skull was examined. It proved to be shattered, dried blood still clinging to the hair, suggesting that the king was killed by a heavy blow to the back of the head.[19]

By whatever means, Henry VI had died and the Lancastrian king was gone. Edward IV was restored to the throne. The French chronicler Philippe de Commines (no slave to punctuation) wrote of the conflict, known then as the Cousins' War:

HAVE we not seen in our own days such examples among our neighbours Have we not seen King Edward IV of England the head of the house of York supplant the house of Lancaster under which his father and he had lived a long time and though he had actually sworn allegiance to Henry VI who was of the Lancastrian line yet afterwards this Edward kept King Henry a prisoner for many years in the Tower of London the metropolis of that kingdom and at last put him to death. Have we not seen the Earl of Warwick the chief manager of all King Edward's affairs after having put all his adversaries to death and particularly the Dukes of Somerset at length turn rebel against his master King Edward marry his daughter to the Prince of Wales son to King Henry VI endeavour to restore the house of Lancaster and return into England where he was defeated and slain in battle himself his brothers and relations besides many others of the nobility of England who not long before had vanquished and put to death their adversaries Afterwards times changed and the children revenged the destruction of their parents It is not to be imagined that such judgments proceeded from anything but the Divine justice But as I observed before England enjoyed this peculiar mercy above all other kingdoms that neither the country nor the people nor the houses were wasted destroyed or demolished but the calamities and misfortunes of the war fell only upon the soldiers and especially on the nobility of whom they are more than ordinarily jealous for nothing is perfect in this world.[20]

The rewards for the Brandon men did not stop at William Brandon's knighthood; throughout the rest of Edward's reign they continued to receive important and profitable positions from the king. The following year, on 7 March 1472, William Brandon was part of a commission of array to muster and fit men within his service for the defence of the realm against the king's enemies, especially the French.[21] This commission was repeated on 10 May, with Brandon specifically named as the one required to muster and arm men for the king's defences.[22] William, along with his brothers-in-law John and Robert Wingfield as well as Thomas Vaughan, were granted 'warranty of the manors of Halfnakyd and Walberton co. Sussex, Chawton co. Southampton and Shillyngham and Hornecote co. Cornwall' from John Bonvyle.[23]

William Brandon was, however, held by a bond of 200 marks, along with his brothers-in-law John and Robert, to pay to William Lord Hastings and Thomas Vaughan by 'the morrow of All Saints, 1474, in the chapel of St. Stephens Westminster'.[24] Just what this bond was for remains unknown, but social advancement in the service of a grateful king did not absolve William from payment of his debts, which may well have increased with the responsibilities of his new social status.

On 3 July 1472, at Westminster in the Chamber of Parliament, William Brandon was among the lords and knights who swore an oath recognising King Edward IV's son, Edward, Prince of Wales, as the next king.

[I ac]knowledge, take and repute you Edward prince of Wales etc. first begotten son of our sovereign lord King Edward, etc. to be very and undoubted heir to our said lord as to the crowns and realms of England and France and lordship of Ireland, and promise and swear that in case hereafter it happen you by God's disposition to overlive our sovereign lord; I shall then take and accept you for the very true and righteous king of England etc. and faith and truth shall to you bear: and in all things truly and faithfully behave me towards you and your heirs as a true and faithful subject oweth to behave him to his sovereign lord etc.: So help me God and halidom and this holy Evangeliste.[25]

After publicly making this oath, Brandon then signed his name underneath, binding himself to the vow he had made. One can only wonder how William Brandon later felt regarding this oath when, in 1483, Edward IV's younger brother, Richard, Duke of Gloucester, ascended the throne instead of his nephew. Brandon served at Richard III's coronation but later fled into sanctuary during 1484 when his sons William and Thomas rebelled. Did William reflect upon the oath he had made to the lost prince in the Tower?

With his star on the rise, William Brandon looked for an advantageous marriage for his oldest son and heir, also named William. William Brandon II married Elizabeth Bruyn of South Ockendon sometime between 1473 and 1476.[26] Elizabeth was the daughter and co-heiress of Sir Henry Bruyn. Elizabeth had first been married to Thomas Tyrell Esq., who had died in 1473. Sir Bruyn had died in 1466, leaving Elizabeth a portion of her father's wealth. Elizabeth would survive the death of her husband William in 1485, and went on to marry William Mallory Esq. Elizabeth lived until 7 March 1494, dying when her son Charles was approximately nine or ten years of age – there are no surviving records of Charles's birth in France to give us a firm date.[27]

William and Elizabeth had at least three children: a first-born son named William after his father, a daughter named Anne, and Charles, the youngest. The exact birth dates remain unknown.[28] It has not been easy to detail the lives of either William or Anne. Anne married Sir John Shilston, and then after his death she married Sir Gawain Carew.[29] However, the date of her death is unknown, and we do not know if she had children.

William's life is also difficult to track, and it is unknown if he married or fathered any children. When his grandmother died on 28 April 1497, the inquisition post-mortem of Henry VII stated that William Brandon III, son of William Brandon II, was one of Elizabeth's heirs. It also stated that he was aged twenty-one or older.[30] This puts William Brandon III's birth year at 1476 or earlier, making him at least nine years older than his younger brother Charles. Where William Brandon III was during the tumultuous events of 1484/85 remains unknown. There are no records of him travelling to Brittany with his father and mother, nor are there any records of him remaining in England. Frustratingly, there are no records of him at all beyond the single reference in the inquisition post-mortem. At twenty-one, as a young man of good stock with family connections to court, it would be highly likely that William Brandon III would be part of the court, and yet there are no records of him being in Henry VII's service. Of all the Brandon men, William Brandon III's life remains the greatest mystery.

Meanwhile, in 1475, Edward IV sought to attack England's old enemy, France, as a continuation of the Hundred Years War and in pursuance of the English claim to the French crown. An invasion of France began on 20 June 1475 when the first soldiers of an 11,500-strong army travelled from England to Calais. On 15 April 1475, Sir William Brandon I had been granted protection by Edward IV for one year to go to France with the king to fight against the French. However, on 18 November this grant was revoked as William had been delayed in the county of Middlesex.[31] This revocation of the grant strongly suggests that instead of travelling to France to fight, Brandon had chosen to remain in England. There is some suggestion that William's son Robert may have gone to France with the king.

In Francis Pierrepont Barnard's book *Edward IV's French Expedition of 1475*, there is an image of an original document which lists a 'Sir Rychard Brandon' as having mustered only himself for the king's army. Next to the name is an image of 'a lyon hede Rafyd gold'. The coat of arms of Sir William Brandon I was a crowned golden lion rampant.[32] Who was this 'Sir Rychard Brandon'? In 1475 Robert Brandon was not knighted; only his father carried the title. However, there is no record of any Richard Brandon being knighted during the fifteenth century. Also, why did this mysterious Brandon carry the same coat of arms as Sir William Brandon? It could be a distant Brandon relative, although no record of him being knighted has been found. It is therefore suggested that this Rychard was, in fact, Robert Brandon and he was incorrectly labelled as Richard and given his father's title of Sir. If so, this would indicate that at least one Brandon travelled to France with the king's army. That would make sense as a sound political strategy.

In France, Edward IV sought to attack the French forces with the aid of Burgundy, but support was minimal, and Edward was essentially alone. With King Louis XI's army ready to attack, Edward turned to his diplomatic skills. The Treaty of Picquigny was negotiated between France and England. France would pay England an initial sum of 75,000 crowns and then a yearly payment of 50,000 crowns. In return, the English army would withdraw, and the two nations would be at peace.[33] There had been no fighting and Edward and his men were back in England by the New Year.

The following year, on 15 November 1476, William Brandon II, son of Sir William Brandon I, was listed as an esquire who was part of a commission of oyer and terminer to explore offences committed by several men in the county of Essex.[34] This is the first mention of the younger William. In the same year, John Mowbray, 4th Duke of Norfolk died without an heir. The title would be resurrected in 1483 when his cousin John Howard inherited the dukedom with the third creation of the title under Richard III. He would later die on the field of Bosworth in 1485 supporting Richard.

Four years later, in 1480, William Brandon II and his wife were taken to court by John Aleyn, who claimed:

> ... William Brandon and his wife Elizabeth Brandon, herself the executor of the will of Thomas Tyrell, owe him £121 by way of a bond which was made between JA and the late TT at London on 10/04/1473 and due on 14/04/1474. JA says that he was not paid this money by the late TT, nor by EB while she was a single woman, nor has he been paid it by WB and EB since their marriage.[35]

Thomas Tyrell was the late husband of Elizabeth (née Bruyn). For their part, William and Elizabeth claimed that Elizabeth was never the executor of the goods and chattels of Thomas Tyrell's will, nor did she administer any goods after his death. Aleyn claimed this was false and that Elizabeth had administered some of her late husband's goods. The case was dismissed until Easter the following year. However, there are no accounts as to whether the case was reheard or, if so, the outcome.

King Edward IV died on 9 April 1483; his successor was his twelve-year-old son, also named Edward. Understanding the turmoil that a young boy might have in his early reign, Edward had left his younger brother, Richard, Duke of Gloucester, as protector to guide the young Edward V in the ways of kingship until he reached the age of majority. To keep the young king and his younger brother, Richard, Duke of York, safe after the death of their father, and to prepare for the coronation, Richard took the boys to the Tower of London. Then, just before young Edward's coronation, Richard had the boys declared illegitimate on the basis that his brother had been precontracted to marry Lady Eleanor Butler and thus the children he had with his wife, Elizabeth

Woodville, were illegitimate. As his brother's only legitimate heir, Richard was asked by Parliament to take the throne and on 26 June 1483 was crowned king.[36] Neither Edward or Richard were ever seen or heard from again. They are known to history as 'the Princes in the Tower'. The debate as to their fate rages to this day.

On 5 July 1483, Richard III rode with great pomp and ceremony through the streets of London to Westminster Abbey accompanied by the dukes of Norfolk, Suffolk and Buckingham, as well as many earls and over fifty knights. One of them was Sir William Brandon I.[37]

In May of that year, Robert Brandon, son of Sir William Brandon I and younger brother to William, had been reappointed as comptroller of the 'great and little' customs, with the 'custody of the cocket' in the port of Lynn.[38] Robert's father had been appointed to such a position in Ipswich. Clearly, the Brandon men were trusted by the new regime to hold such important positions concerning the valuable trade in English wool.

On 1 August 1483, Sir William Brandon I was among several men ordered to assess any subsidies not paid in the county of Suffolk and to organise men to collect the payments.[39] He was also appointed to the commission of peace and oyer and terminer for the county of Suffolk on 18 August.[40] Furthermore, he was appointed to a committee to assess and collect the tax imposed by the last parliament of Edward IV in the county of Suffolk.[41] For now, the Brandons were weathering the change of kings well, publicly throwing their support behind Richard III. This support would last just over a year, before the Brandon men made a significant decision that would ultimately change the fate of their whole family.

4

Hedging Bets

Richard III was now King of England. Yet many believed, rightly or wrongly, that Richard III had murdered the sons of Edward IV, and so they refused to reconcile with him or his new regime. They sought a new king, and many believed there was another man who held a good claim to the throne.

Henry Tudor, born on 28 January 1457, was the son of Edmund Tudor, 1st Earl of Richmond and his wife, Lady Margaret Beaufort. Edmund, who had died of the plague on 1 November 1456, two months before his son's birth,[1] was the oldest son of Owen Tudor and Dowager Queen Catherine of Valois. Catherine's first marriage had been to King Henry V, and their son, Henry VI, was the half-brother of Edmund Tudor.[2] As one of the last male heirs in the Lancastrian line, Henry Tudor therefore had a tenuous claim to the English throne.

Henry, along with his uncle Jasper, Earl of Pembroke, had escaped to Brittany in 1471 when Edward IV had come to the throne for the second time. It was here that Henry and his uncle would spend the next fourteen years, slowly building up support for their eventual return to England.

During the summer of 1483, Henry Stafford, 2nd Duke of Buckingham was in his castle at Brecon on the Welsh border. In his care was Dr John Morton, the Bishop of Ely, who had recently been released from the Tower of London. Morton had been a faithful servant of Edward IV. A persuasive man, he convinced Buckingham to transfer his allegiance to Henry Tudor, to whom Buckingham was related. By leading a rebellion against Richard

III and putting Henry Tudor on the throne, Buckingham would be in the same position as the late Earl of Warwick, who had helped to make Edward IV king and had in the process become a very powerful man. Buckingham agreed, and Morton sent word of the proposed rebellion to Margaret Beaufort, Henry Tudor's mother. She in turn sent word to her son and brother-in-law in Brittany.

At this point it is interesting to note that Sir William Brandon I was an associate of Dr John Morton, their relationship dating back at least four years when Brandon had been granted the honour of sitting with Morton at the high table after his consecration as Bishop of Ely in 1479. In addition to this, Brandon had served on a commission with Morton in 1480.[3] Could it be that in order to muster support for Buckingham's rebellion Morton made contact with Sir William Brandon, reminding him of their association and persuading Brandon and his sons to join the rebellion? While this is only speculation, it must be noted that the Brandon men soon became dissatisfied with Richard III. They decided that the oldest Brandon son, William, and his youngest brother, Thomas, would join the Duke of Buckingham's rebellion.

The rebellion was planned for 18 October 1483; however, rebels in Kent took to arms early and began to march upon London ahead of schedule. Richard III was now alerted to the uprising and sent John Howard, Duke of Norfolk to crush the rebels. It was vitally important that Buckingham and his men were able to meet up with supporters in the west, but the weather was appalling, with constant rain causing the rivers Severn and Wye to break their banks, flooding the surrounding lands and making it virtually impossible for Buckingham to progress. Soon his soldiers began to retreat. Knowing that his cause was lost, Buckingham fled to seek refuge with Ralph Banastre, one of his retainers. However, there was a price upon Buckingham's head, and Banastre betrayed the duke. Buckingham was arrested, and on 2 November he was beheaded in the marketplace at Salisbury. Meanwhile, Henry Tudor had led a force across the Channel, landing at Plymouth. News of Buckingham's failed rebellion quickly reached him, and he and his men, not finding the support they had hoped for, returned to Brittany.[4]

Why did the Brandon men decide to join Buckingham's rebellion? For centuries there have been theories that Richard III, or even

Buckingham, ordered the murders of Edward and Richard, the Princes in the Tower. Had such rumours reached the ears of the Brandon men? Did they truly believe that both Edward and Richard were dead, or was it merely a matter of being unhappy with how Richard III had claimed the throne? Or perhaps Sir William Brandon I remembered the vow he made to the late King Edward IV to accept his son and heir, Edward, as the next king.

On paper, it appears the Brandon men had decided to hedge their bets. With four adult Brandon men, the family chose to align two with Buckingham and Henry Tudor and one with Richard III, while another fled into sanctuary. If Buckingham proved victorious and Henry Tudor took the throne, then the Brandons would support the new king. If the rebellion failed and Richard III remained as king – as happened – then Robert Brandon would still have been seen to support the Yorkist king. Meanwhile, Sir William Brandon I would have been safe. This was a smart move, allowing the family, no matter the outcome, to be on the winning side.

In 1484, brothers William and Thomas Brandon left England and headed to Brittany to join Henry Tudor. The port from which William, Thomas and William's wife Elizabeth left England is uknown. One possibility is that they went from Dover to Calais, and then overland to Brittany. Another is that they left England from a more westerly point such as Southampton. That same year, on 28 March, a general pardon was granted to William Brandon II 'the younger, "gentilman," alias esquire, son of William Brandon of the country of Norfolk, knight, of all offences committed by him before 27 March'.[5]

It is unclear if this pardon was issued before or after William Brandon II left to join Henry Tudor. If it was before, then William may not have trusted the king's words. If the pardon had been issued after William had left for Brittany, it might be that he was unaware of it; alternatively, he might have heard about it but felt it was too late as he had already thrown in his lot with Henry Tudor. Whatever the reason for not accepting the pardon, it is thought that at this time William's wife Elizabeth was pregnant with their second son, Charles.

The Wars of the Roses had brought huge upheaval to England, and now, leaving the country, William and Elizabeth Brandon placed their hope in Henry Tudor and his campaign. Laying claim to the English throne was one thing, but obtaining it was another. Throughout 1483 and 1484, Henry and his ever-growing group of supporters relied heavily upon Francis, Duke of Brittany for support, receiving money from the duke to help pay for their day-to-day upkeep.

In September 1484, it was discovered that Francis's treasurer, Pierre Landais, was planning to hand Henry and Jasper Tudor over to the English king. Henry Tudor managed to escape, and threw himself upon the mercy of King Charles VIII of France, begging for his support in his claim on the English throne. The French king did not disappoint, helping Henry and his supporters purchase resources and collect mercenaries for the campaign ahead.

While in France, the Brandon men were not idle. For his part in the rebellion against the late Edward IV, the staunch Lancastrian John de Vere, 13th Earl of Oxford had been imprisoned at Hammes Castle in the Pale of Calais, which was still under English rule. In 1484, Oxford convinced the captain of Hammes Castle, James Blount, to allow him to escape. Oxford also convinced the captain to come with him, as well as Sir John Gawsein, the Porter of Calais. The men left the captain's wife in charge of the garrison.

Shortly after their escape, the castle was besieged by Richard III's men from Calais. Mrs Blount managed to get a message to her husband. Oxford returned with a group of men, all English exiles from Henry Tudor's entourage, including Thomas Brandon. While Oxford attacked the rear of the castle, Brandon led thirty men into the castle via a secret path through the adjoining marsh.[6] After a short fight, the garrison of Calais agreed to let the men of Hammes go free without any further harm. Many of the men of Hammes then changed their allegiance and joined with Henry Tudor, further bolstering his numbers.[7]

Edward Hall describes the heroics of Thomas Brandon in his book *Hall's Chronicle: Containing the History of England, During the Reign of Henry the Fourth, and the Succeeding Monarchs, to the End of the Reign of Henry the Eighth, in Which Are Particularly Described the Manners and Customs of Those Periods*:

The erle slepyng not this first begonne assaute, sent the earle of Oxenforde with an elected company of souldioures to reise the siege & reskewe the castle: Which at their first arryuynge pitched their campe not farre from their enemies. And while king Rychardes men gaue vigilaunt iye, weytyne least the Earl of Oxforde should take any aduauntage of theim that laie on that side of the Castell. Thomas Brandon with. Xxx. Approued men of warre by a marishe which laie on the other syde entred into the castell. The souldioures within greately animated and muche comforted by this newe succour and aide, greued thenemies by shotyng fro y walles more then they were accustom,ed to do. And they of the Castell vexed their enemies on the forepart: the Earle of Oxenforde no less molested and unquieted theim on the other parte, which was the occasion that king Richardes men offred of their awne mere mocion licence to all beynge within the Castle to departe in sauetie with bagge and baggage nothinge excepted: whiche condiction the earle of Oxenforde commynge only for that purpose to deliver his louynge frends oute of all perell and danger, chief yof all his olde hostesses Jane Blount wife to James Blount the capteine, would in no wise repudiate or refuse. And so leauynge the Castll bare and vngarnyshed both of vitaile and artillery, came safe to the earle of Richmond.[8]

On 27 January 1485, Richard III issued a general pardon for Thomas Brandon and the other thirty-seven men involved in the storming of the garrison at Hammes.[9] Once again, it is unclear if Thomas Brandon knew of this pardon; if he did, it is highly doubtful that he would have accepted anyway – by this time he had firmly thrown in his lot with Henry Tudor.

Two months later, on 24 March, William Brandon II was ordered to forfeit all possessions that had formally belonged to his wife Elizabeth's first husband Thomas Tyrell and return them to Thomas Bruyn. It was claimed that Thomas Tyrell had stolen the possessions from Bruyn and claimed them for his own. Upon his death and Elizabeth's remarriage, these possessions had passed to William Brandon, and he was ordered to return them to Thomas Bruyn.[10]

By 11 April, William Brandon II was being referred to as a rebel in government documents. On this date, Philip Constable, servant of Richard III, was granted all the lands belonging to William

Brandon II in Killingholme, Lincoln and a yearly rent of 20*l* from the residents of Brandon's manor in Southcarleton, Lincoln.[11] On 27 May of the same year, William Brandon II was ordered to return the manor of South Workington and 2 acres of land in Stifford, Essex to John Henyngham. It was declared that the property rightfully belonged to William's sister-in-law Alice Bruyn and her husband John Henyngham. When Alice died, John claimed the land. However, William Brandon 'unjustly expelled' John from the land and claimed it as his own. John had also died, and the manor and land reverted to the Crown.[12]

On 7 July, an Act of Attainder was passed on William Brandon II. The Act stripped Brandon of all his land, manors, property and wealth, which reverted to the Crown. In addition to this, the Act charged Brandon with high treason.[13] As well as losing all his property, land and possessions, Brandon, if captured, would be sentenced to a traitor's death without trial.

For his part, his father, Sir William Brandon I, took sanctuary at Gloucester.[14] Sanctuary was a place within the walls of a church or cathedral where a person could stay out of reach of the law. It is important to note that a place of sanctuary had to have been officially designated as such. A person could not simply walk into any religious building and claim it. It is unclear exactly which church Sir William Brandon I entered, or why he chose to go into sanctuary in Gloucester, a city loyal to Richard III before he was king. Perhaps he was caught travelling in the area either for business or attempting to escape England. Whatever the reason, his hopes of freedom lay either with Richard III forgiving the treasonous actions of his sons or with Henry Tudor's successful claim to the throne.

Meanwhile, Elizabeth Brandon was giving birth to her second son, the future Charles Brandon, Duke of Suffolk. Whether he was born in Brittany or France, Charles Brandon would have been baptised shortly after birth.[15] It is possible that Charles was named after the French king in recognition of the king allowing the various supporters of the claimant to the English throne to live at his court.

After fourteen years of exile, Henry Tudor set sail from France on 1 August 1485 to lay claim to the English throne.[16] He sailed from the port of Harfleur, 6 miles east up the River Seine from the Normandy port of Le Havre, accompanied by approximately 2,000 soldiers.[17] The exact number of men is hard to estimate as different reports record different numbers. What is known is that William Brandon II was by his side.

There are no records of Thomas Brandon travelling to England with Henry and his men in August 1485, or of him participating in the ensuing Battle of Bosworth Field. It may very well be that he did take an active part in the battle, or he may have stayed behind in France with his brother's wife to protect her and his young nephew; if so, then once again we are seeing the Brandons hedging their bets and leaving two Brandon men safely out of the reach of Richard III should Henry Tudor's invasion force fail.

On 7 August, the fleet landed at Mill Bay, 6 miles west of Milford Haven on the Pembrokeshire coastline. When he reached the coast, Henry knelt and kissed the sand, reciting Psalm 43: 'Judge me, O Lord, and favour my cause.' He then made the sign of the cross. At Mill Bay, Henry was met by his half-uncle David Owen, the illegitimate son of Owen Tudor, Henry's grandfather. He then gathered his men and began his march.

Their first stop was the village of Dale, which provided little resistance. Henry camped here with his men, making sure to remind them to cause no trouble. The troops then moved on through Haverfordwest and Henry met with Welshman Arnold Butler, who advised the Tudor claimant that the men of the county of Pembroke were willing to throw their support behind him. The army then marched on to Cardigan and from there northward on a 23-mile journey to Llwyndafydd. After Henry's forces claimed the garrison at Aberystwyth Castle following another northward trek, they turned and marched inland.

On 13 August, Henry's army reached Machynlleth. The next day they journeyed 30 miles across rough terrain to Dolarddyn near Castle Caereinion. Following this, the growing army headed to Long Mountain where they camped overnight. Here Henry met with Rhys ap Thomas, an important man who carried a great deal of sway with the Welsh people. Having been promised the chamberlainship of South Wales, Rhys pledged his loyalty to Henry, bringing approximately 2,000 troops to the Tudor cause. In addition, more Welshmen were arriving throughout the evening with supplies.

On Wednesday 17 August, with his growing number of troops Henry headed to Shrewsbury. When he arrived, the portcullises were closed, and Henry and his men were refused permission to pass. The head bailiff, Thomas Mitton, stated that 'he knew of no king but only King Richard to whom he was sworn, whose life tenants he [Mitton] and his fellows were, and before he [Henry] should enter there he should go over his belly'.[18]

The next day Henry sent a messenger to negotiate with Mitton and his fellow executives. At this point, a mysterious message from an outside source was sent to the head bailiff telling him that Henry and his men could pass. Several men from the town then joined Henry's forces. It was said that for Mitton to observe his oath he lay on his back so that Henry could step over him.

Henry travelled through Shropshire and Staffordshire. It was in Staffordshire that Sir Gilbert Talbot and a troop of about 500 men joined Henry's army. On Friday 19 August, the men marched to the country town of Stafford where Henry met Sir William Stanley, the younger brother of Henry's stepfather. Throughout this time the Stanleys had been sitting on the fence, not making their allegiance clear either to Henry Tudor or Richard III. It is interesting to note that Thomas Stanley, Henry's stepfather, had been following Henry and his men under the pretence of keeping an eye on them for the king. Stanley was another who was hedging his bets. Soon it became known that William Stanley had been the author of the message that convinced Mitton to open the gates to Henry and his men.

From Stafford, Henry and his men marched on to Lichfield where he was met with great fanfare and rejoicing by the people. He then marched a further 7 miles south-west to Tamworth. The next day his men crossed the River Anker to reach Atherstone, where Henry was reported to have had a secret meeting with his stepfather Thomas Stanley. It was at this meeting that Thomas allegedly pledged his formal support for his stepson. Later, in the sixteenth century, the humanist scholar Polydore Vergil wrote of that meeting:

Here Henry dyd mete with Thomas and William [Stanley] wher taking one an other by thand and yealding mutuall salutation eche man was glad for the good state of thothers and all ther myndes wer movyd to great joy After that they enteryd in cownsaylle in what sort to darraigne battayll with king Rycherd yf the matter showld coome to strokes whom they herd to be not farre of A little.[19]

The next day, 21 August, Henry Tudor sent a message to his stepfather asking him to send men to reinforce him. To this Stanley replied that he needed to prepare his men, and he appears to have kept his distance for the time being.[20] On the same day, Henry chose to knight several men who had shown great loyalty to him throughout his time in exile. Among them were Sir Richard Guildford, Sir John Jastoy, Sir John Sisley, Sir John Trenzy, Sir William Tyler, Sir Thomas Milborn and Sir William Brandon II.[21] William Brandon II must have felt that his loyalty to Henry was finally being rewarded, and that if Henry defeated Richard III his prospects would continue to rise as the new king consolidated his hold on the crown.

The Battle of Bosworth Field took place the very next day, on 22 August. It is estimated that Henry had an army of between 5,000 and 8,000 soldiers going up against King Richard III's 12,000 to 20,000 men. Thomas and William Stanley had a combined force of approximately 6,000 men, which had not yet been committed to either side.[22]

Lacking experience in military action, Henry Tudor appointed the veteran Earl of Oxford to command his troops and to lead the vanguard. Sir Gilbert Talbot took the right wing and was ordered to defend the archers and keep an eye on the battle line, while John Savage was to lead the left wing. Henry Tudor was positioned to the rear of the troops with several French mercenaries whom he had brought with him from France. Standing close to Henry was Sir William Brandon II.

Brandon had been appointed Henry's standard-bearer. It is unclear exactly why Brandon was chosen to carry one of Henry Tudor's standards; perhaps it was due to his unfaltering loyalty to the man he hoped would become king, or perhaps it was down to his physical toughness.[23] We have no description of what Sir William Brandon II looked like, but his son Charles grew up to be tall, handsome, well built and extremely suited to physical pastimes such as hunting and jousting – all qualities that he may have inherited from his father.

Facing them, on King Richard's side was John Howard, Duke of Norfolk with Sir Robert Brackenbury leading the Yorkist vanguard. Next came a force commanded by Richard III and comprised of his bodyguard and others. In the rear was the Earl of Northumberland and his men.[24]

When the battle cry went up, arrows flew and the roar of Richard III's artillery filled the air. Oxford's men clashed with the Duke of Norfolk's, the two being old foes. Both sides paused to reorientate themselves. Oxford formed his men into a wedge and charged forward.[25] At this second charge, Henry's French troops attacked Norfolk's vanguard. Soon Norfolk's men were in trouble. Many were killed, including the duke. Others fled while some defected to fight on Henry Tudor's side.[26]

Northumberland and his men did not move into the fight, and it is believed that at some point the earl decided to leave the battle without throwing any of his men into the fray. Amid this chaos, some of Richard III's supporters begged him to flee, but he declared that he would live or die as a king.[27] Oxford's men had pushed forward, leaving a gap, and Richard III now saw an opportunity to get to Henry Tudor directly. He charged with his men, aiming to strike Henry down.

As he advanced, Richard III's lance pierced through Henry's standard-bearer, Sir William Brandon II, and broke in half. History records that William Brandon 'hevyd on high [the Tudor standard] and vamisyd it, tyll with deathe's dent he was tryken downe'.[28] What was racing through Sir William's mind in those last few moments as Richard III and his men came thundering towards him? He had given up his property, his land, his wealth, everything he had to support Henry Tudor. He had bid his wife and infant son farewell to follow Henry to England in the hopes of a better life, not just for himself or his family but for England. It was his sworn duty to protect Henry Tudor with his life, and as Richard III's lance pierced his armour and threw him from his horse, he gave up his life to save the man he believed to be the rightful king of England. Sir William Brandon II had been loyal to his last breath.

Richard III and his men continued fighting their way forward. The battle was fierce and heated, and Henry became separated from the Earl of Oxford and his men. At this point, William Stanley and his men charged down in support of Henry Tudor. At some point, Richard III was killed. Vergil wrote that 'king Richerd alone was killyd fyghting manfully in the thickkest presse of his enemyes'.[29] Despite what people thought of his rule, Richard III fought bravely until the end.[30]

After victory was won, Henry ordered that the dead be given decent burials and that the wounded be treated. Many of those who died were buried at the nearby church of St James the Greater, Dadlington.[31] Sir William Brandon II was the only member of the nobility on Henry Tudor's side killed at Bosworth.[32] Unfortunately, the exact location of his grave remains unknown. For a man who had died so loyally trying to protect his king, it is a pity that his final resting place has been forgotten.

After fourteen years in exile, having marched halfway across Wales and England in just two weeks, and despite being vastly outnumbered, Henry Tudor and his men defied seemingly insurmountable odds and won. Within two short hours of battle, this man with his tenuous ties to the throne had defeated the king and claimed the English crown for himself.

For Elizabeth Brandon and her son, Charles, things were not so happy. Elizabeth had lost her husband, and the one-year-old Charles had lost his father. Yet from these humble and uncertain beginnings, Charles Brandon would go on to forge a life of great responsibility and power at the side of his best friend, King Henry VIII.

5

The Rise of the Next Generation

After Henry Tudor claimed the throne, Sir William Brandon I came out of sanctuary. He had lost his eldest son and heir, but still had two sons and two grandsons to carry on the family name. In 1485, William petitioned the new king, stating that[1]

he was late marshall of the Marshallsie of the King's Bench, and lawfully possessed of the same office for the term of his lyfe, by the gyft of 1485. John, late duke of Norfolk, late marshall of England, the which deceased, in the tyme of the reign of King Edward the Fourth, to whom the gift of the said office of Marshallsie of the King's Bench, ate every voidaunce thereof, thenne belonged. And your said suppliaunt, so being thereof possessed for the true service the which he owed to youre highness, was so put in drede of his lyfe by Richard late, in dede and not of right, king of England the iii, that he was faine, for salvacione of his lyfe, to take tuition and privilledge of the seinctuarie of Glouc, and there abode fro the fest of S. Michell th'Archangell, the seconde yere of the said Richard, late King, unto youre comeing into this reame sovereign lord And for so much as your same suppliant durst not in that tyme come out of the same seinctuerie to occupie his said office in the Courte of the Kinges Bench, as he would have doune, and no deputy durst take upon him to occupie the same office of deputie of youre same suppiant the xi. Dale of Feb the 2 yere of the same late, as is abovesaid, kinge, before the said late kinge, the defaute of your said suppliaunt, sollomnly called in the Courte of the said Bench, was recorded. And thereupon John, late duke of Norffi, the last deceased, by occasione of the letters pattentes of the same Richard, late, as is abovesaid, king, was admitted to the said office, and youre said suppliaunt thereby put oute of his said office ayenst reason and good conscience. He therefore prays to be allowed to hold and occupy the said office of marshall of the Kinges Bench.[2]

Brandon's petition was answered 'Soit fait com il est désiré' – 'is to be done as is desired'. Shortly after, William was reinstated as Marshal of the King's Bench.

It is assumed that after the death of Sir William Brandon II his widow, Elizabeth, returned to England with her infant son. The exact date remains unknown, as does their place of residence. It has been suggested that young Charles went to live with his grandfather, or even his uncle Thomas Brandon, who had fled England along with his brother.[3]

Little is known of Charles Brandon's upbringing. He would most likely have had a tutor or joined other boys of a similar age to be educated. We know that Brandon was able to read and write as he wrote many letters throughout his life; however, his handwriting was of very poor quality. As was usual for the time, his spelling was phonetic;[4] in light of this, it has been suggested that Brandon had a strong Suffolk accent as much of the spelling in his letters reflects such an accent.

With the introduction of the printing press into England, people's access to books and pamphlets was increasing. Such works as *Le Morte d'Arthur* by Sir Thomas Malory emphasised chivalric adventures, personal combat and heroic wars while upholding the knightly value of honour.[5] Brandon may have read stories of chivalry and valour as part of his education. These tales were translated into everyday life in the form of jousting and other knightly skills, such as swordplay, good manners and the protection of the weak. Archery was also an important part of a young man's education, and Brandon would likely have been efficient in using a bow as well as hawking, tennis and possibly wrestling.[6] In time he would grow into an incredibly skilled athlete, the perfect image of a heroic knight: tall, broad-shouldered, strong, and skilled in jousting, hand-to-hand combat and other knightly pursuits. These qualities would draw the future Henry VIII to Brandon. As an adult, Brandon would prove to be a very physical and active young man and he appeared to greatly enjoy sports and outdoor pastimes, activities that were also greatly favoured by Henry VIII.[7]

Alongside some kind of formal education, Charles Brandon would have been brought up in the Catholic faith. He would have confessed regularly and taken Communion at least once a year. Most people attended Mass at least several times a week. He would have been taught about the idea of needing to do good deeds for others and making pilgrimages to pray to God.[8] He would have believed that the Pope was the head of the Catholic Church, chosen by God to be his representative on earth.

The new king was generous to those who had helped him secure his throne. Oxford, who had led Henry's army at the Battle of Bosworth, was made Great Chamberlain and High Admiral and a Knight of the Garter. Henry referred to Sir John Paston III as 'my right trusty and well beloved counsellor' and created him Sheriff of Norfolk and Suffolk.[9]

However, it would be Sir William and his surviving son Thomas Brandon who would ultimately reap the greater rewards for their services and loyalty to Henry Tudor. In September 1486 Thomas became an Esquire of the Body, a position that required him to be close to the king's person. On 4 March 1487, at the Palace of Westminster, Thomas Brandon was also made admiral of the king's navy[10] and was instructed to take command of an armed force and go out to sea to protect England from her enemies.[11] There are no further details of the size or number of ships that Thomas was ordered to take; however, this was a vitally important command. Thomas's standing orders were to patrol the English Channel and other territorial waters to spy out any enemy ships and stop them from invading or attacking England. Thomas would have been required to find seaworthy vessels, ensure that they were stocked with food and supplies, and also that they were manned with the requisite crews. In short, Henry VII had placed his trust in Thomas Brandon to protect England's coastlines.

It is important to remember that at this time Thomas Brandon had not yet received a knighthood and his status was that of 'esquire'.[12] The following month, on 7 April, Thomas's father, Sir William, was part of a commission of array that was appointed to oversee the repair and guarding of the beacons along the coast of Suffolk.[13]

As a reward for 'disportes in the Ilde halle', Henry VII gave Thomas Brandon wine worth 3s 4d[14] (about £110 today).[15] Brandon was himself building alliances, giving patronage to graduates and ecclesiastical people in the West Country and Suffolk.[16]

On 18 January 1486, Henry VII married the late Edward IV's daughter, Elizabeth of York, uniting the houses of Lancaster and York. Eight months later, on 20 September, Henry VII's firstborn son and heir, Arthur, was born. On 24 September 1486, Thomas Brandon participated in Arthur's baptism. He had the honour of guarding the christening font. Three years later, in November 1489, he served the young prince dinner on the eve of his knighting.[17] He was also present at the knighting of young Prince Henry, the future Henry VIII. Thomas regularly participated in court jousts; this and the fact that Charles Brandon was also well suited to jousting suggests that the Brandon men were well built and extremely fit and strong. It is most likely from Thomas that Charles Brandon first learnt about jousting.

In 1501, Thomas took part in the magnificent wedding of Prince Arthur and Princess Katherine of Aragon. He was part of the court delegation that first met Katherine when she arrived in England. At the royal wedding, Thomas wore a gold chain worth around £1,400[18] (approximately £680,000 today)[19] and a black gown that was 'great and massy' and presumably expensive. Thomas Brandon also owned other items of expensive clothing including a gown of 'russet tinsel satin furred with genet' and two gowns of cloth of gold – cloth customarily reserved solely for the use of the royal family.[20]

Henry VII faced multiple threats to his throne. The first came just two years after his victory at Bosworth.

In 1487 a young boy appeared claiming to be Edward, Earl of Warwick, son of the late George, Duke of Clarence, brother to Edward IV. The boy was aided by the staunch Yorkist supporter John de la Pole, Earl of Lincoln, son of Elizabeth, Duchess of Suffolk and sister of Edward IV. De la Pole and the young boy travelled to Wales seeking support for this claim to the throne.

Unfortunately, for de la Pole and the Yorkist supporters, Henry VII had the real Edward, Earl of Warwick, safely locked up in the Tower of London. Henry brought out the real heir, showing him off and publicly proclaiming that the other was a pretender.

Undaunted, the Yorkist army marched south where they were met by Henry VII's army on 16 June 1487. It is estimated that the Earl of Lincoln had raised an army of approximately 8,000 men consisting mainly of poorly trained Irish soldiers and Swiss mercenaries led by Colonel Martin Schwartz. John de Vere, Earl of Oxford led Henry VII's army of 12,000–15,000 battle-hardened men. The clash went down in history as the Battle of Stoke Field. Robert Brandon, the second son and oldest surviving child of Sir William, participated in the battle. Of the battle, Polydore Vergil wrote:

Both sides fought very stoutly and fiercely, nor did the Germans in the forefront, rough men and exercised in arms, yield to the English, just as not many men excelled their captain Martin Schwartz in power of mind and body. On the other hand the Irish, although they conducted themselves with great courage, yet since in accordance with their national custom they fought with bodies unprotected by any armor, they fell more than anybody else, and their slaughter was a great source of fear to the others. The battle was fought on equal terms for more than three hours, when at length the king's first battle-line, by far the strongest and best manned, which alone had joined and continued the fight, made such a vigorous attack on the enemy that first it killed the opposing captains, then turned all the rest to rout, and in the flight these men were killed or captured. But when the battle was finished, then it was more evident how much courage had existed in the enemy army. For their leaders John Earl of Lincoln, Francis Lovell, Thomas Broughton, Martin Schwartz and Thomas Fitzgerald, the commander of the Irish, all died at the posts they had occupied while fighting when alive. About 4,000 men were killed, and among these the five leaders I have named. The king lost less than half as many of his men, who had launched the first attack.[21]

The supposed Edward, Earl of Warwick was captured and discovered to be a boy named Lambert Simnel from Oxfordshire. Henry VII chose to show pity for the manipulated boy and employed him within his kitchens. He eventually became the king's royal falconer.[22]

For his efforts in the battle, Robert Brandon was knighted.[23] The Brandon men were showing themselves to be loyal, strong fighters, having survived the Battle of Barnet, the Battle of Tewksbury, the Battle of Stoke Field and most likely the Battle of Towton. Their trustworthiness and devotion to their king meant they were reaping the rewards.

On 7 April 1487 at Bury St Edmunds,[24] and again on 28 August 1490, Sir William Brandon I and his son Sir Robert were among a number ordered to organise their men to set up beacons along the coast of Suffolk to warn the people of any possible arrival of the king's enemies.[25]

Henry VII's use of the Brandon men continued, and on 15 August 1488, Sir William Brandon was one of eight men ordered to oversee the 'conductors and wafters' who had been instructed to protect fishermen along the coasts of Norfolk and Suffolk. In addition to this Brandon was ordered to levy contributions to pay for the fishermen's protection.[26] This commission was repeated on 24 and 29 August 1490 at Westminster,[27] with the additional responsibility to oversee Edward Lawnson, captain of the ship *Le Carvell of Ewe*, John Nasshe, captain of the ship *Le Kings Berke*, and John Hamond, captain of *le Myghell of London*.[28] Then on 23 December 1488 both Sir William and his son Sir Robert were ordered to muster those of their retainers who were archers on behalf of the king for the forthcoming expedition to support Brittany.[29]

On 28 April 1489, the Earl of Northumberland was killed in North Yorkshire by rebels who were unhappy with the taxes imposed upon them. As a result, the king rode at the head of an army to meet the rebels, and Thomas Brandon was chosen to carry the king's banner, just as his father had done four years earlier.[30] Ultimately, the rebels were pardoned, and they dispersed.

On 21 August 1489, Sir William was appointed to commissions of peace and oyer and terminer in Suffolk, although their purpose was not stated.[31] In the same year, Thomas Brandon was listed as an Esquire to the King's Body, a position which required him to serve the king's person, helping him dress and undress, and guarding him. During this year Thomas was granted cloth of black satin from the king's wardrobe.[32]

On 11 September of the same year, Sir William Brandon I, along with ten other men, were given the duty of delivering prisoners from Ipswich gaol to the judge and then releasing those found innocent and returning to gaol those found guilty. This role required Sir William to ensure their safety and that they did not escape while on the way to trial.[33]

Two years later, on 22 June 1491 at Westminster, Thomas Brandon was granted the keeping of the lands of Margaret Fenys, widow of William Fenys, Lord Saye in the country of Oxford while her son Richard Fenys was a minor. In addition, Thomas was granted the wardship of Richard and the right to marry him to a woman of his choosing.[34] The wardship of young Richard and the keeping of Margaret Fenyn's lands provided Thomas with an annual income which would go into his pocket rather than the hands of Richard Fenys. He was able to marry Richard to whomever he chose, most likely a bride related through family so that the Fenys' income and revenue would stay within the clan. However, in the same year, Thomas had to face the humiliating job of standing as surety for his brother Robert when the latter was arrested and ordered to pay damages for trespassing.[35]

In the same year, Sir William Brandon I died after a long and illustrious career, serving four English kings and using his influence to create wealth and a high position in society for himself and his family. His descendants would serve the Tudor monarchs for a further sixty years. His lands and inheritance went to his eldest son, Robert Brandon.[36] In his will, he stated that he wished to be buried at the parish church of St Peter and St Paul, Wangford.[37]

Service to the king continued for the remaining Brandon men, and in the year of Sir William's death Robert Brandon was created Sheriff of Suffolk and held the post between 1507 and 1509. He was also appointed as a Knight of the Shire of Norfolk in the 1491/92 parliament. He was declared by John, Lord FitzWalter to be 'one of the worshipful of this shire'.[38]

Thomas Brandon took over his father's position as Marshal of the King's Bench prison in Southwark. Thomas, however, did not appear to be as dedicated to the performance of his duties as his father because many prisoners were soon complaining of the high cost of purchasing food, drink and firewood. Between July 1498 and January 1502, forty-four people died from disease within the prison. Many asked that they be transferred to a new prison such as Newgate.[39]

Two years later, on 13 July 1493, William Danvers and Thomas Say were ordered to assemble a jury to inquire if Richard Fenys had come of age. If he had, then Thomas Brandon was to show due cause as to why he should not hand over the lands belonging to Richard through his late father.[40] The results of the said jury have not been recorded and thus the outcome unknown. If Richard was of age, then legally Thomas should have handed the lands of the late William Fenys, Lord Saye over to his son. Brandon may have sought to keep the lands for the revenue they brought in.

The surviving Brandon men, Sir Robert and Thomas, were now looking for marriages. On 7 December 1493, Robert Brandon married Anne, daughter of Sir Henry Ingels[41] and wife of the late John Colvyle. Anne died the following year on 6 July 1494.[42] Robert then married Katherine, who had previously been the wife of John Carew of Haccomb. Katherine outlived her husband and was still alive in 1532.[43] Katherine was the daughter of John la Zouche, 7th Baron Zouche, 8th Baron St Maur, who had been loyal to Richard III. After Henry VII came to the throne, la Zouche had lost his titles and lands and was treated severely by the Tudor king. He eventually managed to earn Henry VII's favour, and his titles and lands were restored to him in 1495. So Robert had married well.

At the end of October 1494, Henry VII invested his second son, Henry, into the Most Noble Order of the Bath. Little Henry was just three years of age. On Wednesday 29 October, young Henry rode through the streets of London to Westminster Palace on a mighty warhorse. The ceremony officially began the following day. First, the young prince participated in a small dinner for his father the king. It was his responsibility to help his father wash his hands before and after the meal. Once the king's hands were washed, Henry would have handed his father a white cloth with which to dry his hands. After the meal was completed, young Henry was taken to the king's chamber where a wooden tub lined with white cloth was waiting for him. Twenty-two other men were also being inducted into the Order that night, and their wooden tubs were lined up within the Parliament Chamber, except for those of Lord Harrington and Lord Fitzwarren who had their tubs in the queen's closet. Once in the warm water, John de Vere, Earl of Oxford and the Great Chamberlain of England, came forward and read the rules and responsibilities of a Knight of the Bath. After this, Henry VII entered and dipped his fingers into the water and made a sign of the cross on his son's right shoulder before kissing the mark. The king then exited the room to repeat the ritual with the other future members of the Order. Henry was then taken from the bath, dried and dressed in coarse robes before being led to St Stephen's Chapel within Westminster Palace where the men confessed their sins and received absolution from the chaplains before hearing Mass. Presumably the three-year-old had no sins to confess. Once this was completed, Henry was allowed to return to his bed and sleep for a few hours.

In the early hours of the morning the three-year-old boy was awoken with the other soon-to-be knights and rode to Westminster Hall. Once there, Henry was carried by Sir William Sandys and presented before the king. Next little Henry had the right spur attached to his heel by the Duke of Buckingham and the left spur attached by the Marquis of Dorset. The king then came forward and knighted his son with his sword. Out of love, it seems the king then picked up his young son and placed him on a table for all to see. The very next day, on Saturday 1 November 1494, young Henry Tudor was created Duke of York in a lavish ceremony.[44]

To celebrate his son's elevation, a series of jousting events were held over three days at Westminster. Thomas Brandon, a skilled jouster, participated. His horse was 'trapped with a demy trapper of gren velvet as the oder a bove enramplished with lions heddys rasyd and crowned gold'.[45] His opponent was Sir Robert Curson, and the pair seemed to be evenly matched.

Sir Robert Curson and Thomas Brandon furieusly and couragieusly ran to gedres and after certain strokkis there swerdes wer enterolosed with the gauntellet of the said Sir Robert that Thomas Brandon with the ploke of Sir Robert was sum what meved of his sadell butt soo well recouverd that the gauntellet with the swerde of Sir Robert felde to the ground or ells hit was thought the said Thomas had ben in juberte to have ben on sadeled but the kyng licenced the said Sir Robert to have his gauntellet a geyn and thenne they bothe turned a geyn like champions and

Sir Robert brake his swerde and Thomas swerde brake in the hilt and eythcr of them had new swerdes and full valiantly aecumplished thair armes.[46]

Thomas and Robert had multiple jousts against one another, breaking several lances in the process, and the contest ended in a draw. For his valiant effort, Brandon was presented with a golden ring containing a ruby.[47]

In 1496, Henry VII paid Thomas Brandon 10s for a hound he had purchased on behalf of the king.[48] Brandon seems to have received several payments from the king. In 1497 he was paid 100s for two falcons he had purchased for the king[49] and 40s for two 'falcons gowns'.[50] The following year Henry VII paid Thomas 6s 8d for finding two hares at 'Wodestok'.[51] In 1499 he received £4 6s 8d for a horse.[52] In this year he had become Master of the Horse, so it is probable that he purchased a horse for the royal stables from his own money and Henry VII reimbursed him. Thomas was also granted 10s for a minstrel.[53] In 1501 he received £6 13s 4d for an unknown item,[54] and in 1503 he was paid £6 13s 4d for '2 Caste of hawks'.[55]

Sometime between August 1495 and May 1496, Thomas Brandon married Anne Finnes,[56] wife of the late William de Berkeley, 1st Marquess of Berkeley, who had died in February 1492. Anne's brother was Thomas Fiennes, 8th Baron Dacre. His wife brought to the marriage five manors in Gloucestershire, two in Essex and one in Somerset; together they were worth between £300 and £450 per annum. Despite representing a considerable leap up the social ladder for Thomas, the marriage did not last long. Anne died in September 1497,[57] her body being laid to rest at St George's Chapel, Windsor.[58]

In the year 1496 Elizabeth Wingfield, wife of Sir William Brandon I, mother of the late Sir William II and the living Sir Robert and Thomas Brandon and various daughters, wrote her will. She died the following year on 28 April, outliving her husband by six years. In her will she stated:

My body to be buried as near as may be to the tomb of my late husband Sir William Brandon I bequeath my manor of Cravens in Henham to Sir Robert Brandon my son and the heirs male of his body remainder to Thomas Brandon my son remainder to William Brandon nephew to the said Thomas remainder to Charles Brandon brother to the said William remainder to Ann sister to the said Charles remainder to Elizabeth Lenthorp aunt to the said Ann my daughter remainder to Eleanor Glenham my daughter remainder to Mary Redinge my daughter remainder to Ann Sidney my daughter remainder to Thomas Brandon my son remainder to Dame Margaret Lovell my daughter remainder to Katherine Gurney my daughter remainder to Anne Loveday my daughter remainder to Eleanor Sidney daughter of Anne Sidney remainder to the right heirs of Sir William Brandon Proved 8th May 1497.[59]

In June 1497, rebellion broke out in Cornwall. Unhappy with the taxes being levied on them, the people headed for London in ever-growing numbers. An army of around 10,000 rebels was led by James Truchet, 7th Baron Audley, Thomas Flamank and Michael An Gof. In response around 25,000 men were gathered under Lord Daubeney and the Earl of Oxford. On 17 June, Daubeney met the rebels at Blackheath near London while Lord Oxford and his men manoeuvred around and attacked from behind. Thomas Brandon was part of the battle, although it is unknown whom he served. The rebels were decisively defeated, and an estimated 2,000 killed. Flamank and An Gof were hanged at Tyburn, while Lord Audley was beheaded on Tower Hill. Afterwards, the heads of all three were spiked upon London Bridge. Thomas Brandon received a knighthood after the battle.[60]

Thomas Brandon, now a Sir, was an active member of the court and even sat on the King's Council on several occasions, as well as acting as a diplomat. Along with his role as Master of the Horse, records also show that he had at least some part in the care of the royal hawks. So efficient was Thomas that after Henry VII's death he would be reappointed as Master of the Horse by Henry VIII in 1509.[61] For this role, Brandon was granted an annuity of £40.[62]

On 20 May 1500:

Thomas Brandon and Robert Brandon, knights of the king's body, to the king. Promise to pay 14*l*. a year for the manor of Southwold co. Suffolk, with all lands and tenements, courts leet, view frankpledge, rents and services from the Annunciation next for a period of ten years with the clause of distraint, so long as the original letters patent granting the same remain valid.[63]

What is most significant about this memorandum is that both Thomas and his older brother Robert are referred to as 'knights of the king's body'. This position showed that Henry VII trusted both surviving Brandon sons to protect him from anyone who might wish to do him harm. Such a position came with great respect and allowed access to the king.

The following year, on 4 May 1501, Sir Robert Brandon, who is stated as being from of Henham in Suffolk, was recorded as owing £80 to John Shaa, knight (alderman, goldsmith, merchant of London).[64]

With such an active and illustrious court career it is no wonder that Charles Brandon followed in his uncles' footsteps and ascended the hierarchy of the royal court to become one of the highest-ranking men in England by the end of his life. Charles Brandon was first recorded as participating in the celebratory jousts that formed part of the celebrations surrounding the wedding of Arthur, Prince of Wales to Katherine of Aragon in 1501. He also had the honour of waiting upon the prince the morning after his marriage.[65] Brandon was following closely in his uncle Thomas's footsteps, because towards the end of Henry VII's reign he became Master of the Horse for Henry Bourchier, Earl of Essex, one of the most prominent nobles at Henry VII's court.[66]

In early June 1500, Henry VII and Philip, Duke of Burgundy negotiated a treaty of friendship. The first part of this treaty was that Henry VII's second son, Henry Tudor, Duke of York, would be promised in marriage to Philip's oldest daughter, Eleanor.[67] The second was that the English king's younger surviving daughter, Mary, would be pledged to marry Philip's son Charles. The treaty did not last long. Events throughout Europe would see constant changes in alliances, and soon Philip was seeking a French bride for his son Charles, namely Princess Claude, the daughter of Louis XII of France. The political winds turned again, and soon Louis XII withdrew from the treaty with Philip and married his daughter Claude to Francis of Angoulême, son of Charles, Count of Angoulême and Louise of Savoy.[68]

In January 1503, Sir Thomas Brandon was part of a select group of ambassadors sent to meet with Holy Roman Emperor Maximilian I in order to discuss the Emperor becoming a member of the elite Order of the Garter, the highest and most prestigious chivalric order in England, and the oldest in Europe. Brandon and a Dr West met with Maximilian on 15 February, only to be told that Maximilian was hesitant to receive the honour and that his council would meet with them the following day. On 16 February, members of the Emperor's council met with Brandon and Dr West and again it was stated that the Emperor did not wish to enter the Order of the Garter. On 18 February, it was finally decided that the Emperor's son, Archduke Philip, future King of Castile, would receive the honour.[69]

Thomas had another mission, which was to persuade the Holy Roman Emperor not to support the staunch Yorkist Edmund de la Pole, 3rd Duke of Suffolk, also known as the 'White Rose'. De la Pole was a contender for the English throne. He was a consistent thorn in Henry VII's side, and the king wanted him brought back to England. Brandon was successful in his mission, and Maximilian signed a treaty stating that he would not support Edmund de la Pole if he ever attempted to invade England.[70] While at Maximilian's court, Brandon was described as 'a distinguished knight'.[71] For his expenses as ambassador, he was granted £66 13s 4d by Henry VII.[72] Brandon would return to Maximilian's court as an ambassador in 1508.[73]

Between August and September 1502, Sir Thomas Brandon married Elizabeth Dynham, sister and co-heir of John, Lord Dynham and widow of first Lord Fitzwarin and then Sir John Sapcotes. Thomas paid Henry VII £100 for a letter of recommendation to Elizabeth for this marital alliance.[74] Elizabeth was a wealthy widow, and the marriage further boosted Thomas's finances.

On 2 October 1503, Charles Brandon was granted protection for one year; for what, however, remains unknown. In the grant, he was referred to as a gentleman.[75] Charles Brandon was also recorded as waiting upon Henry VII at his table in this year.[76]

The following year, on 13 June, a Robert Willoughby and his household were bound by 500*l* to keep the peace against Thomas Brandon, knight, and his household servants.[77] On 26 May 1506, reciprocity: Thomas Brandon and his servants were bound by

500*l* to keep the peace with Robert Willoughby and his servants.[78] The disputes between Willoughby and Brandon were related to lands inherited by Brandon through his new wife.

Four months later, on 21 October 1504, Sir Thomas was granted the office of Parker of Freemantle Park in Southampton, with all relevant wages and an additional five marks per year for expenses in conveying water through pipes to the park and in carts during summer for the deer and game.[79]

However, it was not all smooth sailing for Thomas Brandon. On 14 August 1505, he was bound by 100*l* to the king. We do not know what offence he had committed or under what condition the bond was held.[80] Then, on 27 July 1507, Sir Thomas was further bound by 100*l* to his sovereign; again the nature of the offences remains unknown.[81] On 4 August 1507, Thomas was yet again bound by 200 marks, except this time the bond was cancelled.[82] Despite these punitive bonds for various undefined offences, the Brandon men continued their rise at court.

6

The Fairest Man at Arms

With the death of Prince Arthur in 1502, young Henry was moved to live close to the king and kept under careful supervision as he was now the sole heir to the throne.[1] Charles Brandon, now aged seventeen, also resided at court. Lacking a great deal of freedom,[2] it is possible that Henry lived out many of his fantasies and desires through Brandon. The prince was able to watch the strong, fit Brandon joust and participate at the lists while he was forbidden to participate for fear of injury.

With his imposing size and muscular body, Brandon was perfect for the joust.[3] Tall, well built and extremely skilled, Brandon soon became well known in the lists. In 1505/06 he was appointed as part of the 'King's Spears', a group of men who participated in jousting and courtly displays.[4] In the period from 20 March to 20 July, he was paid £10,[5] a considerable sum for the time. From then on it appears that Brandon frequently participated in various jousting events and celebrations. In addition to all this, Brandon provided young Henry with a good source of gossip about romantic interests – young, accomplished and very handsome, Brandon was becoming quite the lady's man at court.[6]

In the eighteenth century, the Earl of Huntingdon owned a copy of a portrait of Charles Brandon said to having been painted in 1544. Underneath the portrait the inscription reads: 'Charles Brandon, Dvke of Svffolke, Lord Great Master to K. Henrye VIII. The Fayrest man at armes in his tyme, Leftenant to the Kyng in his grettest warres, voyd of despite, most fortvnate to the ende, never to displeasvre with his Kynge.'[7]

As well as several surviving portraits, we are fortunate enough to have multiple written descriptions of Charles Brandon's appearance, as well as details about his personality. Richard Davey, in his rather damning book *The Sisters of Lady Jane Grey and their Wicked Grandfather*, describes Brandon:

> In person, he bore so striking a resemblance to Henry, that the French, when on bad terms with us, were wont to say that he was his master's bastard brother. The two men were of the same towering height, but Charles was, perhaps, the more powerful ... Both king and duke were exceedingly fair, and had the same curly, golden hair, the same steel-grey eyes, planted on either side of an aquiline nose, somewhat too small for the breadth of a very large face. In youth and early manhood, owing to the brilliancy of their pink-and-white complexions, they were universally considered extremely handsome.[8]

Davey also goes on to state that a French chronicler saw Brandon in Paris in 1514 when the duke was there for the marriage of Mary Tudor to King Louis XII:

> He had never seen so handsome a man, or one of such manly power who possessed so delicate a complexion — *rose et blanc tout comme une fille*. And yet he was not the least effeminate, for of all the men of his day, he was the most splendid sportsman, the most skilful in the tilt-yard, and the surest with the arrow. He danced so lightly and so gracefully that to see him was a sight in which even Henry VIII, himself an elegant dancer, delighted.[9]

The ambassador Philippe de Bregilles, writing to Margaret of Savoy in August 1513, stated that Charles Brandon was like a 'second king'.[10] In *Memoirs of the Life of Anne Boleyn*, Elizabeth Benger describes Brandon as 'confessedly one of the most handsome and accomplished cavaliers of the age'.[11] Hume, in his book *Chronicle of King Henry VIII of England*, described Brandon as 'an extremely handsome man, very brave, and one of the best jousters in the kingdom'.[12] And in *Henry VIII: King & Court* Alison Weir describes Brandon as 'the perfect companion for the king who he so resembled in looks and build that some people thought he was Henry's bastard brother'.[13]

In August 1519, Venetian ambassador Sebastian Giustinian described Henry VIII as 'much handsomer than any sovereign in Christendom, a good deal handsomer than the king of France; very fair, and well proportioned'.[14] He also stated that Brandon 'governs, commands, and acts with authority scarcely inferior to the king himself'.[15] This, of course, was not entirely true as between 1515 and 1519, when Giustinian was ambassador in England, Brandon spent some time away from court waiting for the scandal resulting from his marriage to Mary Tudor to blow over.

By all accounts Charles Brandon was an extremely attractive man for his time. In an age where men strived to recreate the Arthurian code of chivalry, Brandon was the perfect example. He strove to present himself well, always dressing in the finest clothing and apparel, even if he could not always afford to do so. Brandon would have been one of the most notable and striking figures at court. The fact that he resembled the king so closely would have only added to his attraction.

Brandon first attracted the attention of Anne Browne, daughter of Sir Anthony Browne, around 1505/06 when Brandon was around twenty-one years of age. Anne would bear Brandon two daughters, although it is unclear if the first, a daughter named Anne after her mother, was born out of wedlock. In 1552, more than forty years after Anne and Charles Brandon were united, Walter Devereux, Viscount Hereford recalled:

He was a page, waiting on the lords' cups in the Court of Henry VII's time, at which time the said duke [of Suffolk] was a sewer [waiter] for the board's end ... and by that occasion they did often dine and sup together, which gave cause of much familiarity ... He knew Anne Browne ... waiting on Queen Elizabeth, at which time waited also Mistress Margaret Wootton and Mistress Anne Green, those at that time being called the three gentlewomen of honour. He saith that he knew the said Duke of Suffolk was in love and resorted much to the company of the said Anne Browne in the said King Henry VII's time, but how long before the death of the said king he doth not certainly remember ... He remembereth well that the said duke had one daughter by the same Anne Browne, before any matrimony solemnized, whose name was Anne ... This deponent saith that he doeth well remember that the said duke and Anne Browne were married in the time of King Henry VIII, at a church in London called St Michael's church in Cornhill, where this deponent gave her at the church door, the said Anne Browne, being then great with child, whereof she was shortly after delivered.[16]

Thomas, third Duke of Norfolk concurred in 1552:

He saith that he knew Charles Brandon ever since he was of the age of 8 or 10 ... He saith that the said Duke of Suffolk did keep the said Anne Browne as his concubine before he was married to her in King Henry VII's days, but how long he kept her so this deponent doth not now remember...[17]

This was not unusual or particularly shocking. It may have been that while he and Anne were not formally married at a church they had committed to one another in a simple, less formal ceremony. During the Tudor period, a marriage could be as simple as a young couple agreeing to marry one another. There would not be the need for a priest. Instead, the young couple would clasp hands and then exchange simple vows, such as 'I take you to be my wife' and 'I take you to be my husband', and from this the couple were married. The couple could have then slept together, conceiving a daughter who was named Anne after her mother.

Brandon soon saw better prospects for himself with Anne's aunt, and he broke off the engagement and made a proposal to Margaret Neville, Dame Mortimer, an older widow of some wealth. On 7 February 1507, Brandon had the licence of Dame Margaret's lands and began to sell them off in quick succession, profiting over £1,000 (around £480,000 today).[18] However, with the land sold and a healthy profit made, Brandon was looking to annul his marriage to Dame Margaret on the grounds of consanguinity, owing to his previous relationship with the Dame's niece and also his being related to the grandmother of Dame Margaret's first husband.[19] Dame Margaret would continue to play a role in Brandon's life for many more years to come as she bitterly fought the annulment of her marriage before eventually, on 20 August 1529, the Pope was forced to step in and grant Brandon an annulment. This, in turn, would see the legitimisation of the children he had with Anne Browne, and also those he had with his third wife, Mary Tudor.[20]

In 1508, Brandon returned to Anne Browne and the couple married in secret at Stepney Church. They later repeated the marriage ceremony publicly at St Michael, Cornhill. In 1510 Anne gave birth to the couple's second daughter, Mary. Anne died shortly after, and Brandon, at the age of twenty-five, was left a widower with two young daughters.[21]

There is some debate as to whether Brandon fathered several illegitimate children during his early years. A Mary, who married Robert Ball of Scottow, and Frances, who married William Sandon and after his death Andrew Bilsby, have both been suggested as illegitimate daughters of Brandon.[22] There seems to be no information regarding who this Mary Ball or Frances Sandon/Bilsby, were; even the names of their husbands are challenging to track down.

One illegitimate child Charles Brandon is known to have fathered is Charles, presumably named after his father. The records within the History of Parliament Trust state that Sir Charles Brandon was the illegitimate son of Charles Brandon, Duke of Suffolk, born on or before 1521. Without a clear date of birth or reference to the mother, it cannot be said that the child was conceived during Brandon's later marriage to Mary Tudor, Dowager Queen of France. While it is possible this happened, it is also equally possible that the son was born between 1510 and 1515 when Brandon was unmarried.

There is no information regarding Sir Charles's younger years, although the records state that in November 1542 he was in command of a garrison of 200 men on the Scottish border. He then served with his father protecting the Northern borders between January 1543 and February 1544. The records suggest that Sir Charles married an Elizabeth Strangways, although this woman's exact identity remains unknown. Sir Charles was made Steward and Constable of Sheriff Hutton in January 1544 and fought in Boulogne, where the king knighted him on 30 September.[23]

Sir Charles is not mentioned in his father's will; however, he inherited one-third of his father-in-law's property in Yorkshire, as well as the manor and castle of Sigston upon the man's death. In addition, he acquired former monastic lands in Yorkshire, including the estates of Appleton Wiske and Unerby.

In 1547, after his father's death two years before, Sir Charles was selected as a senior knight of the shire of Westmorland. He wrote his will on 22 July 1551, perhaps knowing he was a sick man, and died at Alnwick on 12 August of the same year, just a month after the death of his two younger half-brothers.

Sir Charles appears to have been a man of some wealth as he left several bequests including his manor at Sigston to Humphrey Seckford and £10 to Anthony Seckford. With such property and cash going to the Seckfords, it has been suggested that Sir Charles's mother was also a Seckford, perhaps sister to Humphrey or Anthony. However, he also left considerable amounts of cash to others, such as £200 to the dowager Countess of Sussex and £40 to William Naunton. He bequeathed gold bracelets and rings. His will was proved on 16 November 1551.[24]

There is no mention of any children or a son and heir in Sir Charles's will. This indicates that Charles either never had any children or that they had predeceased him. It would seem that the Brandon line, even in illegitimate form, would not continue through this Charles.

Back in the early sixteenth century, on 16 January 1506, Philip I of Castile and his wife Juana were sailing for Spain when a fierce storm blew them off course, and they had to take refuge in England. Never one to overlook an opportunity, Henry VII seized upon the chance and welcomed his royal guests warmly. Sir Thomas Brandon had the honour of being one of the men selected to meet Philip I and his wife when they unexpectedly arrived on English shores.[25] Philip I and Juana were regaled with nearly three months of entertainment and lavish celebrations. While this was happening, Henry VII and Philip I negotiated a new treaty of friendship and once more discussion was broached concerning a marriage between Henry's daughter Mary Tudor and Prince Charles, son of Philip I and Juana.[26] Finally, on 21 December 1507, Maximilian, King of the Romans, Prince Charles of Spain and Henry VII of England signed an agreement of marriage between Charles and Mary.[27] When Philip I and his wife finally left, Sir Thomas Brandon was among the party that accompanied them to Falmouth.[28]

The following year, in October, Sir Thomas Brandon and a number of his servants were sent to warmly welcome Baldassare Castiglione, who arrived in England to accept the Order of the Garter on behalf of his master, the Duke of Urbino.[29]

In April 1507, Sir Thomas Brandon himself was initiated into the Order of the Garter.[30] To add to this impressive list of responsibilities and honours, he was also appointed as Marshal of the Court of Common Pleas.[31] This form of court examined common cases brought by subjects against subjects not concerning the king. This appointment, alongside his roles as the king's Master of the Horse and Marshal of the King's Bench Prison, would have put a great deal of pressure upon Brandon's shoulders. It is therefore reasonable to think that he would have had several men working beneath him, tending to the duties that he was unable to undertake personally.

On 23 December 1507, Sir Robert Brandon along with William Nanson and Sir John Gawsein were appointed attorneys in the counties of Norfolk and Suffolk. They were in charge of collecting all writs, precepts and other warrants and returning them to Chancery.[32]

On 21 April 1509, King Henry VII died at Richmond Palace.[33] His death was kept secret for several days as preparations were made to usher his son Henry to the throne. Naturally, Henry was informed of his father's death and he played along with the charade that his father was still alive until it was proclaimed that the old king had passed and he was succeeded by his only living son.[34] At Henry VII's funeral, Charles Brandon was appointed one of the ninety-three Esquires of the Body in the funeral procession alongside such men as Thomas Knyvett and William Parr.[35] His uncle, Sir Thomas Brandon, as Master of the Horse, 'led a courser trapped in black velvet embroidered with the royal arms, while also having responsibility for fifty men with staves to control the crowd'.[36]

While there was inevitably a great deal of vying for position and power at this time, it seems that the Brandon men passed effortlessly from the service of the old king to the new. With the coronation of King Henry VIII, it looked as though Charles Brandon's prospects were only set to improve.

Sir Thomas Brandon's career also continued to flourish under the new king. As previously stated, he retained his title of Master of the Horse, and on 2 June 1509 was created warden and chief justice of the royal forests south of Trent. On 24 June 1509, Sir Thomas Brandon had the great honour of participating in Henry VIII's coronation procession.[37] According to Edward Hall in his book *The Lives of King Henry VIII*, Brandon was

> ... clothed in tissue, Broudered with Roses of fine Gold, and traverse his body, a greate Bauderike of Gold, greate and massy, his Horse trapped in Golde, leadyng by a rayne of Silke, the kynges spare Horse trapped barde wise, with harneis Broudered with Bullion Golde, curiously [intricately] wroughte by Gold Smithes.[38]

Henry Tudor took Katherine of Aragon, his late brother's widow, to be his wife on 11 June 1509 in a small ceremony in the queen's closet at Greenwich. Unlike his brother's lavish wedding ceremony at St Paul's, this was a low-key affair with only a few attending.[39] There is some debate as to why Henry took Katherine to be his wife when, as a man approaching eighteen years of age and a newly anointed king, he could have had almost any foreign princess he desired. He stated that he chose Katherine to fulfil his father's dying wish, although it could quite simply be that Henry had fallen for the young, cultured, intelligent and extremely beautiful Katherine; and, of course, she was readily available.

While the couple's wedding was a quiet affair, their coronation on 24 June was a magnificent event, heralding not only a new king and queen but also the dawning of a new age. By the end of his reign, King Henry VII had become known as a miser, maintaining tight control of the many notable members of court and heads of influential families. Some historians, such as Nathen Amin in *Henry VII and the Tudor Pretenders*, put some of this change down to the death of his son Arthur, a loss from which he never recovered. He had achieved a great deal – put an end to the Wars of the Roses, made peace with France and Scotland, improved the economy and brought relative prosperity. He even forced the nobility to pay a fairer share of tax. Importantly, he had abolished the right of great nobles to maintain private armies, so no more 'kingmakers' such as Warwick. Now with the knowledge of his end ever in his mind, Henry VII was desperate to ensure the safe passage of kingship to his son. He did not want a repeat of the Wars of the Roses or any challenge to his son's reign. With the coming of a young, extremely handsome teenager who greatly resembled his late grandfather King Edward IV, the people of England held great hope for a new beginning, the ushering in of a new era of prosperity.[40]

Charles Brandon was selected to be one of the six challengers in the grand tournaments held to celebrate the new king and queen's coronation.[41] For a man of just twenty-three or twenty-four years of age and who was only an Esquire of the Body and a member of the King's Spears, this was a huge honour and a sign of things to come. Brandon was also given the position of Chamberlain of the principality of North Wales in November 1509.[42]

The early years of Henry VIII's reign were filled with entertainments and celebrations. The king was young, athletic and found it challenging to keep still. He had little interest in politics and council meetings and thus left the running of his kingdom to his trusted advisers and Privy Council members. Through his love of sports and entertainment the king built up a close group of friends around him who all shared similar interests and skills, notably Edward Howard, Nicholas Carew, Francis Bryan, William Compton, Thomas Knyvet, Henry Guildford and, of course, Charles Brandon. These men formed the inner core of the king's great household and soon became the staff of his privy chamber. They spent a great deal of time with the king, sharing in his love of sports, entertainment, gambling and other pastimes. Many of them, especially Brandon, were extremely talented within the tiltyard and shared a great skill and passion for jousting. It was these men who held the king's ear simply through the amount of time they spent with him. Many of them would spend almost every waking moment with the king and together they would create an Arthurian ethos in which the young Henry thrived.[43] The king showered his close friends with gifts, patronage, and rich, expensive clothing.[44]

With Henry VIII on the throne, Charles Brandon remained an Esquire of the Body.[45] This position meant that he was responsible for such activities as dressing the king each morning and tending to his personal needs. It is easy to imagine Brandon and Henry spending their days hunting, playing card games, gambling, playing tennis, taking part in archery, practising in the tiltyard, observing beautiful women at court or getting up to the general antics that young men enjoy. Both Henry and Brandon were strong and had a natural talent for all things athletic, and it is easy to see how through these endless days of activity and close proximity Brandon formed a close bond with the king, which would go on to span his entire life.[46]

Despite these days of entertainment, laughter and joy, the new king and queen did face a tragic loss in January 1510 when Katherine gave birth to a stillborn daughter. Despite a sharp pain in her knee, there was no other sign that anything was wrong and the death of Henry's firstborn was a great loss for the king. However, he believed that he and Katherine were still young and that they had plenty of time to produce more children – hopefully sons.

Only a few weeks later, on 27 January 1510, Sir Thomas Brandon passed away at Blackfriars. Upon his deathbed, the prior of the Dominicans attended Sir Thomas and was granted £13 6s 8d for repairs to his church for doing so. Thomas Brandon was buried on the 29th at London Blackfriars.[47] At Sir Thomas's funeral, his oldest brother Robert was the chief mourner, followed by Anthony and Humphrey Wingfield and John Brews.[48] Thomas's nephew William Sidney by his sister Anne, whom Thomas had taken under his wing when he was a boy and raised in his household, carried Sir Thomas' Great Banner of Arms.[49] There was a sermon and Masses were said for his soul, and twenty-four poor men were hired to grieve. The church was hung with black cloth, and his arms were on display. There were offerings of sword, shield, coat of arms, helm and crest and afterwards a sumptuous dinner and refreshments including red and white wine, hippocras, malmsey, beer, ale, bread, wafers, dates, currants and prunes.[50]

William Sidney was around twenty-eight when his uncle died and he would go on to have an illustrious career at court, jousting alongside his cousin, Charles Brandon, as well as being created an Esquire of the Body to Henry VIII, accompanying the king to the Field of the Cloth of Gold in 1520, participating in the war against France and being appointed to the household of Henry VIII's son, Edward. With such a grand career, and an upbringing in Thomas Brandon's household, it must be true that young William learnt the skills required to succeed and prosper at court from his uncle.

Sir Thomas named John Roydon as one of the executors of his will. In his own will, Roydon stated that 'he loved Brandon's blood and name before all others'. He also named his nephew through his sister Margaret as his second executor.[51]

Thomas Brandon's will stated:

> My body to be buried in the Church of the Friars Preachers of London as nigh the sepulture of Sir John Wingfield Knight as maybe I bequeath 60l to the Friars Augustines London for a perpetual memory to be had of the Lord Marquess Berkley and the Lady Marquess late my wife, to my brother Sir Robert Brandon to Charles Brandon all my gowns not bequeathed my sister my niece Yaxley my niece Dorothy my niece Katherine my sister Catherine Gorney Charles Brandon my nephew to Lady Jane Gylford widow my place in Southwark with my lease which I have of my Lord of Winchester I will that the marriage of the Lord Say whose wardship I have shall remain to Charles Brandon my nephew during the Lord Say's non age I bequeath all my purchased lands in Norfolk and Suffolk to Lady Jane Gylford for life she to pay to my nephew William Sidney xx marks a year remainder thereof to Charles Brandon and his heirs and I constitute Sir Thomas Lovell Knight and John Roydon Esquire my executors Proved 11th May 1510.[52]

As Sir Thomas had no male heirs of his own body, a considerable part of his fortune was left to his nephew Charles. Sir Thomas's will comprised land, plate and coin totalling almost £1,000 (roughly £485,000 today).[53] To his wife he left plate worth £333 6s 8d and half of the goods she had brought into the marriage.[54] He also held manors in Thorndon and Wattisfield, and after Brandon's death these properties were granted to his brother Robert for life and then to his nephew Charles. To his servants, he asked that his horses and geldings be distributed in addition to a saddle, bridle and harness for each. He also bequeathed one hundred nobles to be given, within three days after he was buried, to a hundred poor householders and those who were bedridden.[55] Sir Thomas left Suffolk Place in Southwark to Lady Jane Guildford as well as a sum of money, thanking her servants for caring for him during his final illness.[56] It is unclear precisely what this 'final illness' was, although it seems to have been short and sudden, as he had participated in Henry VIII's coronation just six months earlier as well as continuing his role as Master of the Horse.

Upon his uncle's death, Charles Brandon was forced to rent Suffolk Place back from Lady Guildford for an annuity of £47 6s 8d[57] (£28,000).[58] It can be assumed that after Lady Guildford's death, Suffolk Place reverted to Brandon as he held the lavish manor until he exchanged it with the king in 1535.

Charles Brandon succeeded his uncle as Marshal of the King's Bench and in November 1511 he also became Marshal of the King's Household. These positions gave Charles control over the prisons in Southwark and helped to make him an influential figure in the borough.

In April 1510, Robert Brandon 'of Henham, Suff., late sheriff of Norfolk and Suffolk' and his associates, his nephew Charles Brandon, 'of Lenne', and a Roger Towneshend, of Reynham, Norfolk were granted a pardon and release in return for paying 100 marks. It is unclear exactly what offence the three men were pardoned for and where they were released from, as there are no records of them being imprisoned.[59] It is very curious how increasing wealth and social status never seemed to put a stop to the Brandons' brushes with the law! However, the indictment against Robert Brandon clearly caused him little harm as the following January he was being referred to as a 'Knight for the Body', as well as being granted

> ... manors of Thorndon and Wattelesfeld, Suff., with a warren in Thorndon, the park of Ryshangles, advowsons of the churches of Thorndon and Wattelesfeld, and all other lands in those places which belonged to Edmund de la Pole, Earl of Suffolk, attainted; with the fair, market, and advowson of the church of Saxmondham, Suff., which also belonged to the said earl.[60]

On 1 January 1511, the great and joyous event Henry had been waiting for finally arrived. At approximately 1.30 a.m. Katherine of Aragon delivered a son, who was named Henry after his father. After eighteen months on the throne, Henry VIII finally had a son and heir. Four days later, the baby was baptised at the Chapel of the Observant Friars at Richmond. His grandparents were King Louis XII of France, Margaret of Austria and William Warham, Archbishop of Canterbury.

An extravagant tournament was held at Westminster to celebrate the young prince's birth, and Charles Brandon had the great privilege of participating in it. The tournament consisted of a magnificent pageant, jousting and then a huge feast. At the joust the king appeared upon one end of the field from his grand pavilion of cloth of gold, his horse draped in the same. At the other end of the field, for the defenders, appeared Charles Brandon. He was wearing a long robe of russet satin and appeared to be disguised in the form of a hermit or some kind of priest. His horse was also draped in the same golden cloth.[61] He entered the arena without pomp or minstrels playing and rode to where the queen was sitting. Brandon pleaded with the queen for permission to be allowed to joust in her honour, saying that if she did not give licence he would depart without further noise. Naturally, the queen permitted him to joust and when she did Brandon threw off his robe to reveal that he was wearing a rich suit of armour. It must have been a sight to behold. Once his true presence was revealed, Charles Brandon rode to the end of the tiltyard opposite the king and was met by several of his servants decked in russet satin.[62]

After this came Henry Guildford, Esquire, wearing cloth of gold and silver surrounded by what appeared to be a small castle. The castle was beautifully decorated with mystical rhymes which were said to evoke blessings upon the young king and queen. Following him came the rest of the men who would joust for the queen wearing cloth of silver, and once permission was granted for them to participate, they made their way to where Brandon was waiting. Then came the Marquis of Dorset and Sir Thomas Boleyn (father of Anne Boleyn), who were dressed in black velvet as though they were pilgrims from St James' shrine. They carried staves and several men also wearing black followed behind them. After this came the Duke of Buckingham and his horse dressed in cloth of silver. The procession finished with several lords dressed in ornate armour.[63]

The joust itself was a spectacular event with many courses run and multiple lances broken. The queen and her ladies cheered and waved their honours while the crowd watched on with great excitement. Naturally, the king won first prize[64] and Brandon came second; he was smart enough not to beat the king!

Tragically, Henry and Katherine's son would die fifty-two days after his birth at Richmond Palace. The cause of his death remains unknown. Despite the great loss, the king was once more hopeful that the Katherine would give him a son and heir.

After being granted the honour of jousting for the queen, Charles Brandon's accolades continued to accumulate. In January 1511, Brandon was named a Justice of the Peace for Surrey[65] and he, along with Sir Thomas Knyvet, Sir Edward Howard and Edward Guildford, was given licence by the king to export 500 sacks of wool from London, Southampton or Sandwich.[66] In April 1512 he was granted for life the office of Ranger of the New Forest, and in May he was also made Keeper of Wanstead in Essex.[67] He served upon the *Dragon* under the captaincy of Sir William Sidney.[68] In January 1513 Brandon was granted a 'pece of tawny cloth of gold upon satten with dammaske containing 19 yards di at 40s the yard the sum of £39'[69] (a staggering £26,000 today).[70] This was a lavish and costly present, most likely a New Year's gift from Henry VIII.

On 9 September 1512, William Burgeys alleged that five of Robert Brandon's servants broke into Burgeys' house in Swafield, Norfolk, and using bows and arrows, bills, swords and bucklers broke open several doors, kidnapped Dyonese Bolt, William's stepdaughter, and then fled to one of Robert Brandon's properties. He went on to claim that Robert kept Dyonese by force and violence and refused to let her go as she was contracted to marry his servant Henry More.

Robert refuted the charges adamantly. He said that the allegations against him were wholly made up and had been created by Christopher Jenny, a lawyer and Justice of the Peace from Great Cressingham, with a grudge against Brandon. William Burgeys retorted that Jenny was merely his lawyer, acting on his behalf.

The whole matter went to court where it was discovered that Robert did send Francis Simpson to Burgeys' house to see if his stepdaughter Dyonese was there. Once it was discovered that she was there, John Atwood and several of Brandon's other servants went to the house and took Dyonese. There was a great struggle over the woman, and it was reported that she cried and made great lamentation. Upon hearing of the brawl, the town constable John Hall came and took Dyonese to Robert Brandon's home on the back of his horse. He stated that Burgeys and his priest could come along if they wished to speak with Brandon.

It was also discovered that Dyonese was Robert Brandon's ward. He had purchased her wardship in 1508 and had allowed her to live with her mother, although he was still responsible for her upbringing and future marriage. William Burgeys was trying to order a marriage for his stepdaughter, and this was not his right or responsibility.

Robert Brandon then went on to state that William Burgeys did come to visit his stepdaughter and found her content and happy living with Robert Brandon and his wife. He explained that his servant Henry More had shown interest in marrying Dyonese and Robert was content with this marriage. More then won Dyonese's affection and the pair were married with Robert's consent.

Most frustratingly, the outcome of this court case is unknown. By the time the case came to court Dyonese and Henry were married, a union that was bound by the Catholic Church. What can be worked out is that some affray had occurred while Robert Brandon's men were trying to bring Dyonese back to Brandon's home. She was his ward, and although Brandon had allowed her to stay with her mother, Dyonese's welfare, her upbringing and especially her marriage were his responsibility. It would appear that William Burgeys had exaggerated the whole story in an attempt to bring some form of dishonour to Brandon's reputation.[71]

Sir Robert Brandon's dealings with the court must not have vitiated him in the eyes of the king, for in January 1513 he was granted the wardship and marriage of John Carew, son and heir of John Carew.[72] This gave Robert control over all of Carew's inheritance, lands, property and income, as well as the right to choose him a wife when he came of age.

Meanwhile, Charles Brandon's career continued to flourish. On 6 October 1513 he was created Master of the Horse, the title that had once been held by his uncle Thomas. This position granted him £60 13s (£29,000)[73] from the chamber and an additional £40 (£19,000)[74] from the exchequer.[75] He was also granted a warrant which allowed him to employ and pay 'embroiderers saddleers silk women & other necessarys'[76] as part of his duties as Master of the Horse.

This role gave him responsibility for the king's horses including those used for hunting and jousting.[77] Naturally, as an accomplished rider, Charles Brandon would have taken easily to this role, and it also gave him more time with the king. Brandon would have assisted the king in choosing which horse he would take out to hunt and then join his master in that hunt. Such closeness gave Brandon even more opportunity to speak personally with the king, and one would love to know what conversations the pair had over the many hours that they were together. It can be imagined they spoke of the lovely women at court, both men young and dashing in their looks and seeing themselves as representatives of the chivalry of King Arthur. It is also possible that they spoke about the upcoming war against France.

Also in 1513, Brandon was granted the old manor and park at Henham, Suffolk that had once belonged to the Yorkist de la Pole family. Brandon built upon the previous manor to create Henham Hall. By 1538, Henham Hall was described as 'a faier newe howse well buylded with tymber and fayer lyghtys and at the cumming in to the Court a faier yate howe of breake newly buylded with iiii turrettes'. Brandon estimated that Henham had cost him £2,000.[78] In the same year, Brandon sold Henham to the king.[79]

7

The King's Favourite

Tensions were starting to mount in Europe. Towards the end of 1508, Pope Julius II created the League of Cambrai, which was joined by most European nations (but not England). The league sought to oust Venice from the mainland territories it had acquired over many years. Pope Julius II vowed to reduce Venice to nothing more than a fishing village for daring to encroach upon papal territory, not to mention their attempts to secure spiritual independence from the Holy See. France played a significant role in this war, stripping Venice of most of its territory. Then King Louis XII of France summoned an ecumenical council which was designed to examine not only the reform of the Church but also Pope Julius II himself, whom the French king thought to be corrupt and self-indulgent. Pope Julius II was livid. Seeing his position challenged, he sought to make a new alliance to crush the French king. As a true Christian monarch, Henry VIII joined the Holy League against France towards the end of 1511.[1]

Henry VIII saw great potential benefits in participating in the Holy League. Most importantly, the Pope had promised him the French crown once King Louis XII was defeated. This would have appealed to Henry's Arthurian side and would have harked back to the tremendous military triumphs achieved by Henry V. The Pope also promised to bestow upon Henry the title of 'The Most Christian King', which had recently been stripped from Louis XII.[2]

In March 1512, Charles Brandon was knighted. However, he had little time to celebrate such an elevation as soon preparations for war were being made. While the royal coffers funded a great deal of the war, many high lords and nobles throughout England had to raise and arm their own men. Much of the planning for the war was left to Thomas Wolsey, a man who would soon become a cardinal and right-hand man to the king. An English/Spanish invasion was planned, with Guyenne in south-west France as the point of entry. King Ferdinand, Katherine of Aragon's father and Henry VIII's father-in-law, would supply his son-in-law with additional cavalry, cannons and wagons to conquer Aquitaine, which had once belonged to the English.[3]

The campaign was to be supported by the English fleet, and Charles Brandon and Henry Guildford were given the joint captaincy of *Sovereign*, one of the king's largest ships. Edward Howard, brother of Thomas Howard, was made admiral. His duty was to ensure that the Channel was kept clear of French warships. Howard sent his fleet to find French ships and capture or sink them. In August 1512 he located several enemy ships at the port of Brest and the English and French ships engaged. As was the style of the time, the ships were designed not to shoot cannons at one another but to lock together so that the sailors could board and fight. The French ship *Marie La Cordeliere* and the English ship *Regent* became locked in battle and somehow *Cordeliere*'s gunpowder store was ignited. There was a colossal explosion, and both ships began to burn fiercely. The men aboard, including Henry VIII's boon companion Thomas Knyvet, either burned to death or drowned.[4]

Two months previously, in June, Thomas Grey, Marquis of Dorset had landed with 12,000 men[5] in San Sebastian, near Biarritz.[6] Without any support from Edward Howard and his fleet, Dorset and his men were trapped at St Jean de Luz. To make matters worse, King Ferdinand reneged on his promise to send the supplies and equipment he had promised. He also tried to persuade Dorset to take his army to the Pyrenees rather than continue with his instructions from Henry VIII, which were to march north and invade Bayonne. Instead of marching forward, Dorset remained in place, and soon his troops became ill with dysentery. Around 1,800 men died and some mutinied. Dorset, too, fell sick and soon he and his men returned home. Once back in England Dorset made multiple excuses not to meet with his irate king. Henry VIII did not wish to offend Ferdinand and publicly accepted his explanation of English incompetence for the failure of the attack, although privately no real punishments were handed out to his men[7] as Henry realised it was Ferdinand's failure to uphold his side of the agreement that caused the campaign to fail.

In early 1513, Charles Brandon had the high honour of being selected to lead an army that was to land on the coast of Brittany; however, the expedition was soon called off in favour of an autumn invasion. Henry VIII decided to invade France personally with an army of 30,000,[8] of which Brandon raised 1,831 men, mostly from his offices in Wales. Brandon was also appointed as High Marshal and lieutenant of the army, meaning he was responsible for discipline (including dispensing the death penalty), selecting campsites and creating knights. This was an extraordinary position for Brandon, as at the time he was a mere viscount, yet he had power over the Duke of Buckingham, earls and more experienced knights and men.[9] He also had the honour of leading the vanguard of the king's ward, which consisted of around 3,000 men.

The English army took the city of Therouanne in Artois without great difficulty and then went on to besiege Tournai. Brandon led the assault upon one of the city gates of Tournai, and the people of the city surrendered on 24 September 1513. When Henry VIII was given the keys to Tournai he handed them to Brandon, who then allowed his men to occupy the city.[10] The king rewarded Brandon by granting him the castle of Mortain.[11]

After this early success, there were several weeks of celebration in which Brandon was to cause a great scandal. Henry VIII and his men met with Margaret of Austria, who was Duchess of Savoy and daughter of Maximilian I, the Holy Roman Emperor. Twice widowed and having vowed never to remarry, Margaret was the Governor of the Habsburg Netherlands and an exceptionally well-educated and influential woman. During these lavish celebrations, it was reported that King Henry VIII suggested a marriage between his best friend and Margaret of Austria. The duchess, unwilling to marry again, deflected any suggestion by saying that it would deeply offend her father.[12] Whether there was any real prospect of marriage remains unclear, but it seems as though Brandon was willing to push the boundaries.

Margaret of Austria wrote of the occasion:

One night at Tournay, being at the banquet, after the banquet he [Brandon] put himself upon his knees before me, and in speaking and him playing, he drew from my finger the ring, and put it upon his, and since shewed it me; and I took to laugh, and to him said that he was a thief, and that I thought not that the King had with him led thieves out of his country. This word *laron* he could not understand; wherefore I was constrained to ask how one said in Flemish *laron*. And afterwards I said to him in Flemish *dieffe*, and I prayed him many times to give it me again, for that it was too much known. But he understood me not well, and kept it unto the next day that I spake to the King, him requiring to make him to give it me, because it was too much known—I promising him one of my bracelets the which I wore, the which I gave him. And then he gave me the said ring.[13]

Brandon knew that he was stepping beyond accepted boundaries and pushing the limits of courtly love. It was not uncommon for a lady to give a man a gift to show her favour, but at this time Margaret was a duchess and an extremely influential and important woman, and Brandon was a mere viscount. Brandon continued to push the limits. Another time, at Lille, Brandon once more got down on his knees before the duchess and took another ring from her finger.[14] Margaret spoke with Henry VIII and begged for the ring back, saying that it was not for the love of the ring but for the fact that Brandon had stepped out of line and acted far above his status. It would seem that Henry was willing to play along with his friend's game: instead of getting Brandon to return the ring he gave Margaret another, more beautiful ring, set with diamonds and rubies.[15]

The whole incident caused quite a scandal. One report from Andrea Badoer, the Venetian Ambassador in England, stated that an agreement of marriage had already been made between Margaret and Brandon.[16] There was some outrage expressed by Maximilian I, Margaret's father,[17] and Henry VIII was quick to deny any inclination to see Brandon married to her. In March 1514 Henry VIII wrote to Maximilian I that he was 'much displeased to hear that there is a common report that the Archduchess of Austria is to be married to the Duke of Suffolk; will make enquiry if it originated in England, that the authors may be punished.'[18]

It is interesting to note that despite this scandal Brandon was not admonished, nor does there seem to have been any punishment handed out to anyone who could have been responsible for spreading rumours about the supposed marriage.[19] Perhaps the whole incident was put down to an overdramatic game of courtly love, or maybe Henry VIII realised that he had let his friend push a little too far and wished for the whole incident to be forgotten.

On a less scandalous note, on 23 April 1513 Brandon became a Knight of the Garter.[20] The Order of the Garter, officially known as The Most Noble Order of the Garter, is the oldest and highest British order of chivalry. It was founded in 1348 by King Edward III[21] and consists of the monarch, their spouse, the Prince of Wales and twenty-four knights. Other members of the Order of the Garter are known as Royal Knights Companions and Extra or Stranger Knights. The members are a small group, and a new member can only be chosen if a vacancy becomes available. A new member is personally selected by the ruling sovereign, and has to be someone who has served him or her faithfully. Sir Charles Brandon had already shown throughout his service not only to Henry VIII but also to the king's late father that he was a loyal and dedicated servant. As a member of the Order of the Garter, Brandon was required to display his banner of arms, helmet, crest and sword as well as a stall plate within the stalls of St George's Chapel.[22] Upon Brandon's death, his banner of arms, helmet, crest and sword were removed, leaving only the stall plate, which can still be seen today.[23]

Also in 1513, Brandon was contracted to marry Elizabeth Grey, Viscountess Lisle. Elizabeth Grey was the daughter of John Grey, 2nd Baron Lisle.[24] When her stepfather, Sir Thomas Knyvet, died in August 1512 she became the ward of Brandon.[25] He had arranged with the king to purchase Elizabeth's wardship for the sum of £1,400[26] (£680,000),[27] which he could pay off over seven years. While this was a huge sum to lay out, Brandon would receive around £800 (£390,000)[28] a year from Elizabeth's lands and would hold her wardship until she came of age, which was at least six years away; thus Brandon would more than make his money back.[29] At twenty-eight years of age, Brandon, ever seeking to enhance his prospects, proposed marriage to the eight-year-old Elizabeth when she came of age. On 15 May, Brandon was created Viscount Lisle and received several grants to signify his new position.[30] He would also have access to the coin and lands that his intended inherited. The marriage between Brandon and Elizabeth never took place, as less than two years later Brandon would create an even bigger scandal than he had with Margaret of Austria.

By the end of 1513, it was clear to everyone at court that Brandon was the king's favourite. Anyone who knew the king or saw Brandon and Henry VIII together recognised the close bond between the pair. Even Margaret of Austria noted 'the great love and trust that the kynge baare and hadd' towards Brandon.[31] Philippe de Bregilles, writing to Margaret of Savoy in August 1513, referred to Brandon as the 'second king'.[32]

Sebastian Giustinian, Venetian Ambassador at the English court between 1515 and 1519, wrote: 'Charles Brandon Duke of Suffolk, nearer than any other to the king in age, tastes, and love of martial exercises, shared much of his confidence, although he was infinitely inferior to Henry in all literary and intellectual qualifications. He is associated with his Majesty, says Giustinian, *tanquam intelligentiam assistentem orbi*, which governs, commands, and acts with authority scarcely inferior to the king himself.'[33]

In *Letters and Papers, Foreign and Domestic, During the Reign of Henry VIII* there is a description of Brandon's relationship with the king:

> ... for the affection which the King entertained for Charles Brandon, afterwards Duke of Suffolk. Henry's partiality to this brilliant nobleman exceeded the bounds of ordinary friendship. He pushed Brandon's fortunes with the affection and assiduity of a brother. But Suffolk managed a war-horse much better than he wielded a pen. He took but little interest in politics.[34]

Lord Herbert mentions how others 'finding now the king's favour shining manifestly on Wolsey applied themselves much to him and especially Charles Brandon who for his goodly person courage and conformity of disposition was noted to be most acceptable to the king in all his exercises and pastimes'.[35]

While Brandon was neither a great politician nor fond of letter writing or academic pursuits, he still possessed many talents and skills that greatly endeared him to the king. Elizabeth Benger in *Memoirs of the Life of Anne Boleyn* describes Brandon as 'endeared to his master by sympathy in tastes, habits and amusements'.[36]

One of the most well-known talents that Brandon possessed, as we have seen, was his jousting. Jousting has a long and rich history that stretches back several hundred years before the Tudor period. Starting around the early 1100s, jousting was initially used as a means for knights to train for warfare. In the latter half of the eleventh century, warfare included mounted cavalrymen with heavy lances who would charge at the enemy in formation. Due to this new strategy, more practice was required to undertake such attacks. Initially, jousting tournaments consisted of mock battles with dozens or even hundreds of men all riding horses and carrying lances. They would attack one another with their lances, swords and maces across a large area of the countryside rather than in a formal arena. From around the mid-1300s the more ritualised style of jousting began, with individual combat, where one man charged at another. Jousting was then used more as a means to refine fighting skills.[37]

Jousting became a popular event to which hundreds of people would flock and in which knights and noblemen would fight for the honour of their king or queen. Henry VIII loved jousting, and during his reign jousting events evolved from simple one-on-one contests into huge spectacles designed to impress and awe spectators. Men would dress up in disguises, magnificent floats and decorations would be created, and competitors would seek to outshine one another. In addition, lavish prizes were granted to winners.

The joust became highly formalised, and in 1514 Brandon would be put in charge of organising a jousting tournament to celebrate Henry VIII's sister Mary Tudor's marriage to King Louis XII. There was a great deal involved in organising such an event. A suitable arena needed to be found and then set up, and champions had to be chosen to represent various members of royalty. The area designated to hold the joust was called the list, a roped-off area where the two competitors challenged one another. Through the centre of the list a barrier was erected to create two lanes for the jousters to ride down. This barrier was initially known as the tilt and was first made out of cloth and then in the early sixteenth century was made out of wood. The tilt also allowed riders to focus more on their opponent rather than steering their horse. Over time the tilt became known as the tilt barrier, and the act of riding down the list was called tilt or tilting.[38]

The rules surrounding jousting are complicated, but the key point was for a participant to strike their opponent upon the shield or armour, or to wield such strength they could dismount their opponent using the lance.[39] Specialised armour was created for jousters, and in many tournaments the participant had to supply their own armour, horses and weaponry. Lances were often blunted, but this did not stop an array of injuries and even deaths occurring. Bone fractures from the blow of the lance or from being unhorsed were common. While infrequent, deaths did happen. For example, King Henry II of France died in 1559 from wounds he received while jousting. Henry VIII suffered several injuries while jousting, one of them after he was hit in the brow by Charles Brandon's lance. The king had forgotten to put his visor down, and splinters went into his helmet and almost blinded him.[40] There are few records of Brandon suffering any serious injuries as a result of his jousting. During the 1514 celebrations he did injure his hand, but there are no records of this being a long-term injury.[41]

Soon Brandon was making a name for himself as one of the best jousters in England, possibly all of Europe, yet the man was not so smart as to think he could vanquish the king. One of Brandon's most significant skills in jousting events was that he could convincingly lose to the king in every contest despite excelling all the way up to the final tilt. Brandon was smart enough to know when to win and when to lose. Ultimately, he did all the legwork to make the king the greatest jouster at the event.[42]

Derek Wilson, in his book *Henry VIII, Reformer and Tyrant*, wrote:

> In the February 1511 tournament Charles Brandon, a talented performer, excelled in all his bouts, until he came up against the king. At the halfway-way point the scores were close but in the last three courses Brandon was careful to miss his target and to allow Henry to break his lance against him and, thus, to emerge as the victor in a 'hard fought' contest.[43]

Not only was Brandon allowing Henry VIII to beat him but he was also displaying his masculinity, a quality greatly admired by the king. Henry VIII lived, or attempted to live, by the code of chivalry exemplified by that mythical English hero, King Arthur of the Round Table. In addition, he was keen to emulate the crushing victories Henry V had won over the French in bygone times. Warfare, jousting and other physical pursuits were closely tied with the code of chivalry and Brandon was able to display his masculinity and his ties to the code through his jousting skills.[44] Being such a skilled jouster and yet always falling at the last hurdle to Henry VIII helped to endear Brandon to his king.

Concerning the codes of chivalry, Henry VIII also expected the nobility around him to act and dress according to their status, and Brandon worked hard to do this. Unlike the dukes of Norfolk[45] and Buckingham,[46] who inherited titles, land and wealth, Brandon did not come from a noble family. The Brandon men had worked hard over the decades to gain status, property and wealth. They were also smart and cunning men, purchasing and exchanging lands and properties to build up their estates.[47] It was clear that Charles Brandon worked hard to maintain his public image. He presented himself as the powerful and influential Duke of Suffolk, and because appearances were extremely important to Henry VIII, Brandon was able to successfully present himself as the perfect image of a loyal, faithful courtier.

Brandon also possessed the ability to befriend or at least to have a good working relationship with almost everyone at court. Naturally, he was very close to the king, but he also appeared to have an easy relationship with many of the other members of the court. There was only one time when it appeared that Brandon had fallen out with those on the council and that was when he caused his greatest scandal in marrying Mary Tudor, the king's sister. Brandon wrote that the whole council was against him, but this general animosity could have been principally generated through the machinations of Thomas Howard, Duke of Norfolk.

All the Council, except my Lord of York [Thomas Wolsey], are determined to have Suffolk put to death or imprisoned. This is hard; for none of them ever were in trouble but he was glad to help them to the best of his power, and now in this little trouble they are ready to destroy him.[48]

Brandon and Norfolk seemed to have had an uneasy working relationship throughout their lives. Norfolk had inherited his title from his father, although it was regranted to him by Henry VIII; Brandon's title of duke, on the other hand, was gifted to him from the king.[49] It is possible Norfolk thought of Brandon as an upstart and he may have been resentful and jealous of Brandon's friendship and position with the king. While the two men disliked one another, and disagreed on many subjects, they were able to work together when required. Both were on the Privy Council, and together they would help to put down the rebellion known as the Pilgrimage of Grace in 1536.

The Duke of Norfolk aside, Brandon seems to have been a well-respected and greatly admired member of the council and court.[50] He did clash with Cardinal Wolsey towards the end of the latter's life, but only when Wolsey failed to obtain for Henry VIII the desperately desired annulment of his marriage to Katherine of Aragon, when Wolsey's fortunes were on the decline. At this point, Brandon was jumping ship to save his reputation. Brandon appeared to have had a close relationship with Wolsey before that, and had sought Wolsey's help after marrying Mary Tudor.

Brandon also had a good working relationship with Thomas Cromwell, even asking the man to be godfather to his son.[51] Cromwell had first worked under Cardinal Wolsey and rose to prominence during the cardinal's fall from grace and subsequent death. Cromwell was a dedicated servant, working long hours to bring about the king's wishes. He was a lowborn man who had risen through the ranks, and although he was not the equal of the likes of the Duke of Norfolk or other members at court, he was soon to become their political superior. In Cromwell, Brandon saw an ally he could turn to for assistance and support should it be needed – if he managed to stay on Cromwell's good side, that is.

In September 1531, Brandon wrote to Cromwell saying that he '[t]hanks him for his faithful and continual kindness; for his pains in ordering George Cornewall; and for his advancement of the duke's treasurer in Oxon and Berks'.[52] Two months later, Brandon once more wrote to Cromwell to thank him for 'his past kindness, and desires its continuance. Asks him from time to time to tell the news to the bearer, his treasurer, who will advertise him thereof.'[53]

In December, Brandon wrote a letter to Cromwell addressing him as 'my kind and loving friend, Mr. Crumwell'.[54] In October the following year, Brandon asked Cromwell to favour a man by the name of Gawyn Carew in the next election of sheriffs at Devonshire.[55]

In July 1535, Cromwell asked Richard Rich to speak with Brandon regarding the king's displeasure about several houses that had fallen into decay and which Brandon claimed to have restored. Cromwell asked Rich

> ... to say somewhat to the saide duke in this matier alledging vnto him that as I am, always haue been, and euer wilbe his graces poure frende so I require him not to stycke with the kings highness in this matier ... I pray you shew him on my behalf that my poure and frendelie aduise is that his grace shal liberally wryte to the kings highness in this matier so that his highness may thereby perceyue thae saide dukes gentilll herte and natural zele towards his maieste aswell in this as in all other things.[56]

The pair hunted together the following month, and Brandon gave Cromwell a stag.[57] In January 1539, Brandon sold Cromwell his manor at Dunsford, Surrey for the sum of 403*l* 6*s* 8*d*.[58]

After Brandon's death, Henry VIII stated that 'for as long as Suffolk had served him, he had never betrayed a friend or knowingly taken unfair advantage of an enemy'[59] and that Brandon was 'truly magnanimous towards his political enemies'.[60] Brandon had the talent and ability to manoeuvre himself at court, being able to further his desires and career while retaining friendships and working relationships with those around him, especially with the king.

Henry VIII had a good eye for using people who possessed the skills he required. For example, he could appreciate the administrative skills demonstrated by both Thomas Wolsey and Thomas Cromwell, and used the two men to carry out a great deal of the tedious administration involved in government. Henry also saw the military skills and abilities that Brandon possessed and put them to use. In 1513 Brandon was appointed as High Marshal of the army in the war against France, and he was also responsible for leading the vanguard of the king's army. Brandon proved himself to be a shrewd, tactically minded and talented military leader, as we know from his actions in the siege of Tournai.

On Candlemas Eve, 1 February 1514, Charles Brandon, Viscount Lisle was formally invested as the Duke of Suffolk. The ceremony took place at Lambeth and was conducted by the king.[61] This was a considerable advancement for Brandon and a signal of his great favour with the king. At the time of Brandon's creation as Duke of Suffolk there were only two other dukes in the realm: the newly created Duke of Norfolk and the Duke of Buckingham. Thomas Howard, Duke of Norfolk, was the second of that name and came from a noble family. His father, Thomas Howard, 1st Duke of Norfolk, had been head of Richard III's vanguard at the Battle of Bosworth[62] and was slain by an arrow through the head while defending his king.[63] Thomas Howard had also fought at the Battle of Bosworth but was injured and captured by Henry VII.[64] Over time, Howard proved his loyalty to the new Tudor monarch and was restored to his title of Earl of Surrey.[65] He continued to display his loyalty and was duly created 2nd Duke of Norfolk on the same day that Charles Brandon was invested as Duke of Suffolk.

The one man equal with the dukes of Suffolk and Norfolk was Edward Stafford, Duke of Buckingham. Buckingham was a descendant of Thomas Woodstock, youngest son of Edward III. His mother was Katherine Woodville, sister of the late Queen Elizabeth Woodville, wife of King Edward IV. Buckingham was the richest peer in England at this time, with an annual income of around £6,000 per year (£2,900,000),[66] and was High Steward of England and a Privy Councillor.[67]

In addition to being created Duke of Suffolk, Brandon was granted custody of the lands and marriage of Roger, son and heir of Sir Robert Corbett. This allowed Brandon to control all the boy's lands and property, around £150[68] (£73,000), until Roger came of age.[69] Brandon arranged a marriage between Roger and Anne Windsor, daughter of Sir Andrew Windsor. Brandon was also granted the manor, castle and park of Donington, Berkshire and an annuity of £40[70] (£19,000).[71] On 28 February, Henry VIII wrote to the Great Wardrobe from Lambeth requesting a saddle and harness for the Duke of Suffolk,[72] a gift for the newly created duke. In January 1515, Brandon was granted a licence to import 300 tuns (283,500 litres) of Gascon wine.

Being created Duke of Suffolk was a huge step up in social standing for Brandon. He was now one of the most powerful men in England. The following year, driven by love, he would risk all he had gained.

8

Journey to France

In 1515, Brandon created the greatest scandal of his career. Indeed, his actions caused such a stir throughout Christendom that his flirtation with Margaret of Savoy, which had caused such outrage at the time, look like a mere hiccup in the prevailing social structure.

Years before, on 17 December 1508, the thirteen-year-old Mary Tudor had been married by proxy to Prince Charles, grandson of Maximilian I, Holy Roman Emperor. Sieur de Berghes had stood in for the young prince. Both Mary and de Berghes had exchanged vows before de Berghes placed a ring upon the middle finger of Mary's left hand. According to the law, Mary and Charles were now married. The twin issues of Charles being underage and the wedding never being legally consummated would cause problems later, but at the time the marriage was a huge achievement for Henry VII. After the proxy wedding there was a lavish banquet and three days of celebrations and jousting,[1] in which Brandon, as one of the King's Spears, would have participated.

By 1509, however, when Henry VIII came to the throne, European alliances were in flux. The Holy League was created two years later, and England went to war with France[2] only to be abandoned by Ferdinand, Katherine of Aragon's father, when he was expected to provide military support. In addition, Ferdinand signed a one-year truce with the French king.[3] At the same time, Pope Julius II died. When Pope Leo X succeeded him, he showed no appetite to continue the Holy League's feud with France.[4] All the while, Thomas Wolsey, Henry VIII's right-hand man, was pressing for England to pursue a peaceful settlement in Europe.

Henry VIII was growing angry with the Emperor for delaying the physical marriage between his sister and Prince Charles. Soon he was looking for an alliance elsewhere, and Mary was to play a vital role. Henry turned his attention away from a treaty between England and the Roman Empire and in its place sought one with France. King Louis XII of France was also eager for an alliance with England as there was a conflict between France and the Holy Roman Empire. Part of this alliance was a marriage between Henry's sister Mary and the fifty-two-year-old Louis XII.[5]

On 30 July 1514, Mary Tudor formally renounced her marriage to Prince Charles of Spain:

> In the royal manor of Wanstead, and in the presence of Thomas duke of Norfolk, Charles duke of Suffolk, Thomas bp. of Lincoln postulate of York, Richard bp. of Winchester, Thomas bp. of Durham, Charles earl of Worcester, and Sir Ralph Vernay, the Princess Mary solemnly renounced her compact of marriage with Charles Prince of Spain.[6]

Only two weeks later, on 13 August, Mary was married by proxy to King Louis XII. The Duke of Longueville, who had been captured in the 1513 campaign in France, acted as a proxy for the French king.[7]

> Duke of Longueville, taking with his right the right hand of the Princess Mary, read the French King's words of espousal (recited) in French. Then the Princess, taking the right hand of the Duke of Longueville, read her part of the contract in the same tongue. Then the Duke of Longueville signed the schedule and delivered it for signature to the Princess Mary, who signed Marye; after which the Duke delivered the Princess a gold ring, which the Princess placed on the fourth finger of her right hand.[8]

Charles Brandon was present at both Mary's renunciation of her marriage to Prince Charles of Spain and her proxy marriage to the French king. By now, Mary was eighteen years of age and reported to be one of the most beautiful princesses in all of Christendom.[9]

Things would move swiftly for Mary after her proxy wedding. No expense was spared for the new French queen's wardrobe, and it is reported that Henry VIII spent something close to an astounding £43,000 (£21,000,000)[10] on clothing, mostly in the French fashion, for Mary and her servants.[11] On 2 October, Mary left Dover for France. As she left, Henry VIII walked his sister down to the waterside, and it was here that Mary made her brother promise that if she should outlive Louis XII then she would be able to choose her second husband for herself. At this time Mary would most likely have been aware that the frequently infirm Louis may not live long.[12] Why did Mary make her brother agree to this arrangement at that moment? Did Mary already have her eye upon Charles Brandon, Duke of Suffolk? Was there some connection between the pair before her French marriage? It is significant that, after Louis' death the next year, when Brandon was sent to fetch Mary back to the English court, Henry made him promise not to marry Mary.[13] It is highly likely that Henry VIII was already aware of a romantic connection between the two.

The journey from Dover to Boulogne was rough and Mary's ships were scattered. The poor queen had to be carried to shore in the pouring rain.[14] On 7 October, Mary set out for Abbeville where she would meet her new husband. Along the way Mary was greeted with pageants and celebrations. Many dignitaries from the towns welcomed the new queen with flattery and gifts.[15]

Mary was not supposed to meet her husband until she officially arrived at Abbeville; however, it seemed the French king was eager to see his young bride. Pretending to be out hawking, the king happened to bump into Mary and her entourage. Upon the sudden meeting, Mary acted the part and initially pretended to be surprised before greeting her new husband warmly. The ageing king was delighted with his new and beautiful bride.[16] Later that day, Mary formally entered Abbeville.

At nine o'clock in the morning on 9 October 1514, Mary was married to Louis XII in the great hall of the Hotel de la Gruthose. She wore a French gown made of gold brocade and trimmed with ermine. She was covered in beautiful jewels and was given away by the Duke of Norfolk and the Marquis of Dorset. Louis XII wore gold and ermine to match his bride. After the wedding, the pair were separated and dined in their apartments before they came together to participate in a lavish ball. Later on, the newly married couple were escorted to their bed for the official bedding ceremony.[17]

The morning after the wedding, King Louis XII dismissed most of the English women in the queen's household. Mary was quite distressed about this and sought advice from Thomas Wolsey. When Brandon heard the news he quickly wrote to Wolsey:

Had met with Dannot at Canterbury, who showed him divers news, which he [Dannot] would tell Wolsey at his coming. Wolsey will perceive what the Duke of Norfolk and his son mean, to whom it was owing that the Queen's servants were discharged because they were of Wolsey's choosing and not theirs. Advises Wolsey to redress it; for if the Queen is not well treated the blame will be "laid in our ne[cks] by them that be the causer and loves neither yo[u nor] me." Requests Wolsey's instructions how to act. Trusts to be at Boulogne by noon, and at Paris to-morrow, with all his harness, leaving his horses to follow softly. He makes the more haste because he would be loth to be returned. "For, me Lor, nhow I am howar (over), yf the Frynche[men] wold for sake thyr challang, as I thynke thay wyll not for scham, et (yet) I may dow the Kyn[g] odder byssenes, and coum the sounar hom. W[here] for, me Lor, I by sche (beseech) you hold your hand fast that I by not sent for bake; for I am suar that the fader and the son wold not for no good I schold styke wyet the Frynche Kyng; bout [so] I troust to doo. And I dowth not bout I knaw hall thyr dryeftes."[18]

Brandon believed that Norfolk went along with the French king as most of the women attending Mary were servants of Wolsey and Brandon, so dismissing them would mean they could not feed information to either man. Brandon also went on to state that if Henry VIII found out how unhappy his sister was, Norfolk would not hesitate to lay the blame on Brandon or Wolsey, or both.[19] It should be noted that at this stage of his career Brandon had a close working relationship with Wolsey and the tension between Brandon and Norfolk, which would continue throughout their lives, was already evident.

Charles Brandon was not present during Mary's journey to France or for her wedding to the French king. Henry VIII chose to keep his friend behind; he had other tasks for the duke. First he was to help organise the jousts to celebrate the marriage of Mary and

Louis XII and also represent the English, but more importantly he was to begin negotiations for Henry and Louis to meet sometime in the spring, hopefully to arrange a mutual attack against Ferdinand of Aragon.[20]

Brandon was sent to France in mid-October, and he first met with the French king at Beauvais on 25 October. Unfortunately, at this time the king was ill and had to meet Brandon while he was on his sick bed. Mary was also present, sitting beside her husband. In their discussion Louis XII warmly embraced Brandon, and the pair spoke of the upcoming jousts to celebrate the marriage.[21]

This Thursday, 25 Oct., my Lord Marquis and he came to Bowoes (Beauvais) where the King and Queen both were, and were brought to their lodging. By the King's request, communicated to him by Cleremond, he went to his Grace alone. Found the King lying in bed, and the Queen sitting by the bedside. 'And so I diede me rywarynes and knyelled downe by hes byed sede; and soo he brassed me in hes armes, and held me a good wyell, and said that I was hartylle wyecoum, and axsed me, "How dows men esspysseall good brodar, whom I am so moche bounden to lowf abouf hall the warld?"' To which Suffolk replied, that the King his master recommended himself to his entirely beloved brother, and thanked him for the great honor and [love] that he showed to the Queen his sister. The French King answered, that he knew the nobleness and truth so much in Suffolk's master that he reckoned he had of him the greatest jewel ever one prince had of another. Assures Henry that never Queen behaved herself more wisely and honorably, and so say all the noblemen in France; and no man ever set his mind more upon a woman on account of her loving manner. As to the jousts and tournays, my Lord Marquis and the writer both thought if they had answered the challenge it were little honor to win, seeing there were 200 or 300 answerers. The King had promised to introduce them to the Dauphin to be his aids. On the Dauphin's arrival he sent for them, expressed his sense of the honor done him by the King of England, said he would not take them for his aids but for his brethren, and so went to supper; where supped the Duke of Bourbon and my Lord Marquis and I, and 'it he tabylles' [at the tables] young Count Galleas and two others. As they sat at supper they talked of Henry's running, 'of which, I ensure you, he was right glad to hear; and as far as I can see he is not so well content with nothing [as to] hear talking of your grace, and to talk of you [him]self.' The challenge, he said, would be in seven days, which was too soon for them to be ready. We agreed that it was; and thereupon he sent for 'Robart tyete' [*Robertet*] and sent him to the King, who was content to respite it 15 days.[22]

Brandon would continue negotiations with the French king over the next few weeks:

Louis can give no certain answer, because he does not know the laws of the kingdom of Spain; but without entering upon this he is willing to join the King in prosecuting his claims and expelling Ferdinand from Navarre, and will raise an army with him for that purpose. But, without disclosing their intentions, each King is to hear the ambassadors of Aragon. England and France shall communicate by their ambassadors upon this matter without concealment on either side. No arrangement shall be made without mutual consent. In return Suffolk is to explain to the King of England the history of the claim of Louis to the duchy of Milan, of which a brief is given; is to request the aid of England in its recovery, and a loan for one year of 200,000 crowns, on good security. He hopes the enterprise will be ready by the month of March.[23]

Louis XII initially pretended to be enthusiastic about a joint attack against Ferdinand, but in truth he was only interested in recovering Milan for France. He welcomed England's support in this campaign but was vague in setting an actual date for a meeting with Henry VIII.[24] Despite Brandon's lack of diplomatic experience and preoccupation with organising the jousting events, he did manage to get the French king to agree to a meeting with Henry (although no actual date was set) as well as to start to discuss some possible strategies for a joint attack.[25] Louis was impressed with Brandon's efforts,[26] stating that 'no prince christened hath such a servant for peace and war'.[27]

On 25 October, Brandon wrote to Henry VIII to inform him of the discussions he had been having with the French king and of the upcoming jousting tournaments. He also wrote, 'I bysche yovr grace to [tell my]sstres Blount and mysstres Carru [the] next tyme yt I wreth un to them [or se]nd them tokones thay schall odar [wre] th to me or send me tokones agayen.'[28]

Brandon refers to Mistress Blount aka Elizabeth 'Bessie' Blount and Mistress Carew aka Elizabeth Carew, wife of Nicholas Carew. Both women were part of Queen Katherine's court at the time; close friends, they were said to be extremely beautiful.[29] At first reading it may be suggested that this letter meant that Charles Brandon was in a sexual relationship with Bessie Blount and/or Elizabeth Carew; however, this may not be the case. Courtly love was a common theme in Henry VIII's court. It was not unusual for a man to send tokens, poems or letters to beautiful women and to receive them in return. It was not expected that a full physical relationship should ensue thereafter; it was simply a means for expressing love and desire at court in emilation of the Arthurian legends of old. It is known that Henry lavished expensive gifts upon both Elizabeth Carew and Bessie Blount and that he began a sexual relationship with Bessie Blount sometime after 1514. It cannot be stated with any certainty that Brandon had a sexual affair with either woman. It seems highly doubtful that he would have slept with the wife of Nicholas Carew, one of his close friends and a member of the king's inner circle.[30]

On 5 November, Mary was crowned Queen of France in Paris.[31] The whole court attended, including Brandon. Afterwards another great feast was held for the new queen. Shortly after, on the 9th, Brandon received a French pension of 1,000 crowns.[32] The official celebratory tournaments began on the 13th.[33] As England's representative, and one who had helped organise the jousts, Brandon naturally took part:

My Lord of Suffolk and he ran three days, and lost nothing. One Frenchman was slain at the tilt, and divers horses. On Saturday the 18th, 'the tournay and course in the field began as roughly as ever I saw; for there was divers times both horse and man overthrown, horses slain, and one Frenchman hurt that he is not like to live. My Lord of Suffolk and I ran but the first day thereat, but put our ayds thereto, because there was no noblemen to be put unto us, but poor men of arms and Scots, many of them were hurt on both sides, but no great hurt, and of our Englishmen none overthrown nor greatly hurt but a little of their hands. The Dolphyn himself was a little hurt on his hand.' On Tuesday, the 21st, the fighting on foot began, 'to the which they brought an Almayn that never came into the field before, and put him to my Lord of Suffolk to have put us to shame if they could, but advantage they gat none of us, but rather the contrary. I forbear to write more of our chances, because I am party therein. I ende[d] without any manner hurt; my Lord of Suffolk is a little hurt in his hand.'[34]

Brandon performed excellently at the jousts and in hand-to-hand combat.[35] In fact, he did so well that there seemed to be few Frenchmen who could compare to him at the tilt. Brandon ran fifteen courses on the first day, thirteen of them as the challenger. On the second day, he unhorsed his opponent on three consecutive occasions.[36] To try and outshine Brandon, the French brought in an enormous German of great strength and skill, but Brandon was not to be beaten. After unhorsing his German opponent, Brandon struck him with the butt end of his spear, causing the German to stagger. The fighting continued. After lifting their visors to draw breath, Brandon and the German continued to fight with blunt-edged swords. Despite his opponent's ferocity, Brandon was more skilful than the German and managed to beat him about the head until 'blood came out of his nose'.[37] Brandon emerged with only a sore hand.[38] Mary would have been present at these events, able to watch Brandon joust and fight. Mary's thoughts about this dashing, athletic thirty-year-old remain unknown, yet one cannot help but wonder if she was secretly cheering for Brandon to win.

Brandon's response to the events was modest. He wrote a short note to Henry VIII: 'My lord at the Writing of this lettre the Justes were doon and blissed be god alle our englissh men sped well as I am sure ye shall here by other.'[39]

Instead of trying to build himself up in the king's eyes, Brandon kept his success to himself, instead choosing to praise the victories of the English in general. Despite such modesty, Brandon's achievement helped to secure support amongst many of the French noblemen just as it further endeared him to the French king.[40]

On 18 November, shortly before he returned to England, Brandon wrote a letter to Cardinal Wolsey informing him that Mary had been crowned queen and also that the Duke of Albany had spoken with him regarding his return to Scotland. Brandon said that he felt he had no power in such a decision and would pass the matter on to Henry VIII. Brandon also writes of a discussion he had with Mary regarding her wishing she had good friends about her; he says that he asked the Duke of Longueville and the Bishop of St Paul's to come and meet with her as they would be 'good and loving to her' and could advise her and provide counsel. Clearly, with Louis XII having dismissed most of Mary's ladies, she was still seeking some support and guidance in this new stage of her life.

Myne owne good Lorde I recommend me unto you and so it is that I have receyved your Letter writen at Grenewiche on Alle Soulen daye the ij le day of Novembre wherby I percey ve that the Kinges Grace was well contented with my writing My Lord this Letter shall be to advertise you of alle suche thinges as I can know syns my last writing the whiche was the iijle daye of Novembre My Lorde so it is that on the Sonday after the writing of my last letter the Quene was crowned right honorably and at after noon we and the Frensh Kinges Counsaill went to geder and determyned according as we wrote unto the Kinges Grace yn a lettre My Lord syns the writing of that letter the Duke of Albany came to my lodging and saide that he was come to speke with me and that it was the King his maisters mynde that he shulde breke with me of a mater and I said that I wold be content to here what the King his maisters pleasure was by hym or by any other body and so apon that he began and saide that the Kinges mynde was that he shulde goo into Scotland and that he trusted that his going shuld doo good for he entended to reduse theym of Scotland to be contented to take such a Peas as shuld be for the King my maisters honour and for the suertie of the children and because that there shuld be no suspecion he had maryed and he wold leve his wife in Fraunce and also he wold come by the King my maister and wold retorne assone as he myght possible for he must goo over the Moun tayns with many othre wordes And so whanne I had herd hym alle that he wolde saye I shewed unto hym that I had no commyssion to medill of suche maters and thenne he said that the Frensh King wold speke with me in the mater and I said that and his Grace did I wold make his Grace suche an answere that his Grace shuld be content and so syns I herd no more of the mater How be it my Lord Chamberlayne and Doctour West shewed me that the Frenshe Kinges Counsaill had bien in hand with thaym upon the going of the said Duke and apon that we and they toke a conclusion to advertise the King therof in all haste and if so were that the Frenssh King wold be in hand with me I shuld doo alle that is in me possible to let his going and I ensure you I woll doo soo for I pro myse you he entendith not well as fer as I can per ceyve My Lorde as touching the othre busynes secrete crete I wolle goo in hand therewith in all the haste I can because I wolde come awaye praying you that I have no more busynes to let me for I ensure you I have many thinges to shew the King that I will not write My Lord it was soo that three daies before my Lord Chamberlayn went the Quene shewed to me and to my Lorde Marques divers thinges the whiche we woll shew you at our comyng wherby we per ceyve that she had nede of some good friendes about the King and so we called my Lord Chamberlayne my Lord of Saint John's and Doctor West and shewed them parte of the mater and we shewed unto them that we thought it best that we shuld sende for my Lord Longuevyle the Busshop of Saint Paules Robert Tete a and the Generall of Normandy and shewed unto theym that the Quene had sent for us and desired us that we wold send for theym and desire theym on hir behalff and in the name of the King oure maister that they wold be good and loving to hir and that they wolde gyve hir counsaill frome tyme to tyme how she myght best order hir selff to content the King wherof she was moost desirous and in hir shuld lak no good wille and bicause she knew well they were the men that the King loved and trusted and knew best his mynde therfore she was utterly determyned to love theym and trust theym and to be ordred by thair Counsaill in all causes for she knew well that thoes that the King loved must love hir best and she theym and so we did And whenne we had shewed theym all this on the Quenes bihalff they were very well contented and said that they wold make reporte unto the King what honorable and lovyng request she had made the whiche they said wold content hym very well And they thankid hir Grace for hir good mynde toward thaym and said that they wold doo in every thing hir request and to accept and take hir as theire Soverain Quene and to counsaill hir on every behalff to the best of thair powers to doo the thing that shuld pleas the King thaire maister Of which maters they have promysed us to assure unto hir Grace whansoever it shal be hir pleasure and within thies ij daies our entencion is to bryng theym unto the Quenes Grace according to our comunicacion and appoyntment My Lord at the writing of this letter the Justes were doon and blissed be God alle our Englissh men sped well as I am sure ye shall here by othre And thus I comyt you to the Holy Ghoost whoo ever preserve you Frome Parise the xviij day of Novembre by your assured CHARLYS SUFFOLKE To my Lorde of Yorke.[41]

After the celebrations, Brandon was recalled home where he was greeted warmly by Henry and Thomas Wolsey,[42] who in 1515 would be created a cardinal by Pope Leo X. The next time Brandon journeyed to France it would be to bring the newly widowed Mary back to England.

Less than three months after their marriage, on 1 January 1515, Louis XII died.[43] He had been sick for several weeks previously, and his death came as no surprise although it was reported that Mary fainted on hearing the news. Mary was sent to Cluny where she wore white, the French colour of mourning.[44] She was to stay in seclusion for forty days so that it could be determined if she was pregnant with an heir to the throne. However, no one believed that she was, and Francis, husband of Louis XII's daughter Claude, was quickly accepted as the next king.[45]

Back in England, on the same day that the French king died, Charles Brandon participated in a masque in Queen Katherine of Aragon's chambers. Eight dancers were involved in the masque, four men and four women. The men were Nicholas Carew, Lord Fellinger, Henry VIII and Charles Brandon. The four women were Elizabeth Carew, Bessie Blount, Lady Guildford and Lady Fellinger. They were dressed in cloth of silver and blue velvet with the letters H and K embroidered on them.[46]

Once the news of the French king's death reached England, Brandon was sent to France to return the dowager queen and hopefully to retrieve as much of Mary's coin, plate and jewels as possible.[47] As metioned previously, before Brandon left it was reported that Henry VIII made him swear not to marry Mary during the journey.[48] Did Brandon swear such an oath? We do not know, but if it were so it would have been a very serious matter, as an oath was not lightly broken. It could have been that Henry VIII did intend to fulfil the promise he made to his sister and, knowing of her affection for Brandon, would allow her to marry him but not until they returned home. It could also be that Henry VIII, ever the wily politician, agreed in principle to the marriage but planned to seek a far more advantageous match for her elsewhere once she was safely back in England. We know that a high-born woman of that age had little control over her life in any event, and Henry could well have been completely indifferent to any feelings or desires Mary might have harboured so long as there was a chance of political gain in her betrothal.

Just before Brandon arrived in Paris to meet with Mary, two friars met with the dowager queen to turn her mind against Charles Brandon. They informed her that the English council would never let her marry him and, worse, that Brandon and Thomas Wolsey had performed witchcraft to bend Henry VIII's mind to their will. They even went so far as to suggest that Brandon's witchcraft caused William Compton, Henry VIII's Groom of the Stool, to fall ill. When he heard this news, Brandon immediately informed Wolsey. He proposed that someone must have been coaching the friars and hinted that this person was the Duke of Norfolk. Once again, the enmity between Norfolk and Brandon is exhibited.[49] However, if it was Norfolk who sent the friars to meet with Mary then the duke must have been aware of some romantic tension between Brandon and Mary. At this stage, then, their feelings towards one another were becoming well known to those at court.

Brandon finally arrived in Paris on 31 January 1515. He met with Mary the same day and reported that Mary was eager to return home so that 'she may see her brother'.[50] Brandon was to face two significant difficulties in the negotiations required before Mary could be safely extricated from the French court and returned to England. The first concerned her jewellery. If the late king had given them to her as queen, then they were to stay in France as the jewels belonged to the future queen. However, if they were given to

Mary as personal presents, then she would be entitled to take them home with her to England.[51] The second difficulty was that the new king, Francis I, was reluctant to let Mary leave. In a meeting with the English ambassadors, Francis I stated that he did not wish for her to depart from France for at least a year.[52]

Mary was only eighteen years of age, young, beautiful and available to marry again. While in France, she was vulnerable as Francis I could use her as a bargaining tool. He could have had her married to some French nobleman to buttress the alliance with England; he could even have arranged her marriage to someone suitably highborn from another country to form some new alliance dictated by French interests. There is also speculation that Francis I feared a new alliance between England and the Holy Roman Empire, with Henry VIII renewing Mary's previous betrothal to Prince Charles as part of the deal. Furthermore, if Mary remained in France, Francis I could keep her jewels and save on her travel expenses.[53] It was even rumoured that Francis had an interest in marrying the beautiful young Mary himself,[54] although that seems unlikely given that he would have had to divorce his current wife, the late king's daughter, to do so. Such complications were to be the least of Charles Brandon's difficulties.

A Marriage of Unequals

Knowing that Mary was now a young, vulnerable widow in a foreign country, Thomas Wolsey wrote frantically to his master's sister:

> Having been informed of the danger of the King her husband, 'and that [in] likelihood or this time he is departed to the mercy of God,' offers his consolation and advice 'how your grace shall demean [yourself], being in this heaviness and among strangers, far from [your] most loving brother and other your assured friends and servants. Touching your consolation I most heartily beseech your grace, with thanksgiving to God, to take wisely and patiently such visitation of Almighty God, against whose ordinance no earthy creature may be, and not by extremity of sorrow to hurt your noble person.' Assures her that Henry will not forsake her; and begs her, for the old service the writer has done her, to do nothing without the advice of his grace, however she should be persuaded to the contrary, and to let nothing pass her mouth 'whereby any person in these parts may have [you] at any advantage. And if any motions of marriage or other [offers] fortune to be made unto you, in no wise give hearing to them. And thus doing ye shall not fail to have the King fast and loving to you, to aitain to your desire [and come] home again into England with as much honor as [queen ever] had. And for my part, to the effusion of my [blood and spen]dyng of my goods, I shall never forsake nor leav[e you].'[1]

Mary Tudor was far stronger than Wolsey had given her credit for, and with such uncertainty surrounding her future, she decided to take matters into her own hands. The young dowager queen proposed marriage to Charles Brandon and the duke accepted.[2] Whether this was a spontaneous decision or thought about for several days, perhaps even longer, we cannot know. However, matters were finally decided, and Mary and Brandon married in secret, without Henry VIII's permission. Although the exact date of their wedding remains unknown, it can be confidently stated that the pair married either on 31 January or on 1 or 2 February before approximately ten witnesses[3] at the chapel in Cluny.[4] This can be verified as on 3 February Brandon wrote to Wolsey regarding a meeting with the French king at which it became clear that Francis already knew of the wedding – Mary had told him. What extraordinary courage she showed, defying the rigid codes that would have been imposed upon her from birth. We can speculate that this was her one chance of happiness – and she took it!

My very good lord,

I recommend me unto you and so it is, I need not write yon of none thing [but only of] a matter secret, for all other matters you shall perceive by the letters sent to the king, the one from me, and the other from my fellows and me. My lord, so it was that the same day that the French king gave us audience, his grace called me unto him, and had me into his bed-chamber, and said unto me 'My Lord of Suffolk, so it is that there is a bruit in this my realm, that you are come to marry with the queen, your master's sister;' and when I heard him say I answered and said that I trusted his grace would not reckon no great folly in me, to come into a strange realm and to many a queen of the realm, without the knowledge, and without authority from the king my master to him, and that they both might be content; but I said I assured his grace that I had no such tiling, and that it was never intended on the king my masters behalf, nor on mine—and then he said it was not so; for then [since] that I would not be plain with him he would be plain with me, and showed me that the queen herself had broken her mind onto him, and that he had promised her his faith and truth, and by the truth of a king, that

he would help her, and to d[o what was possi]bly in him to help
her to obtain her heart's desire. And because that you shall not
th[ink that I do] bear you this in hand, and that [she has not spo]
ke her mind, I will s[hew you some word]s that you had to her
[grace] and so showed me a ware word, the which none alive
could tell them but she; and when that then I was abashed, and
he saw that, and said, because for [that] you shall say that you
have found a kind prince and a loving, and because you shall not
think m[e] other here I give you, in your hand, my faith and truth,
by the word of a King, that I shall never fail unto you, but to help
and advance this Marriage betwixt her and you, with as good a
will as (I) would for mine own [self].'And when he had done this,
I could do none less than thank his grace for the great goodness
that his grace intended to show unto the queen and me, and by
it I showed his grace that I was like to be undone, if this matter
should come to the knowledge of the king my master: and then
he said, 'Let me alone for that; I and the queen shall so instance
your master that I trust that he would be content; and because
I would gladly put your heart at rest, I will, when I come to Paris,
speak with the queen, and she and I both will write letters to the
king your master, with our own hands, in the best manner that
can be devised.'

My lord, these were his proper words; [as I] do advertise you;
not intending to hide [this or] any other matter from yon; praying
yon, with all the haste possible, send me your best [council that
yo]u shall think best that I shall [do in this mat]ter; and if you
shall think good [to advertise his] B grace of this letter, I pray yon
[also to give mi]ne assurances to his highness, that I had [rather,
had I dared, have written] unto him myself.

My lord, after mine opinion, I find myself much [bound] to
God, considering that he that I feared most is contented to be the
doer of this act himself, and to instance the king my master in the
same [where] his 'grace shall be marvellously discharged [as well]
against his council, as all the other noble men of his realm. And
thus mine own good lord, I bid yon most heartily farewell,
trusting to hear from yon in all the haste (possible). My cousin
Wingfield has put me in remembrance of your affairs which be
not forgotten, as you shall well know, by my next letters; and of
one thing be you assured, that the amity going forth between the

two princes, that we both shall be as well entreated of the king here as ever any two in England. By yours assured, written at some haste 10 leagues from Paris, the third day of February.

To my Lord of York. Charles Suffolk.[5]

To this letter, Thomas Wolsey replied that he had

... received his letter written with his own hand, dated Paris, the 3rd. Is glad to hear of the good mind of the French King towards his marriage with the French Queen, and his proposal to write to Henry in its favor. The King is glad to hear of Suffolk's discreet behavior, when the French King 'first secretly brake with you of the said marriage,' and desires that he will procure the said letters, as constant practices are made to prevent the match. Wolsey thinks that he shall bring it to a successful conclusion, and Suffolk will know that he has in him a firm friend.[6]

For the time being Charles Brandon was publicly presenting himself as a loyal servant to his king, keeping his marriage to Henry VIII's sister a secret. On 8 February, he wrote to Henry regarding his journey and his reception at the French court:

Wrote last from Saunt Lyestes (Senlis) on the 4 Feb. 'We' came to Paris the next day, which was Sunday, and on Monday in the morning went to 'the Queen your sister,' to whom they delivered the King's letters, according to their instructions. The Queen was not a little glad, and said she was 'much bounden to God that had given her so good and loving a brother, and now specially in her most need, and prayed she might live no longer than that she might do that thing that should be to his contentation'. To Suffolk's inquiries relative to the French King's conduct, she replied that he had been 'in hand with her of many matters; but on hearing that Suffolk was come, he promised to trouble her no more, and to do for her as he would for his own mother;' and 'prayd ... sche wold not by a knowne of non theng that h[e had spo]ken to her, noder to your grace nor me, for because your grace schold not take non onkyndnes therene.' 'And [moreov] ar he sayd that wher soo ewar her mend war, [that] he wold by glade to helpe her ther[ein from] hes hart; and soo semes he newar ... [other]wyes, bout as he that wold by to her [as to his m]odar; and soo, Sir, I parssayef that he had ... your grace, for I thynke h[e nold] to do ane thyng that schold dyescountent your grace, schold anne an kyndnes in whe[ch] ... your grace, that I thynke that you schall fynd hem ... a fast prynes. ar elles I wyel say that he es the moste [untrue] man that lyes; and nat he ondylle, bout hall the [nobil] men of Fraunes; for I cannot dywyes to have any spyke byettar dyn they do, nor to your honnar.' The peace between the two Kings is not a little to the writer's comfort, and their meeting is desired by all the nobles. Thinks the journey will be to the King as much [honour] as ever any journey was to any king of England, the people here are so desirous to see him. When they have seen him it will be never out of their hearts. As touching the affair of [the meeting], thinks there is nothing the French King will not do if Henry wish him. Dated [Paris], 8 Feb.[7]

Meanwhile, on the same day, Brandon also wrote another frantic letter to Thomas Wolsey saying that he

... writes nothing of the King's business, for which he refers him to letters written to the King's grace, one from himself, and another from him and his fellows together. Had been in hand with the Queen touching the matter she broke to the French King, as mentioned in his last. She had showed him that the French King made such business, that she was 'soo wyrre and soo afyerd' he should go about to undo Suffolk, she thought it best to break the matter to him, and said, 'Sir, I beseech you that you will let me alone and speak no more to me of the matter; and if you will promise me by your faith and truth, and as you are a true prince, that you will keep it counsel and help me, I will tell you all my whole mind'. And he gave her 'his faith in her hand that he would keep it counsel, and that he would help her to the best of his power.' Having told him her mind, and said she could not think 'but the King her brother w[ould be disp]lysed' with her, she besought him to get the King['s consent]. He said he would do 'that was in him possible, and write to the King her brother with his own hand' – which agrees with what Francis himself told him, as mentioned in his last letter. Now that Wolsey knows all, 'beseeches his good offices as all his trust is in him, and requests [an answer?] in all possible haste'. 'Also, my lord, I pray you that you will look to the ...; for I insure you that, and it be made to the honor [of our] master, as I am sure the French King will do none otherwise, it shall be the greatest honor and wealth to the King my master and the realm of England that ever came to it. Will write to Wolsey what their mind is as soon as he can perceive it, before they send it, and begs Wolsey to do the same to him, if he hear it first. Paris, 8 Feb.[8]

In addition to his letter to Wolsey, Charles Brandon and Mary both wrote to Henry:

Since his coming to [Paris], the Queen [Mary] told him that from the first the King was importunate with her in divers matters not to her honor; and also he had divers words with Francis, which made her afraid his [grace] would have done him some ill; to avoid which she brake in hand with him, and desired him, as he was a true prince, to keep her counsel and to help her to her desire; and upon that he made her promise in her hand as he was a true prince he would both keep it 'scekarret' [secret]. 'Upon that she brake unto him, and showed unto him the good mind she bare unto me.' Hearing this, Francis said he would keep his promise, and do as much as he could to the advancement thereof. He had mentioned to Suffolk, what words the Queen had used. At her request Francis had written to the King with his own hand, on a subject which Suffolk did not choose to commit to writing. Begs the King to be good lord to him, as he has ever been, and to [write] to him again with his own hand that he was content with this matter at his ryquy[est], the which shall bind him. 'And, Sir, if your grace should not, he shall be at his liberty and again in his former suttes [suits?], the which I and the Queen had rather be out of the world [than] to abide. And, Sir, as for me, your grace not offended, I had rather be out of the world [than] to see her in that case. Sir, as my poor mind is, there can be no way that should stand more [to your] honnor dyn to consent by desire [of the French King], seeing that you are so special good lord [unto] me that I should obtain the same. As knoweth God, who pressarf your grace,' &c. Pa[ris, ...] February. P.S.—'[Touch]yng hall oddar afyeres and the Quynes, [your] grace shall understand them by a letter [that I] and my fellows does write unto your Grace.' The coming home of the Queen shall tarry nothing but the King's pleasure. Both she and Suffolk beseech him 'for the passion of God' to send for her as soon as possible. As to the meeting of Henry and the French King, the latter has none other joy but to talk of it; 'and therefore, Sir, you must make ... euredie [you ready].' Begs again that the King will send for him, and not suffer him to tarry here.[9]

Brandon starts off the letter by noting that Francis I was not behaving like a true and rightful king towards Mary and that she felt genuinely afraid of him. Brandon then begs the king to be good to him, and Mary pleads with her brother that they should be allowed to return home. Perhaps the realisation of what they had done – Mary marrying again and Brandon committing treason by marrying a member of royalty without the king's consent – was starting to set in. It is unclear if Henry VIII received this letter or if it remained in the hands of Thomas Wolsey.

On the same day, Francis I wrote to Henry VIII informing him of his knowledge of Brandon and Mary's marriage:

[He] has been to visit the queen his 'belle-mère,' Henry's sister, as he used to do, to know if he could show her any attention. On his asking whether she contemplated a second marriage, she confessed the great esteem she had for the Duke of Suffolk, 'que davant t[out] autre ele desyreroyt aveque [la] bonne voulonté et lamye ... maryage dele et de luy se fys[t],' and prayed him not only to give his own consent, but to write to Henry in Suffolk's favor, which he now does.[10]

Brandon again wrote directly to Henry VIII, surely realising the magnitude of his offence. However, it does not appear that Henry received the letter straight away. Instead, it may have rested in the hands of his right-hand man Thomas Wolsey until Wolsey found an appropriate moment to break the news of the marriage to the king.

Has received his letter and [been] in hand to the French King touching the answer ... a letter written with his own hand.

Thanks his grace for his letter. Understands [it is said] 'that and I had don me dywar [my devoir] ar wold do me dewar, the Quyen schold optayn hall her stouf and jowyelles. As tocheyng that and yf I have not don the byest ther[in] and wyell doo the byst ther in, newar by [g]ood lord to me; and that I rypourt me to me fyllowes.' If he had not done his best it were pity [that he] lived: 'for I find you so good lord to me that there is none thing that grieves me but that she and I have no more to content your grace. But, Sir, as she has written to you of her own hand, she is content to give you all that her grace shall have by the right of her wosbound (husband); and, if it come not so much as your grace thought, she is content to give your grace what sum you shall be content to axe, to be paid on her jointure, and all that she has in this world.

Alas, Sir, as I understand it should be thought that I should incline too much to the French King's mind. Sir, if ever I inclined to him in thought or deed otherwise than might stand with your honor and profit according to my truth, [let] me die for it; and if ever I meddled in any matter in word or deed with him other than here ... es, never be good lord to me.' (1.) At first meeting with him, the French King broke to him the matter between the Queen and him, to which he answered as he has [written] before. Second, touching Tournay, he first desired the French King to call his fellows and afterwards excused himself from entering upon it, as he had no commission to do so. He, however, by advice of his fellows, communicated the French King's desire to the King. And because the French King would make Suffolk judge in the matter that Henry might think he would do nothing without instructions, if it were his grace's mind to depart with it, 'Sir, now I will say that never passed my mouth but once to your grace. There is but few of y[our] Council but has been in hand with me and [think] it best you should depart with it, so you might depart with it honorably. Yet, Sir, I insure your grace, that I have not put the French King in none hope of it; in so much [that I have] caused him to leave it out of his instructions given to his ambassadors, to the inte[nt that] he should not do manner [?] any thing that should [not] be to your contentation ("countasseun"), but to refer it [to your] pleasure whether that you would be content [with the] instructions given to me or my fel[lows] ... shall send to his ambassadors or...'

The reason why he would have been satisfied with the French King's proposition was that he thought it more for the King's honor and profit to be judged by his own subject, as his grace might know that to die for it he would not have done otherwise than according to his pleasure; and he fears not but that he has handled himself truly according to his allegiance, whatever his enemies may say. (3.) As to the privy amity, 'there was never ... gyng nor man nor woman that ever spoke to him of it, but it was only my own mind, because I saw the ambassadors soo bysse [busy?] to have the marriage and amity with France that I could ... her cold [?] by non better way than to make ... amity to make them know that they have gone out of the way, and that they should be fain to ... to you. Sir, the was men pour apynneun ([this was my poor opinion], which I trust your grace taking as I ...was none harm.' ... Begs the King not to let his enemies [have an advantage over him], as he never went about to hurt any man in his life; 'and your grace [knoweth] best nor I never sought other remedy [against] mine enemies but your grace, nor never [will]: for it is your grace that has made me of [nothing] and holden me up hitherto; and if your [pleasure] be so for to do, I care not for all the world.

Sir, I beseech your grace to [be good lord to] my servant this bearer, for [he shall advertise] your grace of matters secret; [to whom I be]seech your grace to give credence [as to my]self.

Matters between the French [King and your] grace, if ever you find that ever I ... him, or meddled with him otherwise [than I] have written unto your grace, let me ... it that I have showed him what a man you [are], both in condition and everything, the [wh]ich I [*sic*] delights marvelously to hear and I le[ver] to tell it to him, saying that and he have you ... comes and see you, that he shall find that I am none liar. And therefore, Sir, and it may please God and you, I pray God I may see you two once meet, and then I trust that I shall be found a true gentleman, both of my report of your grace and also of the report that I have written to your grace of him.' Begs to have 'some word of comfort' from the King: 'for I promes your grace that I was newarday holl [sith] esnes I parted from your grace. And, Sir, at the writing of this I was not very well; and [with]out I may hear good tidings from your grace, I pray God that I never live to thyn ... Paris.

Sir, one thing I insure your grace, that it shall never be said that ever I did offend [your] grace in word, deed or thought, but for this [matter] touching the Queen, your sister, the which I ca[n no] lynggar nor wolnot hide fro your grace. Sir, so it is that when I came to Paris the Queen was in hand with me the first day I [came], and said she must be short with me and [open] to me her pleasure and mind; and so she b[egan] and show how good lady [she] was to me, and if I would be ordered by her she would never have none but me. ... She showed me she had wyerelle [verily?] und[erstood] as well by Friar Langglay and Friar Fr ... dar that and yewar sche cam in Ynggyll [and she sho]uld newar have me; and ther for sche ... wr that and I wold not marre her ... have me nor never come to [England] When I heard her say so I showed ... plied that but to prove me with, and she ... would not you knew well that my coming ... it was showed her ... and I axsed her wat [it] was; and she said that the best in France had [said] unto her that, and she went into England, she should go into Flanders. To the which she said that she had rather to be torn in pieces than ever she should come there, and with that wept. Sir, I never saw woman so weep; and when I saw [that] I showed unto her grace that there was none such thing [upon] my faith, with the best words I could: but in none ways I could make her to believe it. And when I saw that, I showed her grace that, and her grace would be content to write unto your grace and to obtain your good will, I would be content; or else I durst not, because I had made unto your grace such a promise. Whereunto, in conclusion, she said, "If the King my brother is content and the French King both, the tone by his letters and the todar by his words, that I should have [y]ou, I will have the time after my desire, or else I may well think that the words of ... in these parts and of them in England [be] true and that is that you are come to tyes me home [?] [to the in]tent that I may be married into Fland[ers], which I will never, to die for it; and so [I posse] ssed the French King ar you cam [?]; and th[at if] you will not be content to follow [my] end, look never after this d[ay to have] the proffer again." And, Sir, I ... in that case and I thought ... but rather to put me ... than to lyes all, and so I gra ... an too; and so she and I was ma[rried] ... and but ten persons, of the which [neither Sir Richard] Wyngfyld nor Master Dyne [Dean] was not [present] on my faith; for she would that I should [not take] them on council, for she said and I did [so] … she thought they would give mo couns[el] to the contrary; and therefore they know not of it, nor that the writing of this letter, on my faith and truth.' Has written word by word, as near as he can, how everything was, and begs the King to forgive him and defend him against his enemies, who will think to put him out of favor.[11]

On 11 February, Brandon heard from Wolsey once more:

My lord, I have received a letter [from Mr.] Wyngfyeld and me Chansseller, wherein [he advertises] me what pain you take daily for my cause [and how] good lord you are to me, for the which and h[all the] goodness that I find in you I heartily thank [you, as] he that shall never fail you during my life. Begs to hear from him from time to time. As for the French King I cannot wyche hem [in better mind] towar[d] the King's grace dyn I her hem spyked (than I hear him speak it) … and as for you and me I trow that nexte the Ky[ng] howar masstar wy had newar scheth a frynd; wyche you shall parsayef her aftar.[12]

On 12 February, Brandon wrote again to Henry, first to inform him of business with the French king and then in a postscript imploring the king to keep him in mind and offering that his heart is always with his sovereign. Noticeably, he does not refer to the marriage, only his loyalty:

This day the French King sent for him by Mons. the Bousse to see him at the tilt, where he saw him run, and five with him, against the Duke of [Lor]rayn, and five with him, 'for a banket;' and [I] insure your grace there was good running. The King himself ran clearly best; for in six courses he broke five staves. Soon after he had done he went to dinner. After dinner Suffolk had an interview with him, for particulars of which he refers the King to a letter written by him and his fellows to my Lord of York. With regard to the meeting, Francis said that if Henry would appoint the time he should be ready. Paris, 12 Feb.

P.S.—Sir, I by scheth [beseech] your grace that I [might hear from your] grace som tyme, for et schold by to [my great] coum fort [comfort]. Sir, I by sche (beseech) your grace that I [may be] most youmbylle rycummanded un to the [Queen's?] grace and to hall me nold (all mine old) fyellowes, bowth [men] and women; and tyll them that I thynke no [little] an kyngnes in thym hall that I newar hard f[rom] non of thym senes I dy partted from y[ou]; bout I thynke the faute has byn in the wy ... [weather ?] and not in thym. Sir, I by sche your grace [that] I be not forgootton amongest your ar..; for daw [though] me bodde by [be] her me hart es wyet yo[u] and you wat whyer.'[13]

In turn, Wolsey wrote back to Brandon on behalf of the king:

After consulting with the Council [on Sunday last], the King called Wolsey apart and bid him write to Suffolk to use all efforts to obtain from the French King his plate of gold and jewels. Doubts not he will succeed if he insist upon it. He would be glad to allow Suffolk to return with the Queen, but not until he has completed her business. Advises him, therefore, 'substantially to handle that matter and to stick thereunto; for I assure you the hope that the King hath to obtain the said plate and jewels is the thing that most stayeth his grace constantly to assent that ye should marry his sister; the lack whereof, I fear me, might make him cold and remiss and cause some alteration, whereof all men here, except his grace and myself, would be right glad.' Encloses copy of the letter the King has written with his own hand to the French King. Could not induce him by any persuasion to write otherwise; 'for his grace thinketh that if he should make plain grant at the first instance of the French King he would think that his grace was agreed to the said marriage before your coming thither, and so consequently the French King might think that ye had not been plain with him'. 'Is to tell the French King that Henry reciprocates his desire for the interview; but, as the amity must first be concluded, Suffolk must, as of his own accord, procure the speedy dispatch of the French ambassadors. He may feel the French King's mind, what pastimes he intends to have and whether he would be content to come to Calais, St. Peter's or some place within the Marches.'[14]

It was clear by this stage that Henry VIII knew of the marriage of his sister to Brandon and that he would only agree to it if Brandon were able to return with as much of Mary's dowry as possible. Henry wanted his money back!

Charles Brandon had made a bold move in agreeing to marry the dowager queen. It was a decision that put a stop to any possible marriage plans the French king might have had for Mary to create an alliance with another country, or even continue the alliance with England. The marriage also removed her as a bargaining chip for Henry VIII. Under the circumstances, Henry was extraordinarily forgiving – thus demonstrating his great affection for the duke.

From Brandon's next letter to Wolsey, written on 5 March, it would appear that neither Mary nor Brandon had heard directly from the king. By now they were playing a waiting game, hoping to gain the king's favour so that they could return home.

My Lord, I am obliged to you next God and my master, and therefore I will hide none thing from you, trusting that you will help me now as you have always done. Me Lord, so it is that when I came to Paris I heard many things which put me in great fear, and so did the Queen both; and the Queen would never let me be in rest till I had granted her to be married; and so to be plain with you, I have married her heartily, and have lain with her, insomuch I fear me lest she be with child. My Lord, I am not in a little sorrow if the King should know it, and that his grace should be displeased with me; for I ensure you that I had rather 'a died than he should be miscontent ... let me not be undone now, the which I fear me shall be, without the help of you. Me Lord, think not that ever you shall make any friend that shall be more obliged to you; and therefore me own good Lord ... help me Lord, they marry as well in Lent as out of Lent, with licence of any bishop. Now my Lord, you know all, and in you is all my trust, beseeching you now of your assured help, and that I may have answer from you of this and of the other writings as shortly as may be possible, for I ensure you that I have as heavy a heart as any man living, and shall have until I may hear good news from you.[15]

The anxiety is palpable; to lose the king's favour could be devastating. Interestingly, by now both he and Mary publicly put the blame for the marriage squarely upon Mary. However they came to this decision, it was a very clever ploy on the couple's part as it would be almost impossible for Henry VIII to punish his sister with imprisonment or any other form of harsh treatment.

Brandon also added in a second letter, perhaps on Mary's suggestion, that a diamond with a great pearl belonging to Mary should be sent to the king and that Henry could have whatever plate, gold and jewels of her dowry he desired.[16] This 'diamond with a great pearl' was most likely the famous Mirror of Naples that Louis XII had given to Mary as a gift. Mary and Brandon knew the way back to the king's heart was through riches.

It is believed that Mary smuggled the magnificent Mirror of Naples back to England to give to her brother to help soothe his anger over her marriage. Francis I was reported to have been 'sore displeased at the loss of the diamond called the Mirror of Naples'.[17] Henry declared that it was 'but a small thing and her own by right'[18] – that the jewel had been given to Mary as a personal gift rather than a gift to the Queen of France. If the jewel had been given to Mary as Queen of France, then it would belong to the next queen. Realistically, there was little Francis could do. He offered Henry thirty thousand crowns for the return of the jewel, but the English king laughed at this, saying it was worth twice as much.[19] Henry is reputed to have worn the Mirror of Naples on his hat at his famous meeting with Francis in 1520 called the Field of the Cloth of Gold because of the splendour and extravagance of the two kings and their retinues. Henry was not above taunting his fellow monarch![20]

Having already secretly known of the marriage, it was time for Henry VIII to publicly make a show of being greatly displeased and deeply disappointed in the man he had thought was a close friend and loyal servant but who had betrayed him; not merely because Brandon had committed treason by marrying his sister, but also because he had broken his promise in a world where a man's word was of great importance.[21] In addition, the king needed to be seen to be in control of all things at all times and Mary's marriage to Brandon, without her brother's permission, showed the king as having no control over his own sister and very little over his favourite courtier. It was vital, then, that Henry appeared, at least on the surface, to be furious over the sudden and unexpected marriage. He needed to show that he was not willing to let it quietly go unnoticed, no matter how much he may love his sister and his dear friend. Henry showed his great displeasure by making them pay a hefty fine for their betrayal. He also demanded Mary's entire dowry and insisted that Brandon should somehow convince Francis to pay 200,000 crowns as part of the dowry previously promised.

Wolsey wrote back to Brandon:

My Lord, With sorrowful heart I write unto you, signifying unto the same that I have to my no little discomfort and inward heaviness perceived by your letters, dated at Paris the 5th day of this instant month, how that you be secretly married unto the King's sister, and have accompanied together as man and wife. And albeit ye by your said letters desired me in no wise to disclose the same to the King's grace, yet seeing the same toucheth not only his honor, your promise made to his grace, and also my truth towards the same, I could no less do but incontinent upon the sight of your said letters, declare and show the contents thereof to his highness, which at the first hearing could scantly believe the same to be true: but after I had showed to his grace that by your own writing I had knowledge thereof, his grace, giving credence thereunto, took the same grievously and displeasantly, not only for that ye durst presume to marry his sister without his knowledge, but also for breaking of your promise made to his grace in his hand, I being present, at Eltham; having also such an assured affiance in your truth, that for all the world, and to have been torn with wild horses, ye would not have broken your oath, promise, and assurance, made to his grace, which doth well perceive that he is deceived of the constant and assured trust that he thought to have found in you, and so his grace would I should expressly write unto you. And for my part, no man can be more sorry than I am that ye have so done, being so encumbered therewith that I cannot devise nor study the remedy thereof, considering that ye have failed to him which hath brought you up of low degree to be of this great honor; and that ye were the man in all the world to be loved and trusted best, and was content that with good order and saving of his honor ye should have in marriage his said sister. Cursed be the blind affection and council that hath brought you hereunto! Fearing that such sudden and unadvised dealing shall have sudden repentance. Nevertheless, in this great perplexity, I see no other remedy but first to make your humble pursuits by your own writing, causing also the French king, the queen, with other your friends, to write: with this also that shall follow, which I assure you I write unto you of mine own head without knowledge to any person living, being in great doubt whether the same shall make your peace or no; notwithstanding, if any remedy be, it shall be by that way. It shall be well done that, with all diligence possible, ye and the queen bind yourself by obligation to pay yearly to the King during the queen's life 4,000 of her dower; and so ye and she shall have remaining of the said dower 6,000 and above to live withal yearly. Over and besides this ye must bind yourself to give unto the King the plate of gold and jewels which the late French king had. And whereas the queen shall have full restitution of her dote, ye shall not only give entirely the said dote to the King, but also cause the French king to be bound to pay to the king the 200,000 crowns, which his grace is bounden to pay to the queen, in the full contentation of the said dote de novissimis denariis, and the said French king to acquit the king for the payment thereof; like as the king hath more at the large declared his pleasure to you, by his letters lately sent unto you. This is the way to make your peace; whereat if ye deeply consider what danger ye be and shall be in, having the king's displeasure, I doubt not both the queen and you will not stick, but with all effectual diligence endeavour yourselves to recover the king's favor, as well by this means as by other substantial true ways, which by mine advise ye shall use, and none other, towards his grace, whom by corbobyll [cordial] drifts and ways you cannot abuse. Now I have told you my opinion, hardily follow the same, and trust not too much to your own wit, nor follow the council of them that hath not more deeply considered the dangers of this matter than they have hitherto done. And as touching the overtures made by the French king for Tournay, and also for a new confederation with the king and him, like as I have lately written to you, I would not advise you to wade any further in these matters, for it is to be thought that the French king intendeth to make his hand by favoring you in the attaining to the said marriage; which when he shall perceive that by your means he cannot get such things as he desireth, peradventure he shall show some change and alteration in the queen's affairs, whereof great inconvenience might ensue. Look wisely therefore upon the same, and consider you have enough to do in redressing your own causes; and think it will be hard to induce the king to give you a commission of trust, which hath so lightly regarded the same towards his grace. Thus I have as a friend declared my mind unto you, and never trust to use nor have me in anything contrary to truth, my master's honor, profits, wealth, and surety; to the advancement and furtherance whereof no creature living is more bounden; as our Lord knoweth, who send you grace to look well and deeply upon your acts and doings; for ye put yourself in the greatest danger that ever man was in.[22]

Upon receiving this letter, Brandon wrote directly to Henry VIII begging his forgiveness for his great offence against him:

Begs the King's forgiveness for his offence in this marriage and intreats 'for the passion of God' that it may not turn his heart against him: 'but punish me rather with prison or otherwise as may be your pleasure. Sir, rather than you should have me in mistrust in your [he]art that I should not be true to you as thys may by accusseun, [str]yke of me hed and lyet me not lyef. Alas! Sir, my Lord of York hath written to me two letters that [it] should be thought that the French King would make ... es hand with your grace, and that a would occupy me as [a]n instrument thereunto. Alas! Sir, that ever it should be thought or said that I should be so; for, Sir, your grace not offended, I will make good against all the world [t]o die for it that ever I thought any such thing or did thing, saving the love and [ma]rrag of the Queen, that should be to your displeasure, [I p]ray God let me die as shameful a death as ever did man. But for this he might have said there was never man that had so loving and kind a master as himself, or master that had so true a servant as the King had in him.[23]

Mary also wrote to her brother seeking to remind him that she had agreed to marry the sickly and ageing Louis XII and that he had promised her that she could take a man of her choosing for her second marriage:

Begs he will remember that she had consented to his request, and for the peace of Christendom, to marry Lewis of France, 'though he was very aged and sickly,' on condition that if she survived him she should marry whom she liked. Since her husband was dead, remembering the great virtue in my Lord of Suffolk, 'to whom I have always been of good mind, as ye well know,' she has determined to marry him without any request or labor on his part. She is now so bound to him that for no earthly cause can she change. Begs his good will. Trusted him as one who had always honorably regarded his word. Has come out of France and is at Calais, where she will wait till she hear from him. Binds herself to give up to him her 'dote,' all such plate of gold and jewels as she had with Lewis, and to give such securities for repayment of her dower as he shall think fit.[24]

She asked Henry to excuse her marriage with Suffolk, stating that 'she had constrained him to break his promise to the king. The two friars had put her in despair of the king giving his consent to the match if he came to England.'[25]

Mary also wrote to Wolsey thanking him 'for the letters my Lord of Suffolk lately received by Cooke, by which she perceives that Wolsey will not abandon her and Suffolk in their extreme trouble'.[26]

Nevertheless, by the end of March, Brandon and Mary were still in France. The decision was now made that Mary and Brandon should marry in a more public ceremony. The reason behind this may be the fact that Mary thought herself to be pregnant. If this were the case, then it would be of vital importance that the child was born in wedlock. The pair married for a second time on 31 March.[27] Of the more public wedding, Louise of Savoy, mother of Francis I, reported '*que presque immediatement apres le mort de ce monarque elle donna sa main a un homme de basse condition*'[28] (that almost immediately after the death of the monarch she gave her hand to a man of low rank). Certainly, it did not go unnoticed that Mary, now a dowager Queen of France, had married a duke, a man far beneath her station. This is intriguing as on 12 March Louise had written to Henry VIII requesting that he allow the marriage between Brandon and Mary to happen and assuring him of Brandon's loyalty.[29]

On the same day, Francis I wrote to Henry regarding Mary's marriage and her great desire to return to England:

Had received Henry's letter thanking him for the great affection he had shown to his sister Mary, 'ma belle mère,' and to 'mon cousin' the Duke of Suffolk, and informing him that the said Queen has lately written with her own hand desiring above all things to return to England, which Henry also desires and prays Francis to allow. Thanks Henry for his assurance that he would hold Suffolk 'pour recommandé' on his account. Queen Mary has again told him that she is more and more desirous that the marriage between her and Suffolk should take effect, and has this day desired him again to write to urge Henry to consent to it, which he not only does in this letter, but has written more at length to his ambassador, Mons. de la Guysche, instructing him what to say to Henry on the subject.[30]

Andrea Badoer, the Venetian Ambassador in England, wrote on 31 March that 'the late Queen of France has been married by the Duke of Suffolk, the same who, less than two years ago, was a familiar in another person's service'.[31] It has been suggested that this other person with whom Brandon was familiar was Margaret of Austria. However, besides allowing that some flirting and overstepping of boundaries had occurred, Henry adamantly denied that there had been any prospect of a marriage between Margaret and Charles Brandon.

Brandon was now desperate to return home, and he wrote to Wolsey in haste asking what jewels and plate they could give to Henry to satisfy him.[32] On 16 April, Brandon and Mary left Paris for Calais. They stopped for a time at Montreuil. It is unknown if some message was given to Brandon regarding his status with the king, but on 22 April he wrote a desperate letter to Henry pledging his loyalty and service:

> Most gracious Sovereign Lord, So it is that I am informed divers ways that all your whole council, my Lord of York excepted, with many other, are clearly determined to tympe your grace that I may either be put to death or put in prison, and so to be destroyed. Alas, Sir, I may say that I have a hard fortune, seeing that there was never none of them in trouble but I was glad to help them to my power, and that your grace knows best. And now that I am in this none little trouble and sorrow, now they are ready to help to destroy me. But, Sir, I can no more but God forgive them whatsoever comes to me; for I am determined. For, Sir, your grace

is he that is my sovereign lord and master, and he that hath brought me up out of nought; and I am your subject and servant, and he that hath offended your grace in breaking my promise that I made your grace touching the queen your sister; for the which I, with most humble heart, will yield myself into your grace's hands to do with my poor body your gracious pleasure, not fearing the malice of them; for I know your grace of such nature that it cannot lie in their powers to cause you to destroy me for their malice. But what punishment I have I shall thank God and your grace of it, and think that I have well deserved it, both to God and your grace; as knows our Lord, who send your grace your most honourable heart's desire with long life, and me most sorrowful wretch your gracious favour, what sorrows soever I endure therefor. At Mottryll, the 22nd day of April, by your most humble subject and servant, CHARLES SUFFOLKE.[33]

Brandon's letter is emotional and dramatic. He throws himself on Henry's mercy, acknowledging that he was and is nothing without all that Henry had done for him. He also recognises that he has committed a great sin by breaking his promise to Henry not to marry Mary. Most important of all, Brandon places Henry VIII, his master, above all others. By marrying the sister of a king, Brandon has put himself into a incredibly dangerous position, not only because he has committed treason but because such actions could be perceived as his trying to set himself up as the next king. At this time Henry VIII had no living male heir, and if Brandon could produce a son with Mary then their child could be next in line. But by professing his loyalty to Henry, Brandon calculatedly adopted a pose of submission and weakness to demonstrate to the world that he had no intention of ever betraying Henry or the trust the king held in him.

Brandon writes that he is willing to take any punishment given to him by Henry, but at the same time he hopes that Henry will not punish him 'because of the evil words and malice of others'. This is clever. We know of Brandon's perpetual feud with the Duke of Norfolk, with whom he competed for position, and who also opposed the French alliance, which Brandon and Wolsey supported.[34] Perhaps Norfolk whispered to the other members of the council and sought to turn them against Brandon; or maybe they were genuinely astounded that Brandon would be so presumptuous as to marry the king's sister.

From Montreuil Mary and Charles travelled to the English-held town of Calais where they had to await permission from Henry to board a ship.[35] The couple returned home a fortnight later and landed in Dover on 2 May. They were met by Henry and a great retinue at nearby Birling House. The king greeted the couple warmly and accepted his younger sister's explanation that it was she who was responsible for the marriage and not Brandon.[36]

In return for the king's blessing, Brandon and Mary were ordered not only to return Mary's full dowry, as well as all her plate and jewels, but to also pay £24,000 (£12,000,000)[37] in yearly instalments of £1,000 (£483,000).[38] Mary wrote publicly of her surrendering her plate and jewels:

> Be it known to all manner persons that I, Mary Queen of France, sister unto the King of England, Henry the VIIIth, freely give unto the said King my brother all such plate and vessel of clean gold as the late King Loys of France, the XIIth of that name, gave unto me the said Mary his wife; and also, by these presents I do freely give unto my said brother, King of England, the choice of such special jewels as my said late husband King of France gave me: to the performance whereof I bind me by this my bill, whereto with mine howne hand and signed with my name, and to the same have set my sawlle.[39]

Brandon was also required to give up the wardship of Lady Lisle.[40]

While this was a staggering sum that would have certainly brought Brandon close to beggary (given that marriage to a royal princess would certainly not have been good for his finances anyway), records show that by 1521, six years after their marriage, the couple had only repaid £1,324[41] (£640,000).[42] Henry VIII was more interested in making a show rather than enforcing the regular repayments.

Having gained the king's acceptance of their marriage, Brandon and Mary were formally married at Greenwich on 13 May in front of Henry VIII and Queen Katherine of Aragon.[43] Andrea Badoer and Sebastian Giustinian, the Venetian ambassadors in the English court, described the delicate situation:

On the 13th instant the espousals [*le sponsalitie*] of Queen
Mary to the Duke of Suffolk at length took place; there were no
public demonstrations, because the kingdom did not approve of
the marriage. Wishing to ascertain whether this marriage had
been concluded with the King's consent, were assured by great
personages that it had first been arranged between the bride
and bridegroom, after which they asked the consent of King
Henry, who, however, had maintained his former friendship for
the Duke, which would appear incredible, but is affirmed by the
nobility at the Court. Have, therefore, abstained from paying any
compliments either to the King or to the bride and bridegroom,
but have determined to visit his Majesty in a day or two, and
congratulate him on his sister's arrival. Should they understand
that the great personages of the Court intend to make public
mention of the event, and that it was celebrated, they would
then offer congratulations in the Signory's name on the marriage,
but not seeing it solemnized as becoming, would keep silence,
to avoid giving offence.[44]

Although the king consented to the marriage of his sister to
the Duke of Suffolk, not all in England were happy with the
unconventional marriage.

Against this marriage many men grudged, and said that it was a
great loss to the realm that she was not married to the Prince of
Castile; but the wisest sort was content, considering that if she
had been married again out of this realm, she should have carried
much riches with her; and now she brought every year into the
realm nine or ten thousand marks. But whatsoever the rude people
said, the Duke behaved himself so that he had both the favour of
the king and of the people, his wit and demeanour was such.[45]

Whatever some people might have said of the marriage, it was
clear that many adored the dowager French queen and her
second husband. As an example, when Mary and Brandon visited
Yarmouth in the latter part of 1515 they were warmly welcomed by
the town and entertained for three days. They were so impressed
with the 'urbanity of the people and the situation of the town, that
they promised to prevail on the king to pay a visit to Yarmouth'.[46]

10

Return to Favour

In 1516, Charles Brandon would become a father once more. On 11 March, between ten and eleven o'clock at night, Mary Tudor gave birth to a healthy baby boy at Bath Place, London, a house belonging to Cardinal Wolsey.[1] There is some question as to why Mary gave birth at Bath Place rather than Suffolk Place. It may be that her labour came upon her suddenly and she did not have enough time to go into her lying-in, whereby custom dictates she would have removed herself from the world for several weeks before giving birth. Or it may merely be that due to the duke's relationship with Wolsey, and all the cardinal had done for them in seeing their favour restored with the king, Bath Place was offered to Mary for the birth of her first child. Either way, Brandon now had a son and male heir.

The baby boy was christened Henry after the king. The christening ceremony took place in the hall at Suffolk Place and was conducted with great splendour and ceremony. The hall was lavishly decorated with wall hangings of red and white Tudor roses, torches were lit, and the christening font was warmed for the occasion. John Fisher, Bishop of Rochester, performed the christening assisted by Thomas Ruthal, Bishop of Durham. The king attended the ceremony as did Cardinal Thomas Wolsey, the Duke of Norfolk and other important members of the court. The king and Cardinal Wolsey stood as the godfathers, while Catherine, the dowager Countess of Devon, a daughter of the late King Edward IV, was godmother.[2]

After the ceremony, Lady Anne Grey carried Henry to his nursery and Sir Humphrey Banaster, Mary's Vice Chamberlain, carried his train. After this spices and wine were served by the Duke of Norfolk and presents given in celebration. The king gave Charles Brandon a salt cellar and a cup of solid gold and to Mary two silver-gilt pots. Notably, Mary was not in attendance as she had not yet been 'churched'. The whole event was full of pomp, ritual and lavish celebration, which signified the importance of the birth of the king's nephew, as well as proof that Brandon was in his majesty's good graces.[3]

It should be noted that with his complex marital history, Charles Brandon worked hard to ensure the legitimacy of his children and his marriage to Mary Tudor. He appealed to Pope Clement VII to issue a bull stating the legitimacy of his marriage and in turn of his children. It was not until 20 August 1529 that a bull was finally granted legitimising Brandon and Mary's marriage. The bull stated:

> That Suffolk in the days of Henry VII had married Margaret Mortymer alias Brandon, of London diocese, on the strength of a dispensation which was not valid, and with her had cohabited although he had previously contracted marriage with Ann Browne, and was related to the said Margaret in the second and third degrees of affinity. Besides, the said Anne and Margaret were related in the second and third degrees of consanguinity, and Suffolk's grandmother was the sister of the father of a former husband of Margaret's (ac etiam ex eo avia tua et genitor olim conjugis dictæ Margaretæ frater et soror fuerant). For these causes, feeling that he could not continue to cohabit with Margaret Mortymer without sin, he caused his marriage with her to be declared null by the official of the archdeacon of London, to whom the cognisance of such causes of old belongs. After this sentence Suffolk married the said Anne, and had some daughters by her, and after her death he married Mary queen dowager of France. The bull ratifies this sentence, and supplies all defects both of law and fact, and visits with ecclesiastical censure all who call it in question.[4]

Two months after the birth of his son, on 19 and 20 May, Brandon participated in another spectacular jousting event. Henry, Brandon, Carew and Essex were to be on one team, with Kingston, Capell, Sedley and Howard on the other. On the first day both Brandon and Henry scored well, the king edging it slightly. Brandon continued to gain high scores on the second day, ending up with the highest total. The king had not done as well but his opponents were not on a par with his skills.[5] Frustrated, the king vowed, 'never to joust again except it be with as good a man as himself'.[6] It is perhaps significant that when Brandon returned to court and jousting events, he returned as the king's opponent rather than on the same team.

After this, Brandon was away from court until May 1517. With tensions running high between Holy Roman Emperor Charles V and Francis I of France, it appeared that Wolsey thought it best to keep Brandon, who was clearly pro-French, away from court. Brandon was aware that his high position was entirely reliant upon retaining the king's favour, and he was also concerned about what those around the king were saying about him. He was most worried that the Duke of Norfolk had free access to Henry and could be whispering lies about him. Brandon wrote to Wolsey on 14 July 1516 that 'though he is far off by the king's commandment, his heart is always with him'.[7]

Brandon need not have worried. During Henry VIII's summer progress that year he stopped to visit the Brandons at Donnington, which brought the duke great comfort.[8] In addition to this, the king bestowed upon Brandon the wardships of one of Sir Thomas Knyvett's illegitimate sons. (Knyvett had died on board the ship *Regent* in 1512.)[9]

When Brandon returned to court at the beginning of May 1517, Francesco Chieregato wrote to the knight Vigo da Campo San Pietro:

The Duke of Suffolk had arrived at the Court, to be present on St. George's Day at the festival, as a Knight of the Garter. He was very well received by the King and also by Cardinal Wolsey, who, by reason of his vast ability, rules everything.

Had visited the Duke on behalf of their Lord the Marquis [of Mantua], and made the statement enjoined him. The Duke was beyond measure gratified, and sent hearty remembrances, saying he was very anxious for the coming hither of one of the Marquis's sons, that he might be enabled to show the son how much goodwill he bore the father. He was most grateful for the present of horses now in preparation, and said he would requite the Marquis with most excellent dogs and hobbies, not for the value of the horses, but as a mark of courtesy. During his stay here the Duke went daily to Cardinal Wolsey's house to take and accompany him to the Council, and by following this course his affairs will prosper. Yesterday he departed for his estate, where the Queen his wife is; and within a month she is expected here.[10]

To be warmly welcomed by both Wolsey and the king reassured Brandon of his return to favour. Brandon was soon so well back in the king's good graces that a rumour was spread by Anthony Irby from Lincolnshire that 'it is a wonder to see the king how he is ordered nowadays; for the Cardinal and the Duke of Suffolk, which the king hath brought up of nought, do rule him in all things even as they list; whether it be by necromancy, witchcraft or policy, no man knoweth'.[11]

This was dangerous speculation. It is unknown if the king heard of the rumour or if it was quickly quashed. Such a suggestion could have been extremely damaging for both Brandon and Wolsey. Brandon had nevertheless now resumed his usual position with the king and attended council meetings (although sporadically). In July 1518, he wrote to Wolsey reminding him of his loyalty and asking Wolsey not to believe any false words against him:

Has always striven to do Wolsey's pleasure. They who reported otherwise have maligned him. They should be brought forth to see if they will persist in their untrue surmises. Is glad to find Wolsey does not credit them. Is anxious to see him, and explain everything. Hopes, at the beginning of next term, to satisfy the King and Wolsey of their debts.[12]

Now back at court, Brandon would participate in regular jousting events but always as the king's leading opponent rather than his teammate.[13] In the jousts of July 1517, a man by the name of Sagudino wrote the following account:

The King jousted with Suffolk, and tilted eight courses, both shivering their lances at every time, to the great applause of the spectators. The jousts lasted four hours, but the honor of the day was awarded to the King and the Duke. Between the courses the King and other cavaliers made their horses jump and execute acts of horsemanship, to the delight of everybody. Under the windows were the Queens of England and France.[14]

Francesco Chieregato, Apostolic Nuncio in England, wrote to Isabella d'Este, Marchioness of Mantua saying that the king and the duke 'bore themselves so bravely that the spectators fancied themselves witnessing a joust between Hector and Achilles'.[15]

Chieregato also wrote to the Marquis of Mantua: 'The Duke of Suffolk had regained his former favour with the king, by means of the person who degraded him. The duke was then resident at the court, and the queen his wife was expecting her confinement within a month.'[16]

Mary was indeed pregnant again. In July she set out on a pilgrimage to Walsingham, most likely to pray for the safe delivery of her child when her labour came upon her quite suddenly. She was forced to stop and stay at Hatfield with Bishop West of Ely, and on 16 July between two and three o'clock in the morning she gave birth to a healthy baby girl. The girl was named Frances as she was born on St Francis Day, but her name also allowed Mary and Brandon to pay tribute to King Francis I, who had supported them in their marriage several years earlier.[17]

Despite the suddenness of the labour and birth, Frances' christening was no less grand an affair:

The road to the church was strewed with rushes; the church porch hung with rich cloth of gold and needlework; the church with arras of the history of Holofernes and Hercules; the chancel, with arras of silk and gold; and the altar with rich cloth of tissue, and covered with images, relics, and jewels. In the said chancel were, as deputies for the Queen and Princess, Lady Boleyn and Lady Elizabeth Grey. The Abbot of St. Alban's was godfather. The font was hung with a canopy of crimson satin, powdered with roses, half red and half white, with the sun shining, and fleur de lis gold, and the French Queen's arms in four places, all of needlework. On the way to church were eighty torches borne by yeomen, and eight by gentlemen. The basin, covered, was borne by Mr. Sturton, the taper by Mr. Richard Long, the salt by Mr. Humphrey Barnes, the chrism by Lady Chelton. Mrs. Dorothy Verney bore the young lady, was assisted by the Lord Powes and Sir Roger Pelston, and accompanied by sixty ladies and gentlemen, and the prelates Sir Oliver Poole and Sir Christopher, and other of my Lord's chaplains.[18]

In March 1518, Mary fell ill. Brandon wrote to Wolsey to excuse himself from attending court:

My lord, Whereas I, of a certain space, have not given mine attendance upon your lordship in the king's council, according to my duty, I beseech your lordship to pardon me thereof. The cause why, hath been that the said French queen hath had, and yet hath, divers physicians with her, for her old disease in her side, and as yet cannot be perfectly restored to her health. And, albeit I have been two times at London, only to the intent to have waited upon your lordship, yet her grace, at either time, hath so sent for me, that I might not otherwise do but return home again. Nevertheless, her grace is now in such good amendment, that upon Tuesday or Wednesday next coming, I intend, by God's grace to wait upon your lordship. From Croydon the 16th day of March.[19]

The court physician, Master Peter, was sent to deliver relief to Mary and it appeared that for a time she felt better. In April, Brandon wrote to Thomas Wolsey thanking him for 'the King's fueseunes (physicians) take marvellous good heed unto her, and the king's kindness takes away a gryth par of her payne'.[20]

However, it soon became apparent that Mary was very ill. Brandon wrote once more to Wolsey:

My lord, So it is that the French queen has been sick, and so upon that, she sent for Master Peter, to whom she had a great mind unto, and so since, she is worse than she was before; insomuch that now she has taken such a phantasy that she thinks that she should not do well, with out she should come up to London for remedy; insomuch that she weeps every day, and takes so on that I am afraid it should do her harm; and for the eschewing thereof, I intend, with all diligence possible, to bring her up; and, my lord,

I insure you it is need, for her disease sheweth that it must ask great counsel, as you shall know at her coming up.

My lord, now since it is so far that she must needs come up, I beseech you, as her and my only trust is in you that you, will be so good lord unto her and me, as to be means unto the king's grace, that she may have a lodging in the court; an it be but one chamber, because it shall not be said that she is now in worse favour than she was at her departing. My lord, all her trust and mine is in you, and therefore she nor I will make none further labour for this matter.[21]

Happily, Mary recovered and returned to court. She would go on to bear Brandon two more children.

Oddly there are very few details about the birth of Charles Brandon's next child, a daughter named Eleanor, who quite possibly was named to honour Charles V's favourite sister. Eleanor was born sometime between 1518 and 1521, although there are no records surrounding the circumstances of her birth, its location or her christening. It can be assumed that she was christened – all babies were at the time – and that godparents were appointed.[22]

Despite being the Duke of Suffolk and now married to the dowager Queen of France and the king's sister, Brandon's financial base was fragile. Compared to the dukes of Buckingham and Norfolk, he had little land from which he could draw revenue. Without Mary's plate, jewels or coin, which she had signed over to her brother, Brandon's new wife was relatively poor and relied heavily upon her pension from France.

Between 1515 and 1519, Brandon's income was around £3,000 (£1,140,000)[23] a year, yet upon his marriage to Mary Tudor he lost the title of Viscount Lisle and the wardship of Elizabeth and thus all the lands that went along with that. This reduced his income to around £1,500 (£570,000)[24] a year. Holding various offices would still have brought in revenue from other areas, but this is hard to calculate and certainly would not have amounted to any more than £1,500 (£570,000)[25] a year. He would have also received his French pension, although payments seem to have been sporadic. Brandon was paid 875 livres tournois on 1 May 1516, 1 November 1518, 1 May 1519, 1 November 1519, May 1520 and 1 May 1521.[26] In addition, Brandon would have received his wife's dowager payments from France which amounted to £4,000 (£1,520,000)[27] a year; thus Brandon's financial income would have been around £7,000 (£2,660,000)[28] a year if all payments were received.[29]

Brandon also drew upon his Welsh holdings as well as the £40 a year (£19,000)[30] he was granted at his creation as Duke of Suffolk. Brandon could draw upon the de la Pole estates in Suffolk that had been given to him by the king in February 1515. (Richard de la Pole had been a constant thorn in Henry VIII's side as he had a distant claim to the English throne. He had fled to Europe and was at times used by the French as a possible means to take the English crown.)[31] The king may have granted Brandon some of the de la Pole estates to quash any further thoughts of an uprising in the area and to ensure a man he trusted oversaw events in Suffolk.

By 26 March 1517, no payments had been made toward the £24,000 the couple ostensibly owed the king. Therefore, an indenture of agreement was written, which clearly outlined what Brandon and Mary had to pay and when. In addition to their fine from Henry, the couple had to pay £600 for Mary's stay at the royal household, and £26,901 1d as arrears for the royal manors of Bromefield Yale and Chirklond. £20,000 of that sum was Mary's debt, with the rest belonging to Brandon. By next Michaelmas, 29 September, Mary and Brandon had to pay £666 13s 4d and then each Easter and Michaelmas the same sum had to be paid until £14,765 31s 4d of Mary's debt was paid. It was noted that if Mary was to die before this sum was paid then Brandon did not have to make any more payments, and if Brandon died before the sum was reached then Mary was to hand over any jewels, plate, hangings and other such items to pay off the debt. The indenture did, however, note that only Brandon's part of the debt was to be repaid if war with France caused Mary's dower payments to stop.[32]

The war with France in the 1520s did greatly affect both Mary and Brandon's French pensions. The payments had been coming intermittently throughout this period, and Brandon was constantly chasing his and his wife's arrears. Brandon wrote that his wife's payments 'restith much of her honour and profit, and mine also'.[33] Brandon was heavily reliant upon Mary's dowager payments for his financial stability. Without regular receipts, Brandon was forced to borrow £12,000 (£4,555,000)[34] from the Crown in 1515/16 and an additional £3,000 (£1,140,000)[35] from the revenues of his offices in North Wales.[36] However, in 1525 Brandon lost his position as Chief Justice of North Wales under a new scheme by Thomas Wolsey whereby the 'council in the marshes' was incorporated into the council of Princess Mary. Brandon's position was granted to his deputy and although he was compensated with the castle of Ewelme, it was not so much the loss of income but the loss of military status that affected the duke. No longer would he be the one to call upon the people in the North to march to war.[37]

In December 1526, Mary still owed her brother £19,333 6s 8d and Brandon owed the king 6,519l 13s 11d. A new agreement was made in which £500 would be paid every December and June, two-thirds of that for Mary's debt and a third for Brandon's.[38]

Brandon was living beyond his means. His wife's standing meant she had a reputation to live up to. She required clothing and servants suitable for her position and all of this cost money. In 1524, Brandon had fifty-one servants who earned 26s 8d each. His physician, Master Leonard, was the highest-paid member of his household, earning £20 (£7,600)[39] a year.[40] Mary had more than double this number of servants. While this is not a large number for people of their status, it did put pressure on the Brandons to see everyone clothed, fed and paid appropriately, and he was spending around £1,000 (£380,000)[41] a year just on his servants. Mary paid her servants from her pension from France.[42]

Brandon also had a reputation to live up to; he was a duke and brother-in-law to the king. Cloth suitable for a duke was expensive, and in addition to this Brandon sought to extend his lands and build up his power base. In the late 1510s, Brandon extended his late uncle Thomas's house in Southwark and turned it into a large brick palace decorated with terracotta. Then, in 1527, Brandon decided to build a similar palace in East Anglia, which would become his main country residence. It was to be called Westhorpe Hall and was a moated brick house of considerable size, which had terracotta plaques and battlements built around an open courtyard 126 feet square.

A main feature of the manor were the corridors, which contained large windows allowing residents and visitors to look into the central courtyard, which was designed in the French fashion by Mary Tudor herself. On the south side of the manor were four main rooms. On the east was the Great Hall, around seventy feet in length, again with windows that looked into the courtyard. Next to this was a dining chamber. Above the Great Hall was Charles Brandon's Great Chamber. On the north side of the manor was a tower, of which only the foundations remain to be seen today. It was here that Mary Tudor lay in state after her death in 1533.

There were additional buildings on the eastern side of the manor which are believed to have contained the kitchens, pantry, wet and dry larder and the boiling house. Westhorpe Hall also had beautifully decorated chimneys, a chapel with cloisters that contained a magnificent stained-glass window, oak-panelled rooms and even a statue of Hercules![43]

Brandon stated that the building costs for Westhorpe Hall were £12,000 (£3,870,000),[44] much of which would have come from Mary's French pension.[45] The surrounding parks were well stocked with deer for hunting. Brandon loved to hunt and in 1538 it was recorded that 'the park at Westhorpe held 100 Red deer and 200 Fallow deer.'[46]

Tragically, Westhorpe Hall was demolished in the 1760s. A historian at Thetford named Martin witnessed the destruction:

I went to see the dismal ruins of Westhorpe Hall, formerly the seat of Charles Brandon, Duke of Suffolk. The workmen are now pulling it down as fast as may be, in a very careless and injudicious manner. The coping bricks, battlements and many other ornamental pieces, are made of earth, and burnt hard, as fresh as when first built. They might, with care, have been taken down whole, but all the fine chimnies, and ornaments were pulled down with ropes, and crushed to pieces in a most shameful manner. There was a monstrous figure of Hercules sitting cross-legged with his club, and a lion beside him, but all shattered in pieces. The painted glass is likely to share the same fate. The timber is fresh and sound, and the building, which was very lofty, stood as when it was first built. It is a pity that care is not taken to preserve some few of our ancient fabrics. To demolish every piece of old architecture is quite barbaric.[47]

From 1519, Henry VIII was starting to 'grow up' and moving away from his old chivalric ideals. He was no longer the fun-loving sportsman who filled his time with entertainment and left the running of the kingdom to his advisors, specifically Thomas Wolsey. Now he showed more of an interest in politics, both personal and public. He was competing on a political stage against the likes of Francis I, King of France, and Charles V, who had recently been created Holy Roman Emperor. Both men were younger than Henry and had achieved great military successes. Henry had little to show for the first ten years of his reign – neither military glory nor the male heir he so desperately desired.

In addition to this, the king's coffers, which had been overflowing when he came to the throne, were starting to run low and the common people did not want to be taxed even more heavily just so the king could go to war. Thomas Wolsey endeavoured to persuade his king that instead of seeking military glory he should seek to make peace across Europe, and that this could be his legacy.[48]

In 1520, Henry VIII, ever fearful of treason, wrote a secret letter to Thomas Wolsey: 'To this that followeth I thought not best to make [the messenger] privy, nor none other but you and I, which is that I would you should make good watch on the Duke of Sufolk, on the Duke of Buckingham, on my Lord of Northumberland, on my Lord of Derby, on my Lord of Wiltshire and on others which you think suspect.'[49]

Despite what the king might have thought at the time, Brandon went on to prove that he was always a faithful and loyal servant.

Hostilities between France and Spain had been simmering throughout the past year, and both Francis I and Charles V were seeking the support, or at least the neutrality, of Henry VIII and England.[50] In 1518, the Treaty of London was signed between the major European nations including France, England, Spain, the Holy Roman Empire, the Papacy, Burgundy and the Netherlands. The treaty stated that no signatory should attack another, and that doing so would cause all the other signatories to protect the victim of the aggression.[51]

To solidify the Treaty of London, a magnificent (and fantastically costly) event was organised between King Henry VIII of England and King Francis I of France. The Field of the Cloth of Gold was organised for the period from 7 June to 24 June 1520. The meeting was held between the English stronghold of Guînes and the French town of Ardres, on a piece of land which was referred to (and is still known as) as the Field of the Cloth of Gold.[52]

While the purpose of the meeting between these two mighty kings was to solidify the Treaty of London and strengthen relations between the two countries, it ended up as a means for each king to try to impress and outdo the other. Henry VIII spared no expense and sought not just to impress but to overawe the French.[53]

In the months leading up to the meeting, Henry ordered many lavish furnishings to be gathered, expensive clothing to be made, events to be organised and a magnificent pavilion to be created, which the king would occupy throughout the meeting. The royal coffers paid for many of these expenses, but the majority of the noblemen and noblewomen who attended would have been left in no doubt they were expected to pay their own expenses. This included their clothing, which was designed to impress, and those who participated in jousting events had to pay for their weapons and armour. Some nobles even mortgaged their estates, sold manors and property and organised loans to have the funds to attend the magnificent event. Approximately 5,000 men and women accompanied the king across the English Channel, with around 3,000 horses.[54]

Of course, as the Duke of Suffolk and one of the leading men of the court, Charles Brandon was required to go to the meeting. More than this, it was expected he would make a great impression. Mary was also invited to attend the meeting between her brother and her 'step-son', Francis I.

On 16 March 1520, Brandon replied to a letter written by Wolsey in which he was asked how many horses and people Mary would be taking with her to France. Brandon replied that he should 'take the peyne to ordre the same as ye shall think shall stonde moost with the kinges pleasur and her honor'.[55]

The document listing Mary's attendants no longer survives but it is known that Brandon took with him five chaplains, ten gentlemen, fifty-five servants and thirty horses. All of these would have been paid for out of Brandon's pocket, and the expense of transporting, feeding and clothing them would have been extremely high. In addition, Brandon brought along his own armour for jousting[56] and ordered cloth of gold and silk to wear.[57]

On Thursday 7 June, Henry VIII and Francis had their first meeting. In a small valley between the English-held Guisnes and the French Ardres, the two kings rode towards each other. Both men were clearly set on impressing one another. Henry VIII wore cloth of silver with costly jewels and white plumes, while Francis I wrote cloth of gold frieze, precious jewels and a bonnet with white plumes. When the kings approached each other, they removed their bonnets and then embraced before dismounting and embracing once more; they then went to an English pavilion to talk.[58]

Over the next seventeen days, various events and entertainments were held in an attempt to display the skill and splendour of each country. These included jousting, archery, wrestling, singing, exotic and magnificent feasts and the exchange of extravagant gifts.[59] Brandon participated in multiple jousting events where he represented his king and the English:

> The field was 328 ft wide and probably 900 ft long, surrounded by a ditch and bank and double railing. The main spectators' gallery was on the other side, but less lavishly equipped. The two kings armed themselves in wooden chambers and tents inside the lists, while other combatants had small encampments linked to the lists by a bridge over the ditch. The 'tree of honour' was also within the lists.

Henry VIII also participated in the jousting events. It was reported that one day he was so eager to do well that by the evening his horse was dead! In all, more than 327 lances were broken during the jousts. After this came the tourneys where men fought on foot with blunted spears and swords.[60]

On Thursday 14 June, Brandon ran a staggering twenty-four courses, in the process breaking eighteen staves and scoring three hits. This was a remarkable result and records state that Brandon did marvellously well and was deserving of the prizes he received.[61]

Another notable event of the meeting between the two countries was a wrestling match between Henry VIII and Francis I. Henry VIII challenged Francis; unfortunately, Francis I tripped

Henry and the English king lost. It was reported that the two kings nearly came to blows over this event but others were able to calm them down; perhaps Brandon was even one of those men who had to intervene and help calm his sovereign.

One of the most magnificent displays at the Field of the Cloth of Gold was the splendid pavilion built to house Henry VIII. It consisted of a series of wood and canvas tents which could be separated by hangings of rich cloth to create separate rooms, including chapels and private apartments. The pavilion was made out of red cloth with a fringe of gold, decorated with Tudor roses and fleurs-de-lis. Upon the eaves was a frieze bearing the royal mottoes *Dieu et mon droit* and *semper vavat in eterno*. On top of the pavilion, poles supported models of the king's beasts (lions, greyhounds, dragons and antelope).[62] It has been suggested that around 6,000 workers were employed to build the king's and the other English quarters.[63] Brandon had the honour of staying with his wife Mary in one wing of this grand pavilion.[64]

On 24 June, the lavish meeting came to an end. Both kings departed. Before Henry returned home to England, however, he went to Gravelines to meet with the Holy Roman Emperor, Charles V, to discuss a possible alliance. At the end of May, only a few days before the Field of the Cloth of Gold, Charles V had travelled to England and met with Henry VIII and his wife, Katherine of Aragon. Henry and Charles also rode to Canterbury where they feasted and most likely discussed a possible treaty.[65] At Gravelines, Brandon was appointed to tend to the king with several other members of the nobility.[66] More discussions were held, but a treaty of friendship was not finally agreed upon until 1522.[67]

While Charles Brandon participated in the magnificent Field of the Cloth of Gold, Robert Brandon and his wife Katherine granted their nephew Charles a sixty-year lease and appurtenances in Cravens, Henham, Blythburgh, Bolecampe, Brigge, Sotherton, Dunwich, Wangford, Roydon, Brampton, Westhale and Blyford in Suffolk. In return, Charles Brandon would pay his uncle and aunt 600 marks and then 100 marks per year for the remainder of Robert and Katherine's lives.[68] This grant would provide Brandon with much-needed funds.

In 1522, the secret Treaty of Bruges was signed between Charles V and Thomas Wolsey on behalf of Henry VIII. By this treaty,

Henry would support Charles V in the war against France. In May, England officially declared war on France.[69] So much for the pageantry and amity of the Field of the Cloth of Gold! This was a problematic situation for the pro-French Brandon. His wife had been the Queen of France and was receiving a pension of £4,000 (£1,520,000)[70] a year as a result.[71] Brandon himself was also receiving a pension from Francis I,[72] and both Brandon and Mary owed a great deal to the French king for supporting their marriage. When Charles V visited England, Brandon had the honour of hosting Henry VIII and the Emperor at Suffolk Place where the men dined and hunted. Ever the opportunist, when war with France was declared and his French pension stopped, Brandon was able to secure an imperial pension.[73]

On 21 July, Brandon was ordered by the king as

... Chief justice of North Wales, steward of the lordships of the Holt, Bromefeld and Yale in Chirklond, and steward of divers lands of spiritual and temporal persons within the realm, to assemble the King's tenants and others in cos. Anglesea, Carnarvon, and Merioneth, N. Wales, in the said lordships, in the borough of Southwerk, Surrey, and in all lordships of which he is steward, and muster them for war.[74]

At the end of August, Brandon was appointed Lieutenant-General[75] and sent to Calais at the head of an army of 10,000 men.[76] Brandon was to be paid 100s a day while footmen received 6d a day and men on horseback 8d a day.[77] Brandon reached Calais on 24 August but there were difficulties with supplies, and a plague in the area infected some of the men.[78] The campaign finally started on 1 October.[79] Brandon's initial aim was to head to Boulogne; however, on 26 September Henry VIII, with support from Thomas Wolsey, ordered Brandon and his men to march straight for Paris.[80] The aim was for a three-pronged attack upon the capital. The rebel Duke of Bourbon would attack from the south, Charles V and his army would attack from the east, and Brandon and his men would move in from the north. After receiving Burgundian reinforcements, Brandon's army took the French stronghold of Belle Castle and utterly destroyed it. Then, between 18 and 20 October, they went on to destroy the riverside crossing at Bray. On 28 October, Brandon's army captured Montdidier.[81] Other towns also surrendered along the way, and despite marching such a considerable number of men and hauling huge amounts of supplies, Brandon was soon within eighty kilometres of the city of Paris.

Events did not turn out as planned, however. It seemed that Charles V was more interested in securing his Pyrenean frontier, and focused much of his time and supplies upon the war in northern Italy. Once Charles had captured Fuenterrabia, he stopped his army. The Duke of Bourbon's revolt fell apart, and the aid that Margaret of Savoy had previously offered did not materialise.[82] Suddenly Brandon was left at the head of 10,000 men with no reinforcements or further supplies – and with men dying of the plague. (It was common for armies to suffer more casualties from plague and dysentery than they did from enemy action – especially if they were halted, when conditions swiftly became insanitary.)

By November, winter was upon the English army. There was heavy rain followed by an intense frost. Many men died from the cold or the plague and Brandon had the choice of digging in for the winter just outside of Paris or returning to Calais. He chose the latter, despite being ordered by Henry VIII to remain for the entire month of December.[83] By mid-December Brandon and his men were in Calais waiting to sail back to England. Brandon returned to England in the New Year. Of the 10,000 men who had left for the campaign in August, less than half returned.[84]

Henry openly blamed the Duke of Bourbon for the failure of the attack, and no fault was laid upon Brandon. In fact, despite the setback, Brandon had proved himself a shrewd military expert. He had deferred to his war council at times but had also made crucial decisions regarding the invasion which had proved valuable. His military efforts showed the king once again that Brandon was a competent, skilled and trustworthy military commander.[85]

Another military expedition was tentatively planned for April 1524, and once more Brandon was named as the commander. He was enthusiastic for another campaign against France and sent his man Sir Richard Jerningham to the Low Countries to start organising the necessities. However, final sanction was never granted and the whole idea came to nothing.[86]

War with France was once again proposed in early 1525. In February of that year, the French troops had suffered a devastating loss against the Imperial army of Charles V outside of Pavia. To make matters worse, the French king had been captured in the battle and was now a prisoner of Charles V. When the messenger brought the news of Francis' capture to Henry, the king was reported to have been likened to the Archangel Gabriel, such was his happiness and excitement at hearing the news. Henry VIII, ever the opportunist, saw another chance at military glory and quickly proposed a new war against France. The English king persuaded himself that God had blessed the idea to go to war and now he had visions of reclaiming the French throne for England.[87]

However much the king desired to go to war, his coffers had been nearly emptied by the previous unsuccessful campaigns in France.[88] A lot of money was needed to fund a war, and it was needed quickly. Thomas Wolsey immediately proposed an 'Amicable Grant', hoping to gain an estimated £800,000 (£304,000.00)[89] for the proposed war.[90] However, this 'Amicable Grant' was not passed through Parliament; instead it was proposed as a means by which people would give monetary 'gifts' to fund the king's war.[91] People did not have a say in donating to the king's war fund; the grant was an 'amicable' demand for coin.

Clergy were ordered to pay a third of their income if it was more than £10 (£3,800)[92] a year, or a quarter if it was less.[93] The laity were required to pay 3s 4d in the pound if they earned more than £50 (£19,000)[94] a year, while those earning between £20 and £50 a year (£7,600–£19,000)[95] were required to pay 2s 8d and those earning less than £20 a year had to pay 1s.[96] Naturally, neither laity nor clergy were impressed. These so-called offers to fund the war were nothing of the sort. They were demands upon people who more often than not struggled to make ends meet. In addition to this, in 1522–23, a huge loan of £250,000 (£95,000,00)[97] had been forced upon the people and as yet had not been paid back.[98]

Discontent quickly spread through the country. People claimed that they could not afford to pay the tax and that it was unconstitutional as it had not been approved by Parliament, while the clergy protested as they had not agreed to such a tax in convocation.[99] Soon there were widespread rumblings in Essex, Kent, Norfolk, Warwickshire and Huntingdonshire.[100] However, the greatest protests were in Lavenham where around 4,000 people gathered to protest against the grant.[101] The king quickly sent Brandon and the Duke of Norfolk to try and deal with the protesters but the rebels greatly outnumbered their army. While Brandon waited for the Duke of Norfolk and his men to arrive he began to burn bridges in an attempt to stop the rebels. He also informed Wolsey that the troops would defend him against all perils but that he doubted that they would fight against their countrymen.[102] Luckily for Brandon and his army, the rebels did not turn up and several leaders of the rebellion returned with Brandon and the Duke of Norfolk to London. They were quickly put in the Fleet Prison.

Henry, ever conscious of the opinion of his people, quickly turned face. Organising a council meeting, the king stated that that 'his mynd was neuer, to aske any thyng of his commons, whiche might sounde to his dishonor, or to the breche of his lawes'.[103] With the realisation that it was not possible to gather such funds from the people, and with the threat of rebellion, the Amicable Grant was dropped. The king claimed that he knew nothing about the grant[104] and that he had not authorised it. A general pardon was granted for the rebels and those held in the Fleet were released. In the end, Wolsey took the blame for the whole affair and the idea of going to war with France was dropped.[105]

Once more Brandon had handled himself and his army well, serving his king faithfully and suppressing a possible rebellion.

11

Family Matters

For most of Charles Brandon's life, England was a Catholic nation. During his formative years, he would have been taught all the essential aspects of the Catholic faith including the Mass, the Eucharist, transubstantiation, confession and repentance. He would have been taught about the idea of needing to do good deeds for others and the concept of making pilgrimages to pray to God. He would have been taught that the Pope had been appointed by God, and that his word was law.

In 1517, things began to change. Martin Luther, a professor of theology at Wittenberg University in Germany, nailed his 'Ninety-five Theses'[1] to the door of the local church. The theses attacked the Catholic concept of salvation through good deeds and argued that the way to salvation was through Christ by faith and repentance. Confession alone did not mean repentance. He also attacked the sale of indulgences and emphasised that the Pope had limited powers upon earth. These ideas were drastically different from what the Catholic Church taught, and caused a great deal of upheaval not just in England but throughout Europe.

Henry VIII was outraged by such ideas, and in 1521 wrote (with the help of leading theologians and churchmen) his *Assertio Septem Sacramentorum* (Defence of the Seven Sacraments), which he sent to Pope Leo X and which earned him the title *Defensor Fidei* (Defender of the Faith).[2] However, over the next decade Henry's religious views and opinions would begin to change.

Also in 1521, Edward Stafford, Duke of Buckingham, was executed. He was accused of wishing the king's death and seeing himself on the throne. With royal blood running through his veins and an arrogant attitude, Buckingham had been a regular member at court but often made those around him uncomfortable.[3] When he applied for a licence to raise 400 armed men, Henry was immediately suspicious and Buckingham was arrested. At his trial at Westminster, Charles Brandon stood as one of the judges.[4] On 17 May, the Duke of Buckingham was executed upon Tower Hill.[5]

Tragedy was soon to hit the Brandons. Sometime during 1522 their first-born son, Henry, died.[6] There are no details surrounding the boy's death. At just five or six years of age, the little boy could have died from any number of illnesses or accidents. One can only imagine how devastated Brandon must have been over the loss of his son and heir. However, Mary was pregnant for the fourth time, and during 1522 she gave birth to another son. He was named Henry, once more after the king, although no further information about his birth or christening survives.[7] One can imagine that, like the first Henry, the newborn was christened with some pomp. It could even be suggested that once more the king stood as godfather.

As well as having three children with his third wife, Brandon also had to think of his other two daughters by his first wife, Anne Browne. By now, Anne was sixteen years of age and Mary was twelve. Brandon's attention turned to finding suitable marriages for his daughters, and by March 1525 Anne married Edward Grey, Lord Powis.[8] Brandon had purchased Grey's wardship sometime in 1517 for the sum of £1,000[9] (£380,000).[10] Previously Anne had been at the court of Margaret of Savoy, with which Brandon was very familiar, to further her education. At the insistence of Mary Tudor, Anne had been recalled to England.[11]

Brandon's other daughter with his first wife, Mary, was married to Thomas Stanley, Lord Monteagle, sometime in 1527 or early 1528. As with Edward Grey, Brandon had purchased Thomas Stanley's wardship for an unknown sum. Stanley would be appointed as a Knight of the Bath during the coronation of Henry VIII's second wife, Anne Boleyn. Ironically, he also took part in the trial in May 1536 which found Anne Boleyn guilty of treason. Mary gave her husband six children: sons William, Francis and Charles, and daughters Elizabeth, Anne and Margaret. Mary would also go on to serve as a lady in waiting to Henry VIII's third wife, Jane Seymour.[12] During her marriage, there was some allegation from

Grey of misbehaviour by Mary, although the particulars of the allegation are lost to time.[13]

Brandon was to have difficulties with his son-in-law throughout his life. Thomas Stanley proved unreliable with his money, and on 16 September 1534 Brandon was forced to intervene in Stanley's financial business and had to pay the sum of £1,452 (£468,000)[14] to clear his debts. Brandon also had to cancel debts Stanley owed to him, which amounted to half of the total. However, only fifteen days later, Stanley asked to borrow another £300 (£96,630)[15] from Brandon. Stanley clearly could not cope, so Brandon took charge of his finances. He declared that Monteagle's debts were to be paid in regular instalments and that he would oversee his son-in-law's expenditures from now on.[16] It was also ordered that Stanley was to 'manage his estates and fortune according to a book drawn up by Charles Brandon'.[17] In addition to this, Stanley had to promise to 'honestly handle and entreat the said lady Mary as a nobleman ought to his wife'.[18] This promise may also suggest that Stanley was not treating his wife fittingly and that his financial mismanagement was affecting her.

Curiously, Brandon continued to indulge his son-in-law (perhaps to ensure better treatment of his wife), and on 27 September 1534 he granted Stanley and Mary the lavish and costly gifts of 'an egg of diamonds, with 90 great pearls at 20s., and 14 diamonds at 40s., 118*l*.; a "lasce" of 23 rubies at 20s., and 11 score 7 pearls at 10s. the score, 28*l*. 13s. 6*d*.; a pattlett with 17 diamonds, two rubies at 20s., 216 pearls at 5s. the score, 22*l*. 5s. 4*d*. A pattlett of 19 score pearls at 5s. the score, and other jewels, of which one chain is in the hands of the countess of Worcester, amounting in all to 523*l*. 19s. 9*d*. 25'.[19]

For his son, Brandon sought a greater marriage. Little Henry, after all, was the only legitimate male heir to the English throne at this time, and Brandon needed to find a future wife befitting such a position. In March 1528, he would purchase from the king the wardship of Katherine Willoughby, daughter and heiress of the late Lord Willoughby de Eresby, who had died in October 1526. It cost Brandon a staggering £2,266 13s 4*d*[20] (£860,381).[21]

By 1522, Henry VIII and his queen had only one living child, a daughter named Mary born in 1516. The queen had lost five children, three sons who were either stillborn or died shortly after birth and two daughters who had both been stillborn. Previously, on 15 June 1519, Henry VIII's mistress Bessie Blount had given birth to a healthy young boy who was named Henry Fitzroy, after his father. Fitzroy is a Norman French surname meaning 'son of the King', and it was common for illegitimate children of the king to receive this name. Henry VIII publicly acknowledged the boy as his own, and his godfather was Cardinal Thomas Wolsey.[22] Henry was still hopeful of the birth of a legitimate son and heir.

On 18 June 1525 at Bridewell Palace, young Henry Fitzroy was created Earl of Nottingham and additionally given the double dukedom of Richmond and Somerset. During the investiture, the young boy came out and knelt before the king. Once created Duke of Richmond and Somerset, he took his place on the dais beside his father. On the same day, Henry Brandon, now two or three years old, was created Earl of Lincoln[23] with an annuity of £20 from the profits of the counties of Lincoln and Buckingham.[24] The title was prestigious for the young boy, and may have been granted to him as it was closely associated with the Poles. By giving the title to Brandon's son, the king may have been further distancing not only the title but also the people of East Anglia from the rebellious de la Pole family.

With the elevation of Charles Brandon to Duke of Suffolk in 1514 and his son to Earl of Lincoln in 1525, there was some hushed talk that if anything should happen to the king and he died without a legitimate male heir then Brandon would seek to put his son upon the throne as he was the nephew of the king and born in wedlock. In addition to this, it was suggested that Brandon would rule through his son until the boy came of age. There was no truth to these rumours, and they were quickly suppressed. Brandon was proving himself a loyal friend and courtier to Henry VIII, and, after all, the king had no intention of dying without a male heir.

During the previous year, in 1524, Brandon's uncle Sir Robert had died. He had written his will in February 1523, stating that he wished to be buried at St Peter and St Paul Church in Wangford, next to his first wife, Anne, between the two pillars. He bequeathed the church 66s 8d in tithes and another 20s for repairs. He also promised a boll of barley and half a boll of wheat to every church in Norfolk (in which he held land) for repairs, and requested that the executors of his will pay the Guild of St Peter at Wangford and the Guild of Our Blessed Lady at Newton (in both of which Brandon was an alderman) between £3 and £4. He directed that his current wife deliver a Mass book to the church of Newton and that 20s be given to the church of Worsted in Norfolk for repairs and 40s for an orbit which was to be kept at Norwich Cathedral.

The will goes on to say that Sir Robert Brandon granted the prior of Blyborough 26s 8d for tithes and rents that he had not paid. His manors and lands of Tunstead and Happing in Norfolk and all other goods and chattels he gave to his wife. She was then to pay all of his debts and do with his soul what she thought 'most pleasing to God'. The will was proven at the prerogative court of Canterbury on 28 November 1524.[25]

Sir Robert's will does not refer to any children, with all his remaining goods going to his wife. There are no records of Robert having children with either his first or second wife, so it can be assumed that in 1524 any hopes for the next generation of Brandon men lay firmly with Charles Brandon and his son.

There are no records of Robert Brandon's internment, so we do not know if his nephew Charles attended the funeral. St Peter and St Paul Church in Wangford still survives today. Several pillars remain, and it may be that Sir Robert Brandon, his first wife and his father rest beneath the floor to this day.

In his will Robert Brandon also left his manor at Henham, which Charles Brandon added to his existing estates in East Anglia.[26] Charles continued to purchase estates and manors within this area with the aim to become one of the largest magnates in East Anglia, although he never quite managed to secure all the Pole estates. His chancellor Oliver Pole and his attorney Humphrey Wingfield also spent £100 (£48,377)[27] on four manors in Suffolk in an attempt to secure his power base in Suffolk.[28]

It is on record that the people of the area greatly loved the Duchess of Suffolk and welcomed her warmly wherever she went, and this must have enhanced Brandon's status. In addition to this, in December, the Bishop of Ely made Brandon steward of the estates of the diocese, which added to his prestige.[29] It is interesting to note that Brandon's reputation grew throughout East Anglia over the next few years. In the Norwich episcopal registers for

Right: 1. Coat of arms of Sir William Brandon I. (Courtesy of Richard Goddard)

Below right: 2. King Henry VI (1421–1471). (Courtesy of Yale Center for British Art)

Below: 3. King Edward IV (1442–1483). (Courtesy of Yale Center for British Art)

4. Caister Castle. Sir William Brandon I was part of an army of 3,000 men sent to besiege the castle for the Duke of Norfolk in 1469. (Author's collection)

5. Site of the Battle of Tewkesbury, 4 May 1471. William Brandon I was knighted by Edward IV after the battle. (Courtesy of Peter Bryson)

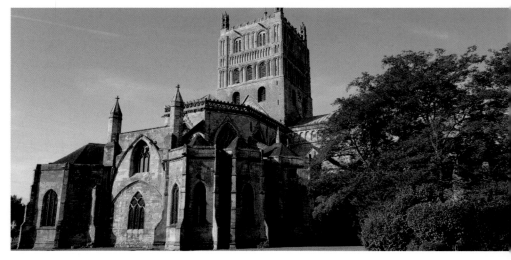

6. Tewkesbury Abbey. (Author's collection)

Right: 7. King Richard III (1452–1485). (Courtesy of Yale Center for British Art)

Below right: 8. King Henry VII (1457–1509). (Courtesy of Yale Center for British Art)

Below left: 9. Models of Henry Tudor, Earl of Richmond and Sir William Brandon I at the Battle of Bosworth from the Bosworth Battlefield Heritage Centre. (Author's collection)

Representing the Tudors

Henry Tudor, Earl of Richmond, and his standard bearer, Sir William Brandon

Left: 10. St Peter and St Paul Church, Wangford. (Author's collection)

Below: 11. Inside St Peter and St Paul Church. Sir William Brandon I was buried within the church. His son, Sir Robert Brandon, also requested to be buried within the church, between the two pillars. In his will he also gave the church 66*s* 8*d* in tithes and 20*s* for repairs. (Courtesy of Peter Bryson)

12. Coat of arms of Sir Thomas Brandon, Master of the Horse. (Courtesy of RS-nourse under Creative Commons 2.0)

13. King Henry VIII (1491–1547).

14. Henham Park. In 1513 Charles Brandon was granted the old manor and park at Henham, Suffolk. He built upon the previous manor to create Henham Hall. Nothing remains of it today. (Author's collection)

15. Charles Brandon, Duke of Suffolk and Mary Tudor, Dowager Queen of France and Duchess of Suffolk. (Courtesy of Yale Center for British Art)

16. The 1511 Westminster Tournament Roll depicting Henry VIII participating in a jousting tournament to celebrate the birth of his first son. Both Sir Thomas Brandon and Charles Brandon, Duke of Suffolk were avid and highly skilled jousters. (Courtesy of the College of Arms)

17. A jousting lance reported to have belonged to Charles Brandon, Duke of Suffolk, at the Tower of London. (Author's collection)

18. The Tower of London. (Courtesy of Duncan Harris under Creative Commons 2.0)

19. Surviving coat of arms of Charles Brandon, Duke of Suffolk from Westhorpe Hall, Suffolk. Westhorpe Hall was built in 1527 by Charles Brandon and demolished in the 1760s. (Courtesy of Peter Bryson)

20. Original bridge at Westhorpe Hall. (Courtesy of Peter Bryson)

21. Embellishments from the bridge at Westhorpe Hall: Charles Brandon, Duke of Suffolk's lion rampant and the Tudor rose. (Author's collection)

22. Westminster Hall, Westminster. During Anne Boleyn's coronation on 1 June 1533, Charles Brandon, Duke of Suffolk acted as Lord High Steward and Constable. He rode through the hall on a charger covered in crimson velvet, wearing a doublet covered in pearls. (Author's collection)

23. Grave of Mary Tudor, Dowager Queen of France and Duchess of Suffolk, third wife of Charles Brandon, Duke of Suffolk. St Mary's Church, Bury St Edmunds. (Author's collection)

24. Katherine Willoughby, Duchess of Suffolk, fourth wife of Charles Brandon, depicted in a miniature by Hans Holbein.

25. Grimsthorpe Castle, acquired by Charles Brandon, Duke of Suffolk through his marriage to Katherine Willoughby. Brandon moved his family to Grimsthorpe in 1537. (Author's collection)

Left: 26. Tattershall Castle, granted to Charles Brandon, Duke of Suffolk in 1537 by Henry VIII for the purpose of overseeing the happenings in Lincolnshire. (Author's collection)

Below: 27. St George's Chapel, Windsor Castle, Windsor. Burial location of Charles Brandon, Duke of Suffolk and Henry VIII. (Author's collection)

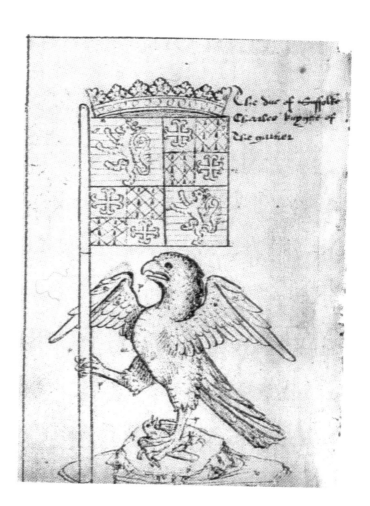

28. Banner, beast and coronet of Charles Brandon, Duke of Suffolk.

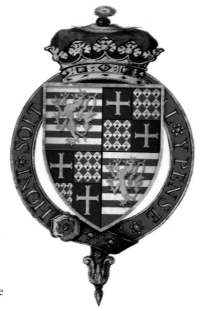

29. Coat of arms of Charles Brandon, Duke of Suffolk based on the duke's Knight of the Garter stall plate in St George's Chapel, Windsor Castle. (Courtesy of RS-nourse under Creative Commons 2.0)

30. Miniatures of Charles Brandon, Duke of Suffolk's sons Henry Brandon (left) and Charles Brandon (right) by Hans Holbein.

31. King Edward VI (1537–1553). (Courtesy of the Metropolitan Museum of Art)

Right: 32. Mary Brandon, Lady Monteagle, daughter of Charles Brandon with his first wife Anne Browne, after a sketch by Hans Holbein.

Below: 33. Frances Grey (née Brandon), daughter of Charles Brandon with his wife Mary Tudor, pictured with her second husband, Adrian Stokes. (Courtesy of Yale Center for British Art)

34. Buckden Towers, Cambridgeshire. Both Henry and Charles Brandon died from the sweating sickness at Buckden Towers within half an hour of one another on 14 July 1551. (Author's collection)

35. The grave of Henry and Charles Brandon. (Author's collection)

1517 Brandon was referred to as 'the Duke of Suffolk'. However, by 1524 he was 'the most powerful man, Charles Duke of Suffolk, great marshal of England' and in September of the same year he was 'the noble and most powerful prince, Charles Duke of Suffolk and Great Marshal of England'.[30]

As well as lavishing such titles upon Brandon, the people of East Anglia recognised the influence he could wield, and they were soon calling upon him to present their requests and causes to Wolsey or the king. An example of this is when there was a grain shortage in January 1528, and the people begged Brandon for support. In return, he wrote to Wolsey: 'The inhabitants of the Suffolk coast, who are destitute of grain fit for man's use, have asked him to request Wolsey for a licence for them to carry white and red herrings and sprats to Flanders, to barter for corn.'[31] It is unclear whether Brandon's intervention had any effect, but it is significant that the desperate and hungry people of the Suffolk coast had pleaded with Brandon for support, knowing that he would be able to take their cause to Wolsey and hopefully obtain the help they required.

In addition to an unwanted tax and the threat of rebellion, in 1524 Henry was to suffer a life-threatening jousting accident, caused by Charles Brandon himself. Brandon and Henry VIII were the two best jousters in all of England. Their skills and abilities were well known, and both men shared a mutual love for the sport. They had been jousting together and against one another for years, and, fatefully, on 10 March that year Brandon was set to joust against the king. With one man at each end of the tilt, the signal was given to start and both men urged their horses forward. Brandon was wearing a helmet that gave him very little vision, and, alarmingly, the king had forgotten to lower his headpiece. People cried for Brandon to halt, but unable to hear and with limited vision, he surged forward and struck the inside of the king's helmet, sending splinters exploding over the king's face.

In his chronicle, Hall recounts the incident in more detail:

The 10th day of March, the king having a new harness [armour] made of his own design and fashion, such as no armourer before that time had seen, thought to test the same at the tilt and appointed a joust to serve this purpose.

On foot were appointed the Lord Marquis of Dorset and the Earl of Surrey; the king came to one end of the tilt and the Duke of Suffolk to the other. Then a gentleman said to the duke, 'Sir, the king is come to the tilt's end.' 'I see him not,' said the duke, 'on my faith, for my headpiece takes from me my sight.' With these words, God knoweth by what chance, the king had his spear delivered to him by the Lord Marquis, the visor of his headpiece being up and not down nor fastened, so that his face was clean naked. Then the gentleman said to the duke, 'Sir, the king cometh.'

Then the duke set forward and charged his spear, and the king likewise inadvisedly set off towards the duke. The people, perceiving the king's face bare, cried 'Hold! Hold!', but the duke neither saw nor heard, and whether the king remembered that his visor was up or not none could tell. Alas, what sorrow was it to the people when they saw the splinters of the duke's spear strike on the king's headpiece. For most certainly, the duke struck the king on the brow, right under the defence of the headpiece, on the very skull cap or basinet piece where unto the barbette is hinged for power and defence, to which skull cap or basinet no armourer takes heed of, for it is ever covered with the visor, barbet and volant piece, and so that piece is so defended that it forceth of no charge. But when the spear landed on that place, it was to place the king in great jeopardy of death, in so much that the face was bare, for the duke's spear broke all to splinters and pushed the king's visor or barbet so far back by the that all the king's headpiece was full of splinters. The armourers for this matter were much blamed and so was the Lord Marquis for delivering the spear when his face was open, but the king said that no-one was to blame but himself, for he intended to have saved himself and his sight.

The duke immediately disarmed himself and came to the king, showing him the closeness of his sight, and swore that he would never run against the king again. But if the king had been even a little hurt, the king's servants would have put the duke in jeopardy. Then the king called his armourers and put all his pieces together and then took a spear and ran six courses very well, by which all men might perceive that he had no hurt, which was a great joy and comfort to all his subjects there present.[32]

Naturally, Brandon was alarmed; after all, his actions might have killed the king. Luckily, Henry was not severely hurt and laid no blame upon Brandon. Their friendship remained intact. Brandon swore that he would never joust against the king again, although this oath did not last. In December of the same year, the pair challenged each other to another joust, coming out disguised in silver beards. However, Brandon was only an occasional participant in jousting events after the accident, and only joined those in which the king also chose to take part.[33]

Brandon did continue to take part in courtly events, and in November 1527 was recorded as dancing with the king. In addition to this, he had the honour of being allowed to wear three ostrich feathers in his cap when all others were allowed only two. Brandon was still high in the king's favour.[34]

By 1526, Katherine of Aragon had still failed to give Henry VIII a living male heir. At forty-one, she was now well past her childbearing years. With the birth of Henry Fitzroy the king had shown that he was capable of fathering a healthy son, so in his mind the problem lay with his wife. Moreover, his attention had turned to another. His eye fell on Anne Boleyn, an intriguing woman who had received an excellent education at the French court. While not classically beautiful, she had dark and compelling eyes that could captivate a man. As Henry fell in love with Anne Boleyn, he became obsessed with separating from Katherine of Aragon. He wanted to marry Anne, whom he was sure could give him a male heir. To do so, however, Henry would need an annulment of his marriage, which could only be granted by Pope Clement VII. This would not be straightforward.

The tale of Henry VIII's 'Great Matter', and his desire to seek an annulment of his first marriage in order to marry Anne Boleyn, has been told many times over in countless books. However, Brandon's role can be glimpsed at times in this complicated affair.

Pope Clement VII was reluctant to grant Henry VIII his heart's desire. In early June 1527, Rome had been ransacked by the imperial army of Katherine of Aragon's nephew Charles V. Pope Clement had been captured,[35] and could not be expected to arrange for his captor's aunt to be removed from her position as Queen of England. However, continual pressure from Thomas Wolsey and Clement's eventual release led him to send a papal legate to England to decide upon the matter. Cardinal Campeggio was chosen for the task, albeit he was under instructions to stall the hearing for as long as possible.[36] Campeggio was an old man riddled with gout, and his journey to England was slow and painful, much to the frustration of the English.[37] Campeggio finally arrived in London on 7 October where he was lodged overnight at Brandon's home in Southwark, before being taken to Bath House the next evening.[38] The hearing for Henry VIII's Great Matter officially started on 31 May 1529.[39]

The hearing, which both Henry VIII and Anne Boleyn hoped would secure the annulment of Henry's marriage, did not go as planned. Cardinal Campeggio and Cardinal Thomas Wolsey were to conduct the hearing, and despite Wolsey's strong desire to serve his king, things were not to go his way. After almost two months of debate, with Henry VIII's hopes relying heavily upon his right-hand man, on 23 July 1529 Cardinal Campeggio announced that he could not give a final judgement until he had discussed the matter further with Pope Clement VII. He then adjourned the court indefinitely.[40]

Henry VIII was furious. All his hopes of having a quick annulment of his marriage to Katherine of Aragon so that he could marry Anne Boleyn and produce a legitimate heir had just been dashed. It would seem that Brandon was equally furious. He had attended the hearing that day, sitting with the king in a gallery above the door. After the king stormed out in anger, Brandon rose and shouted from the gallery, 'By the Mass it was never merry in England whilst we had cardinals amongst us!' Cardinal Thomas Wolsey promptly replied, 'If I, a simple cardinal, had not been, you should have had at this present time no head upon your shoulders wherein you should have a tongue to make any such report in despite of us!'[41]

Wolsey's retort was straight to the point; and indeed, it was Thomas Wolsey who had interceded with Henry when Brandon had committed treason and married the king's sister without permission. Brandon did not reply to Wolsey's remark, and quickly hurried out in search of his king. Interestingly, this is not the first time that open animosity had surfaced between Brandon and Wolsey. On 4 February of the same year, the Spanish ambassador Mendoza had written to his king to state that he believed Anne Boleyn thought Thomas Wolsey was trying to hinder the trial rather than aid it. He also noted that he believed Brandon had joined with the Boleyns and the Duke of Norfolk to bring about the fall of Wolsey:[42]

> This suspicion [of the lady] has been the cause of her forming an alliance with her father [Viscount Rochford], and with the two Dukes of Norfolk and Suffolk, to try and see whether they can conjointly ruin (*desbaratar*) the Cardinal. Hitherto they seem to have made no impression on the king, save that the Cardinal is no longer received at Court as graciously as before, and that now and then king Henry has uttered certain angry words respecting him.[43]

Brandon was smart enough to see which way the wind was blowing. Henry VIII was desperate for an annulment, and he had put all his faith in Thomas Wolsey. Wolsey had failed, and although Brandon had so far supported the cardinal, he did not wish to be brought down with him. It was perhaps not so much that Brandon was against Wolsey but that he was wise enough to side with his king when he saw the writing on the wall.

Meanwhile, in May talk began of a possible peace treaty between Francis I and Charles V. Desperate to see England represented, the king sent Brandon and Sir William Fitzwilliam across the Channel. After a short briefing, the pair left on 17 May to disrupt the peace talks by offering Francis troops and money for a campaign against Charles.[44]

Upon arriving in France, Brandon and Fitzwilliam were entertained lavishly in an attempt to stop them from attending the talks.[45] It is important to note that Brandon alone was sent with another, far more secret mission. He was to seek out Francis I's thoughts regarding Wolsey, specifically whether Francis thought that the cardinal was obstructing Henry's divorce. Brandon communicates Francis' reaction in a letter to his king:

> Campeggio told Francis he was going to England and afterwards to Spain by commission of the Pope. On which Francis asked him how he could go into Spain, and yet do what the king of England wished for the divorce, and he replied that he did not think that the divorce would take effect, but should be dissembled

well enough. Thinking that the king was deceived, he told the bishop of Bath what the Cardinal had said, desiring him to advertise you of it. I then proceeded to inquire of him, promising that what he said should never be revealed, What say you of the cardinal of England in this matter? and he replied, When he was with me, as far as I could perceive, he desired that the divorce might take place, for he loved not the queen; but I advise my good brother not to put too much trust in any man, whereby he may be deceived, and the best remedy is to look to his own matters himself;—saying further that the cardinal of England had great intelligence with the Pope and with Campeggio, and, as they are not inclined to the divorce, it is the more needful for the king to have regard to his own affairs.[46]

In the end, both Brandon and Fitzwilliam were recalled from France as it had become clear that a peace treaty between Francis I and Charles V was inevitable.[47] However, gleaning the French king's thoughts on Wolsey had made the trip worthwhile.

In time Henry VIII would have the annulment of his marriage, but Thomas Wolsey would not live to see it. On 9 October 1529, Wolsey was officially charged with 'praemunire', asserting the power of papal jurisdiction over the supremacy of the English monarch, in this case Henry VIII. The cardinal was also stripped of his role as Lord Chancellor.[48] He was sent to Esher in Surrey and was officially arrested in early November 1530. He died on 29 November on his way to London for trial.[49]

There are no records of Brandon's thoughts regarding the arrest and death of Thomas Wolsey. Brandon had owed a great deal to the cardinal in 1515, when he had desperately sought his help and support after his treasonous marriage to Mary. Brandon had begged the cardinal for assistance and had openly stated that he felt Wolsey was the only one who could help him, yet fourteen years later he had turned against the cardinal. He knew better than to be associated with Wolsey when the man faced ruin, especially since his rival the Duke of Norfolk was in the hostile camp. Brandon's position at court relied heavily upon the king's good graces, and if the king was against Wolsey then so too was Brandon. Political expediency trumped any other consideration.

Brandon received his share of the spoils. He was granted Wolsey's prize mules as well as the manor of Sayes Court in Deptford, and took in the clerk of Wolsey's kitchen.[50] He was appointed president of the King's Council, a role that suited him well as he was one of the king's closest friends. However, his attendance was sporadic; a Venetian ambassador reported in 1531 that he 'has the second seat in his Majesty's Privy Council, which he rarely enters, save for the discussion of matters of a certain importance, passing his time more pleasantly in other amusements'.[51]

Henry got his way. He turned from the Pope to his own parliament, and from October 1529 to April 1536 the Reformation Parliament sat. This parliament was created on the idea that there was only one supreme head in England, the king, and that all matters of Church and State needed to be referred to the monarch and not the Pope. It enforced the idea that no foreign power could dictate law in England and that any laws administered by the monarch were binding.

The king accused the clergy of supporting Thomas Wolsey. In return, the clergy offered the king a bribe of £100,000 (£32,210,000)[52] to drop any charges against them. Then, on 7 February 1531, the king demanded that he be known as the 'Supreme Head of the English Church'. The clergy was naturally opposed to such an idea, but the king was insistent. After some argument, the clergy granted the title with one slight alteration. On 11 February, Convocation granted Henry VIII the title of 'Singular protector, supreme lord, and even, so far as the law of Christ allows, supreme head of the English church and clergy'.[53] By the end of 1532, Parliament was the only legal legislative body in England. Henry VIII could have his annulment.

12

The Tempestuous Years

Over the next decade, what is today known as the Reformation would sweep across England, changing the face of religion in the country forever. Henry VIII was orthodox in his beliefs, and his faith would remain devout throughout his life, but he grew increasingly interested in the running and organisation of the Church. With his new right-hand man, Thomas Cromwell, he would oversee the Dissolution of the Monasteries, whereby religious houses that were hundreds of years old were compelled to surrender to the king. They were closed, pulled down and their wealth absorbed into the king's coffers. Henry VIII then sold much of the land formerly belonging to the monasteries to his courtiers. Charles Brandon would be one of those who benefited from the project. He purchased Vaudey Abbey and its land and used the demolished building to extend his castle in Lincolnshire.

It is challenging to assess Brandon's personal religious beliefs during this time of upheaval in England. On 28 October 1537, Sir Richard Bulkeley wrote to Thomas Cromwell on the subject:

My cousin Doctor Arthur Bulkeley, of the number of the Arches, has been chaplain to the duke of Suffolk this seven years. He now desires 'to appertain to your Lordship, to do you service at his Grace's request'. And as Mr. Bedell who was of your spiritual council is now dead, he would be the rather glad to do you service because of his former acquaintance with your goodness. I pray that at my request he may be the more acceptable.[1]

From this letter, we can assume that Arthur Bulkeley was chaplain to Brandon from around 1530. It is unclear when he left Brandon's services, but Bulkeley was appointed Bishop of Bangor in 1541 and was consecrated 19 February 1542. He died on 14 March 1553.[2] In addition to having Bulkeley as his chaplain, Brandon also adorned his chapel with statues of saints, and hired Nicholas Cutler to be the master of six choirboys attached to the chapel.[3] Brandon was also known to be the patron of former monks.[4] However, towards the end of his life, John Parkhurst, a reformer, was also briefly a chaplain to Brandon and his fourth wife, Katherine Willoughby.[5]

Willoughby was known to have strong reformist beliefs and would become close friends with Queen Katherine Parr, Henry VIII's sixth and final wife, who also shared similar religious beliefs. Parkhurst too had reformist friends such as Miles Coverdale.[6] Willoughby was also known to have a dislike of Bishop Stephen Gardiner, a staunch Catholic who was adamantly opposed to the new reforms happening across England. On one occasion she famously dressed her dog up in white robes and referred to it as Gardiner.[7] On another, Charles Brandon was hosting a dinner at his home and suggested a dance in which each lady should select the man they loved best for their partner. Brandon had taken himself out of the selection, and thus Katherine selected Gardiner as her partner, stating that 'forasmuch as she could not sit down with my lord whom she loved best she had chosen him whom she loved worst'.[8]

Unfortunately, we do not know Brandon's thoughts on Gardiner. However, a conversation was overheard in which he and Archbishop Thomas Cranmer, a reformer, were heard talking about Gardiner. Brandon is reported as stating, 'We of the council had him once at a good lift, and should well have dispatched him of his authority, if the king's majesty our master had stayed himself from admitting him to his presence, as then his highness was content that we should thoroughly have sifted and tried him.'[9] This statement may have been more of an attack upon Gardiner personally than any indication of Brandon's personal religious beliefs. Ultimately, the duke had both reformist and conservative people within his service. It may very well be that Brandon was conservative in his personal religious views but preferred to follow the religious will and desires of his king when it came to public displays.

Despite siding with the Duke of Norfolk and the Boleyns against Thomas Wolsey, Brandon was opposed to the king marrying Anne Boleyn. His wife, Mary Tudor, had been close friends with Katherine of Aragon, and when the king openly separated from her in 1531 Mary excused herself from court.[10]

Eustace Chapuys, ambassador to Charles V, wrote to his master that Anne 'had been accused by the Duke of Suffolk of undue familiarity with a gentleman who on a former occasion had been banished on suspicion'.[11] This gentleman was Sir Thomas Wyatt, poet, courtier and long-time friend of the Boleyn family. Judging from his poetry, it is quite probable that Wyatt had romantic feelings towards Anne. However, there is no evidence to suggest that the feeling was mutual. With the rumour never corroborated, a furious Henry banished Brandon from court for a time. In a riposte to the accusation, meanwhile, Anne Boleyn made one of her own, declaring that Brandon was sleeping with his daughter Frances.[12] This did not teach Brandon a lesson; later in the year, he spoke with William FitzWilliam, Treasurer of the King's Household, floating the notion of persuading the king not to marry Anne Boleyn.[13]

In 1532, Mary Tudor spoke publicly about her opposition to the marriage and made it clear where her loyalties lay, talking about Anne Boleyn in unfavourable terms. This resulted in a quarrel between some of Norfolk's men (the duke being Anne Boleyn's uncle) and Brandon's men. On 23 April, Carlo Capello reported:

At the moment of his arrival at the Court, one of the chief gentlemen in the service of said Duke of Norfolk, with 20 followers, assaulted and killed in the sanctuary of Westminster Sir (D'no) William Peninthum (*sic*) chief gentleman and kinsman of the Duke of Suffolk. In consequence of this, the whole Court was in an uproar, and had the Duke of Suffolk been there, it is supposed that a serious affray would have taken place. On hearing of what had happened, he (Suffolk) was on his way to remove the assailants by force from the sanctuary, when the king sent the Treasurer [Thomas Cromwell] to him, and made him return, and has adjusted the affair; and this turmoil displeased him. It is said to have been caused by a private quarrel, but I am assured it was owing to opprobrious language uttered against Madam Anne by his Majesty's sister, the Duchess of Suffolk, Queen Dowager of France.[14]

Thomas Cromwell then went to the king and informed him that he had heard rumours that the Duke of Suffolk's servants were seeking revenge. Upon hearing this, Brandon wrote frantically to Cromwell, addressing the letter 'to my loving friend, Master Crumewell':

> Sent five or six days ago his servant, John Caundishe, to Court, where my lord of Norfolk showed him that one Threishwell and a servant of my lady of Norfolk had informed Cromwell that several of Suffolk's servants had bound themselves by oath to him to be revenged on Southwell, if ever in their lives they should meet him. My lord of Norfolk said he would not have spoken about it, believing it, as it is, untrue, if Cromwell had not showed it to the king before he knew. One wonders he could act in such an unfriendly manner. If any such thing had been done before his face, remembering his promise to the king, he would have sent his servants up to his Highness with their words, or ordered them so that Southwell should have no fear of them. Ewelme, 20 July.[15]

The murderers were pardoned, but tensions still simmered between Norfolk and Brandon. The following year, Norfolk demanded that Brandon relinquish to him the office of Earl Marshal, which Brandon had held since the death of Norfolk's father in 1524. The king complied with this request, and in mitigation granted Brandon the position of warden and chief justice of the royal forests south of Trent.[16] To further pacify Brandon, Cromwell wrote to the duke suggesting that he should work to keep the peace with Norfolk:

> The king hears that [Suffolk] is content to surrender his patent of Earl Marshal, and has accordingly granted it to the duke of Norfolk, whose ancestors long held it, in place of which he shall have the justiceship of the Forests on this side of the Trent for life. The king is pleased with him for so kindly parting with the office, and that he has more zeal to nourish kindness and love between Norfolk and himself than to that or any other office. Advises him to come to Court, as Norfolk is shortly going "towards his great journey in ambassade.[17]

Unhappy with this turn of events, Brandon and his wife removed themselves from the court. It took the influence of Thomas Cromwell, and even a visit from the king, to smooth things over.[18] Brandon must have learnt a lesson, as when he returned to court he made sure to keep his thoughts and opinions to himself rather than risk losing the king's favour once more.

During this time Brandon appears to have been everywhere at court and yet not directly involved with anything. Various people petitioned Brandon for help, but he did not seem to play any direct role in the happenings of court throughout the early 1530s. He continued to entertain the king and take part in various forms of entertainment and pastimes, but, tellingly, when the king required any real business to be done, he turned to Cromwell.[19]

It could very well be that Brandon had been uncomfortable with the missions that Henry had sent him on concerning the annulment of his marriage to Katherine of Aragon. Brandon also had a poor relationship with Anne Boleyn and the Duke of Norfolk. With his wife adamantly opposed to her brother's remarriage, Brandon may have thought it prudent to appear at court to keep his presence known and maintain a friendship with the king while at the same time distancing himself from the political events unfolding around him.

To close out 1532, on 25 October Francis I elected Brandon and the Duke of Norfolk as Knights of the Order of St Michel,[20] the French equivalent of the English Order of the Garter, to which Brandon had been elected in April 1513.[21]

The year's 1533 to 1535 were tempestuous for Charles Brandon. In two short years, he was forced to act against his conscience, lost a great deal of cash and property, and tragically lost both his wife and his son.

On 25 January 1533, just before dawn, Henry VIII married Anne Boleyn at Whitehall Palace.[22] Unfortunately, records do not state precisely who was in attendance. If Brandon did attend the wedding, then he would have been sworn to absolute secrecy as at the time many still believed that Henry was still legally married to his first wife.

After Henry's marriage to Anne, it was left to the dukes of Norfolk and Suffolk to carry the news to Katherine of Aragon. They met with the queen on 9 April 1533 at her residence at Ampthill and informed Katherine that she was no longer Queen of England, but from that day forward had to style herself as Dowager Princess of Wales. Katherine took the news with grace but refused either to use the new title or to believe that Henry's marriage to Anne was valid.[23] On 3 July, Katherine was given the papers stating that her marriage to Henry VIII had been annulled and that the king was lawfully married to Anne Boleyn. As the king could not have two wives, it was essential that Katherine now style herself as Princess Dowager.[24] This time, an outraged Katherine declared that she did not recognise any judgement made except that of the Pope.[25]

In December, Brandon was once more sent to try and convince Katherine that she was no longer to style herself Queen of England and that she must be moved from her present lodgings to Somersham. Eustace Chapuys wrote to Charles V that 'the duke of Suffolk himself, before he left this city on such an errand, confessed and partook of the Communion, as his own mother-in-law sent to inform me, declaring at the time of his departure that he wished some accident might happen to him on the road that should exempt him at once from accomplishing such a journey and mission'.[26]

The duke was not looking forward to the task ahead, already having been on the receiving end of Katherine's fury. When he arrived and told Katherine of her upcoming move, she stated that she would rather be hewn into pieces than be called Dowager Princess and that she absolutely refused to go to Somersham. The door was slammed in Brandon's face. The duke was left standing outside, imploring Katherine to see reason and to accept her new position. He then went on to question Katherine's servants, who also refused to refer to her as Dowager Princess and insisted that she was queen. Five days passed, in which time Brandon's men removed the furniture and hangings from the house as well as dismissing most of Katherine's servants. All the while Brandon continued to try and persuade Katherine to leave, but she insisted that the only way she would go was if he broke down the door – an action Brandon clearly would not undertake for fear of the ramifications.[27] At a complete loss, Brandon wrote to Henry explaining the situation and even went so far as to say that he thought the only way they could transport Katherine was if they bound her with ropes. He requested the king's guidance.[28] Brandon had to wait until 31 December, when he received instructions from the king that he should leave Katherine where she was and return to court.[29]

The whole situation was uneasy and uncomfortable for Brandon, and while he thought Katherine was stubborn, he was also well aware of her failing health and the ever-declining living conditions that she was forced to endure. He was not unsympathetic to her cause, and he conveyed to the king news of the poor health that Katherine was suffering from when he returned to court.[30] This information had no effect upon the king and Brandon was left once more in the difficult situation of having to harass the former queen while secretly being sympathetic to her cause.

Later in the year, after Anne Boleyn gave birth to baby Elizabeth, Brandon was also instructed to take Katherine of Aragon and Henry VIII's daughter Princess Mary to meet her new half-sister. Eustace Chapuys wrote of the event:

[T]he Princess, attended only by two maids in waiting, was conducted by the Duke of Suffolk to the residence of the king's bastard daughter. Arrived there the duke asked her if she did not like to see and pay her court to the Princess [of Wales]. Upon which she answered that she knew of no other princess in England but herself; that the daughter of Madame de Penebrok (Pembroke) was no princess at all. True, if the king, her father, acknowledged her as his *daughter*, just as he called the duke of Richmont his *son*, she could treat the latter as brother, and her as sister, but in nowise as princess of Wales. Before taking leave the duke asked her whether she had any message for the king. To which she replied: 'None, except that the princess of Wales, his daughter, asked for his blessing;' and upon the duke observing that he would not dare take such a message to the king, she interrupted him by saying; 'Then go away, and leave me alone.'[31]

When he returned to court Brandon was reprimanded by the king for treating Mary too mildly. The duke was in the difficult situation of having to serve his king while also feeling sympathy for Katherine and her daughter. He was damned if he did, and damned if he didn't.

While these events were unfolding, Brandon and his wife Mary also managed to find time to organise the wedding of their eldest daughter, Frances. Now legitimised, the couple's children were highly prized within the marriage market. Previously a marriage between the Duke of Norfolk's son Henry Howard, Earl of Surrey, and Frances Brandon had been proposed, but Norfolk turned it down due to Frances' small dowry. This was another sign that Brandon's financial status was still quite precarious, despite him being Duke of Suffolk and a leading man at court. However, another marriage prospect soon arrived. In October 1530, Thomas Grey, Marquis of Dorset, had died, leaving his son Henry Grey as his heir. Brandon sought the approval of the dowager marchioness and then bought Henry Grey's wardship for 4,000 marks. The young couple married in May at Suffolk Place in a spectacular wedding attended by the king. It was to be Mary Tudor's last public appearance.[32]

On Saturday 12 April 1533, Anne Boleyn was finally presented at court as queen. She attended Mass dressed in robes of estate and wearing beautiful jewels. Following this, on 28 May, Archbishop Cranmer declared that Henry VIII's marriage to Katherine of Aragon had been invalid and his marriage to Anne was lawful. Now there would be no doubt as to who was the rightful Queen of England, at least in Henry and Anne's minds. Sadly, Brandon's private thoughts about this declaration go unrecorded.

Anne Boleyn's magnificent coronation was set for Sunday 1 June. Wearing a gown of crimson velvet edged in ermine and a purple velvet mantle with her hair loose and hanging down to her waist, Anne Boleyn made the journey barefoot from Westminster Hall to Westminster Abbey under a canopy of cloth of gold. Brandon's duty was to walk before the future queen carrying her royal crown and then, during the coronation, to stand close to the queen holding a white staff of office.[33] Afterwards, a great banquet was held at Westminster Hall, where Brandon acted as Lord High Steward and Constable. It was his responsibility to organise all the details of the coronation, including Anne's procession through London the previous day. Wearing a doublet covered in pearls and riding a charger covered in crimson velvet, Brandon rode through the banquet, which hosted eight hundred people who were served approximately thirty-two dishes.[34] Whatever Brandon's thoughts on the marriage, he performed his duties to the fullest. Anne Boleyn's procession through London, her coronation and her lavish banquet afterwards were greatly opulent affairs, with no expense spared.

In January 1534, Brandon gave to the king 'a book garnished with gold, having therein a clock'[35] as a New Year's present.

The cost of such a lavish item is not recorded, but it must have been expensive. One cannot help but wonder if it was a means for Brandon to maintain the king's good graces. Previously, in January 1532, Brandon had gifted the king 'a gold ball for fume' for New Year's.[36]

To secure Anne Boleyn's place as queen, and to see the 'heirs of her body' as legitimate successors to the throne, Henry VIII had Parliament pass the Act of Succession on 23 March 1534. The Act stated that any heirs born to Anne Boleyn would become first in line to the throne and that Mary, Henry's daughter with Katherine of Aragon, was a bastard and no longer able to inherit the throne. The Act also necessitated the swearing of an oath recognising the Act as well as affirming the fact that Henry was now the Supreme Head of the Church of England (so far as the law allowed). Anyone disagreeing with the Act or refusing to take the oath would be charged with treason. Charles Brandon, along with the other important and high-ranking members of Parliament and clergymen, signed the oath on 30 March 1534.[37] Whatever Brandon's thoughts regarding the marriage, his signature was now attached to the oath stating that he not only believed in the marriage but would also uphold it, as well as the king's right to be the Supreme Head of the English Church. Once more, Brandon was showing his loyalty lay first and foremost with his king.

Despite the great triumph and majesty of Anne Boleyn's coronation, the absence of Henry's sister and Brandon's wife, Mary Tudor, could not be missed. Some have suggested that Mary's non-attendance was a firm statement against the new queen. It was common knowledge that she openly opposed her brother's desire to seek the annulment of his marriage to Katherine of Aragon. Brandon had at first spoken similar words, but he quickly learnt to keep his thoughts to himself and to toe the line at court.

However, it was most likely that Mary simply wasn't well enough to attend the magnificent event. The dowager queen had been ill for some time, and in May 1533 Brandon had travelled back to Westhorpe to visit her. Tragically, it would be the last time he would ever see her alive. Before long, Brandon was recalled to London to continue the organisation of Anne's coronation, and it was likely that he was there when Mary died between seven and eight o'clock in the morning on 25 June 1533.[38]

Mary's cause of death is unknown. It has been suggested that she may have suffered from angina. She had been ill for some time, and several years earlier had complained of constant pain in her side. Another suggestion for Mary's death was the grief over her brother's dismissal of Katherine of Aragon and marriage to Anne Boleyn.[39] However, it would seem that despite the rift Mary still loved her brother, and she wrote him a letter in June shortly before her death stating that she 'has been very sick "and ele ates" (ill at ease). Has been fain to send for Master Peter the physician, but is rather worse than better. Trusts shortly to come to London with her husband. Is sure, if she tarries here, that she will never "asperre the sekenys." Will be glad to see the king, as she has been a great while out of his sight, and hopes not to be so long again.'[40] Whether it was the pain in her side, angina or something else, Mary's death would shake Brandon's world.

As Dowager Queen of France and Duchess of Suffolk, Mary Tudor was remembered with a lavish funeral. Her body was embalmed and for three weeks her coffin, draped in deep blue or black velvet, lay in state at Westhorpe, candles burning day and night. On 10 July, King Henry ordered a Requiem Mass to be held for his sister at Westminster Abbey. A delegation was sent from France for Mary's funeral, arriving on 20 July 1533. Mary was to be interred at Bury St Edmunds, and her chief mourner was her daughter Frances, who was accompanied by her husband, Henry Grey, and her brother, Henry, Earl of Lincoln. Also attending the funeral was Mary's youngest daughter, Eleanor, and her ward Katherine Willoughby.[41]

For the journey from Westhorpe to the abbey church at Bury St Edmunds, Mary's coffin was placed upon a hearse draped in black velvet embroidered with Mary's arms and her motto, 'The will of God is sufficient for me.'[42] The coffin was covered in a pall of black cloth of gold and atop this was an effigy of Mary in robes of state, holding a crown and a golden sceptre that signified her status as Dowager Queen of France. The hearse was drawn by six horses wearing black cloth, and the coffin covered by a canopy carried by four of Brandon's knights. Surrounding the coffin, standard-bearers carried the arms of the Brandon and Tudor families.[43]

At the head of the procession walked one hundred torchbearers drawn from the local community who had been paid to dress in black for the funeral. Next came members of the clergy who carried the cross. After them came the household staff, followed by the six horses pulling the hearse. Behind the hearse followed the knights and other noblemen in attendance followed by one hundred of the duke's yeomen. Lastly came Mary's daughter Frances, the chief mourner, and the other ladies including Eleanor and Katherine Willoughby. Along the way, the funeral procession was joined by other members of the local parishes.

At two o'clock in the afternoon, Mary's coffin was received at Bury St Edmunds by the abbot and the monks. The coffin was then placed before the high altar and surrounded by the mourners in order of precedence and a Mass was said. Afterwards, a supper was held for the noble members of Mary's funeral entourage.[44]

Eight women, twelve men, thirty yeomen and some of the clergy were appointed to watch over Mary's body overnight. The following day a Requiem Mass was sung and Mary's daughters, her two stepdaughters, her ward Katherine Willoughby and Katherine's mother brought palls of cloth of gold to the altar. William Rugg conducted the funeral address and the officers of Mary's household broke their white staffs and, finally, Mary was interned. Five years later, the monastery that Mary had been interned was dissolved and she was moved to St Mary's Church nearby. Her body lay peacefully at Bury St Edmunds until 1784; her remains were disturbed again when her altar monument was removed because it obstructed the approach to the rails of the communion table. A slab on the floor now marks her resting place.[45]

The people of Suffolk dearly loved Mary, and after her funeral alms of meat, drink and coin were given to the poor.[46] As was custom, neither Mary's brother nor her husband attended the funeral, although since Mary had been a Dowager Queen of France and Princess of England, a funeral at court was required. Therefore, on 10 and 11 July, another funeral was held at Westminster with all official duties being performed despite the absence of a body. It is believed that Brandon attended this funeral for his wife.[47] We do not have any record of his feelings over the death of his wife of eighteen years, but we can imagine his sense of loss. He had risked all, even facing treason charges and the possibility of death, by marrying a member of the royal family without the king's permission. He must have felt something strong towards Mary, be it love or a sense of close companionship.

With the death of Mary Tudor, Dowager Queen of France and Duchess of Suffolk, Charles Brandon was left in quite a precarious financial situation. Mary's dowager payment, worth a staggering £4,000 (£1,288,400)[48] a year, was no longer available, and Brandon had three children to raise as well as loans from the Crown to repay. In addition to this, he had the status of a duke to keep up. The king did step in, and cancelled £1,000 (£322,100)[49] of Brandon's debt as well as providing him with the fruits of the vacant see of Ely for the year 1533/34, which amounted to around £2,000[50] (£644,200).[51] But Brandon was still strapped for cash, and he needed to look elsewhere for financial assistance. Fortunately, he did not need to look far.

Brandon turned his gaze upon Katherine Willoughby. Born on 22 March 1519, Katherine was the daughter of William, 11th Baron Willoughby, and his wife Maria de Salinas, one of Katherine of Aragon's ladies who had come with her from Spain in 1501. At the tender age of just seven, Katherine lost her father. With no male son surviving, Katherine became his heir.[52] In March 1528, Brandon had bought the wardship of Katherine from the king with the intent to marry her to his son Henry.[53] She had then come to live with the Brandons.

To be sent to live with a prominent member of the court or someone of importance, and to become their ward, was quite common during the Tudor age. For example, Anne Boleyn gained a position within the Duchess of Austria's court to learn the skills required to be an intelligent and dutiful woman.[54] Brandon himself had sent his eldest daughter, Anne, to serve Margaret of Savoy for some time before she was recalled in 1515.[55] To be taken in as a ward was helpful to the ward's family as they no longer had to provide food or clothing for the child, nor pay for the child's education. Another example of this is when Mary Boleyn's husband, William Carey, died in 1528. She was left in a precarious position, and, with little money and two children to raise, she gave her son, Henry, into the wardship of his aunt Anne Boleyn. It would have been Anne's responsibility to see the boy clothed and educated, and this helped to relieve the financial burden on Mary Boleyn.[56]

Life with the Brandons would have granted Katherine the opportunity to learn many skills, including how to run a household. She did not have to wait long to put these valuable lessons to use.

A mere three months after the death of his third wife, Brandon married Katherine on 7 September 1533.[57]

There has been some debate over Brandon's actions at this juncture. Originally, he intended to have Katherine marry his son Henry, who at the time was only eleven years of age. However, he needed cash quickly and he could not afford to wait until his son came of age. In addition, if young Henry had married Katherine then Brandon would not have acquired the properties and financial benefits that were left to her by her father; instead, these would have gone to his son. Brandon, ever the opportunist, and in desperate need of funds, was not going to lose this chance.[58]

At the time of the marriage, Brandon was forty-nine and Katherine a mere fourteen. Looking back with a modern perspective, this can seem quite horrifying. However, it was not entirely unusual at the time for an older man to marry a much younger woman. Despite this, there were still some mutterings surrounding Brandon's behaviour, and people were well aware of the real reasons for the marriage.[59]

Eustace Chapuys reported that 'on Sunday next the duke of Suffolk will be married to the daughter of a Spanish lady named lady Willoughby. She was promised to his son, but he is only ten years old; and although it is not worth writing to your Majesty the novelty of the case made me mention it.'[60] He also went on to say that 'in contracting such a marriage, the duke will no doubt please the ladies of this country, who, imitating his example, will no doubt take their revenge, when accused of marrying again immediately after the death of their husbands, as they are in the habit of doing'.[61]

As well as the couple's marriage on 7 September, another, more important event took place that day. In the queen's apartments at Greenwich, Anne Boleyn gave birth to a baby girl at approximately three o'clock. Anne had retired to her chambers only a short time before and had undertaken the traditional lying-in duties, including covering the windows and floor with tapestries and rugs as well as excluding men from the birthing chamber. While the birth of a daughter was not what Henry and Anne had so desperately longed for, the fact that the little girl was born healthy and that Anne recovered quickly gave hope that soon the couple would have a son.

The baby girl was named Elizabeth, and on 10 September she was christened at the chapel of the Observant Friars. Neither Henry nor Anne attended the christening; it was not tradition for the father to participate, and Anne had not yet been 'churched', the process whereby new mothers were cleansed by the Church and allowed to enter public life once again. Brandon, however, did attend the christening and had the great honour of escorting the baby girl along with the Duke of Norfolk. Archbishop Thomas Cranmer conducted the christening and was one of the baby girl's godparents, along with the Dowager Duchess of Norfolk, the Dowager Marchioness of Dorset and the Marquess of Exeter.[62]

Brandon's financial troubles were not so easily swept away by gaining his new wife's inheritance. The duke would have to battle for two more years before he was able to settle the majority of his debts. Katherine's uncle Sir Christopher Willoughby challenged his niece's inheritance and claimed that before Katherine's birth his brother had stated he was to inherit some of his properties upon his death. Brandon and Katherine's mother, the Dowager Lady Willoughby, joined forces to contest this, and after interference by the king Brandon was able to retain much of Katherine's inheritance.[63] Katherine's lands only brought in approximately £900 a year[64] (£289,890),[65] and even with this new income Brandon's financial woes were not over as at the time he was not entitled to the full amount. Katherine's mother still had control of much of her lands and income, and it was not until after her death 1539 that Brandon was able to obtain the full £900 and incorporate it into his finances.[66]

On 19 July 1535, Mary's debts were cancelled[67] but Brandon still had to pay the staggering sum of £6,700 (£2,158,070).[68] In an attempt to pay off this debt, Brandon handed over a great deal of plate and jewels amounting to £4,360 (£1,404,356)[69] as well as exchanging some of his lands and properties with the king. Brandon lost his Oxfordshire and Berkshire manors as well as his house at Westhorpe. In return, he gained land in Lincolnshire worth a mere £175 (£56,367)[70] a year, a manor in Essex, a house in London as well as £3,183 (£1,025,244)[71] in cash and the final cancellation of his debts.[72]

Brandon also wrote to Nicholas de St Martin in an attempt to obtain his French pension, which at the time of his wife's death was four months overdue:

> I have written to Sir John Wallop to speak to the Great Master that I may have the arrears due to me at May last; trusting that the French king and his council will not stop my dues, if the king forbear his. If Sir John Wallop cannot obtain this from the Grand Master he is to speak with the king, and advertise you of the result. The king (of England) intends to send one of his Council shortly to Francis. When he arrives in Paris, you are to declare to him the effect of my business, and be ordered accordingly, as I wish to have all my causes determined. At the coming of the king's ambassador send me word, that I may give you directions.[73]

Unfortunately, it seems that the duke's efforts came to naught. Despite having revenues of around £2,500–£3,000 (between £800,000 and £1 million)[74] a year, Brandon still owed money to the Crown.[75] He also continued to live beyond his means as he was required to keep up appearances as one of the highest-ranking peers of the land. It seemed that the duke's financial issues would follow him all his life.

Tragically, Brandon's son Henry, Earl of Lincoln, died on the morning of 1 March 1534[76] just six months after his father's marriage to Katherine Willoughby. He was eleven years old. Rumour at the time had it that Henry died of a broken heart after having his wife stolen from him. It has been suggested that young Henry may have been sick for some time leading up to his death. Whatever the cause of the young earl's death, Brandon was left with four daughters and no male heir to succeed him. Anne Boleyn is reported to have said that 'My Lord Brandon Kills one son to beget another'.[77] If there is any truth in this, then clearly Anne still held a great deal of resentment towards the duke for trying to break up her engagement to the king. Probably wisely on the duke's part, any thoughts he had on the queen's comments went unrecorded.

Just over a year later, Brandon wrote to Cromwell advising him of the birth of his first child with Katherine – a son. He also asked if Cromwell could be one of the godfathers: 'It has pleased God to send me a son. I beg you will ask the king to be so good to me as "to make a Corssten solle," and that you also will be one of the godfathers.'[78] The boy's birth is recorded as having occurred on 18 September 1535.[79]

A short time later, the baby boy – named Henry after the king – was christened. King Henry, along with Thomas Cromwell, stood as one of the godfathers.[80] This was a great honour for Brandon. The happy king even gave the midwife and nurse £4 (£1,288)[81] for their efforts.[82]

In December 1535, the king granted Brandon the manors of 'Burwell, Muckton, Anthorpe, Calceby, Anderby, Huttoft, Sutton, Hagnaby, Thoresthorpe, Theddlethorp, Mablethorpe, Ludford and Sloothby with 100 messuages, 500 acres of arable, 100 acres of meadow, 50 acres of pasture, 100 acres of wood, 50 acres of heath and £40 rent charges'.[83] It is highly likely that such lavish grants were given to Brandon to celebrate the birth of his son.

After three years of ups and downs, Charles Brandon was once more a married man with a newborn son and heir. Things were finally settling down for the duke. Perhaps he even hoped for some peace. If this was the case, he was to be mistaken. The next two years would be among the most turbulent of Henry VIII's reign, and Brandon would be drawn into events with powerful force.

13

The King's Man

In 1536, England was to face the deaths of two queens and the arrival of a third, and was rocked by a major rebellion that almost changed the course of English history. Amid such tumult, the king turned to his most trusted friend: Charles Brandon.

On 7 January, Katherine of Aragon died.[1] Katherine's death had a considerable impact on both Henry and Anne Boleyn, as they now considered themselves to be free of the woman who had always cast a shadow over their marriage. Although Henry considered his first marriage to be annulled, the Church and the Pope had not shared the view. Now, with Katherine out of the way, all parties had to accept that Henry's first marriage was truly over.

No records state how Brandon reacted when he heard the news. Henry and Anne both donned yellow and appeared to celebrate, Henry carrying his young daughter Elizabeth and showing her off at court.[2] It has been suggested that yellow was a colour of mourning, but it is more likely that the couple were simply happy to be free of Katherine.

The next major event to send a shock through court came on 24 January when Henry VIII, a passionate lover of the joust, fell from his horse while in full armour and was crushed under the weight of the animal.[3] Eustace Chapuys reported the accident: 'On the eve of the Conversion of St. Paul, the king being mounted on a great horse to run at the lists, both fell so heavily that everyone thought it a miracle he was not killed, but he sustained no injury.'[4] The accident, which has been likened to a car crash at 40 miles per hour,[5] reopened troublesome ulcers in Henry VIII's legs, and it has been proposed that it may also have caused some form of brain damage, affecting his mood and personality. Although there are no records of Brandon attending the joust, as a member of the court and a skilled jouster it is most likely that he was present. Although the king survived this major incident, he would never joust again.[6]

The next major event was Anne Boleyn's miscarriage. On the very same day that Katherine of Aragon was laid to rest at Peterborough Abbey (now Peterborough Cathedral), Anne Boleyn miscarried.[7] Eustace Chapuys, always ready to take up his pen, reported on the development:

> On the day of the interment the concubine had an abortion which seemed to be a male child which she had not borne 3½ months, at which the king has shown great distress. The said concubine wished to lay the blame on the duke of Norfolk, whom she hates, saying he frightened her by bringing the news of the fall the king had six days before. But it is well known that is not the cause, for it was told her in a way that she should not be alarmed or attach much importance to it. Some think it was owing to her own incapacity to bear children, others to a fear that the king would treat her like the late queen, especially considering the treatment shown to a lady of the Court, named Mistress Semel, to whom, as many say, he has lately made great presents.[8]

Whatever the reason for Anne Boleyn's miscarriage, Henry's expected son and future heir was not to be. The king would have no more children with Anne.

It is interesting to note that Brandon's daughter Eleanor and his wife Katherine Willoughby were the chief female mourners at Katherine of Aragon's funeral.[9] This may have been due to their high status at the time, or it could be because Willoughby's mother, Maria de Salinas, was a lady-in-waiting and devoted friend to the late queen.

While these events were unfolding around him, Brandon had time for a swap with the king, trading Suffolk Place in Southwark for Norwich Place, also known as York House.[10] Suffolk Place was a large mansion fronting Southwark High Street. The front was ornamented with turrets and cupolas and also had beautifully carved work. The back had several buildings which formed a courtyard. Suffolk Place also went by the names 'Dukes Palace' and 'Brandon's House'. On 18 December 1535, Brandon had made an inventory of the gold and silver plate he owned at Suffolk Place. The total came to the staggering sum of £1,457 (£580,000 today).[11] Once the king obtained Suffolk Place, he renamed it Southwark Place and eventually turned it into a mint.[12] It was a good exchange for Brandon; while he already had his principal residence at the Barbican, Norwich Place allowed him to stay close to Whitehall Palace, a frequent residence of the king.[13]

Meanwhile, things were starting to unravel for Anne Boleyn. She argued with Thomas Cromwell, right-hand man to Henry, over the profits from the Dissolution of the Monasteries. Cromwell wished for the money to return to the king's coffers, while Anne wanted them to be put towards the founding of universities.[14] With her recent miscarriage and her disagreements with Thomas Cromwell, it would seem that Anne's position at court was starting to crumble.

Worse still for Anne, Henry's eye had been caught by another woman. Jane Seymour was the daughter of Sir John Seymour and Margery Wentworth; her brothers Thomas and Edward were also up-and-coming men of the court. Jane was a lady-in-waiting to both Katherine of Aragon and Anne Boleyn, and it was through her time serving Anne that Henry became aware of her.[15] With Henry growing dissatisfied with his current wife's inability to bear him a son, the Seymours, as the Boleyns and the Howards before them had done, saw an opportunity to further their fortunes and eagerly encouraged the king's interest in Jane.

The events that led up to Anne Boleyn's arrest and execution are far too detailed to describe here, having filled countless books already. Whatever motivated Henry VIII to turn his back on his second wife, events moved swiftly, and Charles Brandon played a major role in them.

On 24 April 1536, two commissions of oyer and terminer were set up at Westminster by Thomas Cromwell and Lord Chancellor Sir Thomas Audley. A jury of noblemen, including Charles Brandon, was presented with purported evidence of various offences against the king committed by Anne in Middlesex and Kent. Having examined these offences, the jury declared itself satisfied that there was indeed damning evidence against Anne Boleyn, and therefore it could only conclude that Anne had indeed committed illicit affairs with Sir Henry Norris, Sir Francis Weston, Sir William Brereton, Mark Smeaton and her brother George Boleyn, Lord Rochford, as well as plotting to have her husband killed.[16]

Did the jury truly believe that Anne was guilty of these offences? After all, while each instance of infidelity was possible in isolation, taken together they were implausible and practically impossible on a logistical level. That the 'evidence' was so readily and conveniently available at the time would surely have troubled the minds of even the most loyal servant of the king; unfortunately, we shall never know Charles Brandon's thoughts on Anne's downfall.

Anne Boleyn was arrested on 2 May 1536 and taken to the Tower of London. She was housed in the queen's apartments, where she had stayed on the eve of her coronation.[17] In the following days, Sir Henry Norris, Sir William Brereton, Sir Francis Weston, Mark Smeaton and Sir Thomas Wyatt were arrested. Wyatt blamed his arrest on Brandon; the two had disliked one another ever since Brandon informed the king of Wyatt's feelings for Anne Boleyn. From here, events began to unfold rapidly.

On 11 May, the jury at Westminster Hall wrote an indictment against Anne Boleyn. They determined that she had committed incest and adultery on multiple occasions as well as plotting the king's death.[18] The next day, Sir Henry Norris, Sir William Brereton, Sir Francis Weston and Mark Smeaton were brought from the Tower of London to Westminster Hall to stand before a jury. Brandon was part of the jury, which gave sentence upon each man's life.[19] The evidence gathered accused all four men of having illicit affairs with the Queen of England and plotting with her the downfall of the king.[20] The indictments of the previous two days were damning, and left little room for anything but the verdict that the four men were guilty.

But it was not just the evidence that went against these four men; it was the worries and fears of the men chosen to be the jurors. What man could stand up and say Smeaton, Norris, Weston and Brereton were innocent when their king wanted them to be guilty? What man in his right mind would go against the iron will of the King of England in this matter? Brandon was no fool; he had challenged Henry VIII before and knew of the punishments that could be inflicted upon anybody who defied the king, be they high or low.

There is no record of Brandon's thoughts on the actual guilt of each man, but we can speculate, and indeed this would not be the first time his conscience appeared to be flexible. Desiring not only to keep his head but also to exploit his current position in Henry's good graces, he would certainly not defy his king in this matter.

It is thus not surprising that Mark Smeaton, Sir Henry Norris, Sir Francis Weston and Sir William Brereton were all found guilty of treason and adultery with the Queen of England. As traitors, they were sentenced to be hanged, drawn and quartered, their manhood cut off in front of them before they were beheaded. It should be noted that only Mark Smeaton confessed to being guilty before the grand jury – Norris, Weston and Brereton all protested their innocence.[21] Mark Smeaton, being a lowly musician and a commoner, would most likely have been put to torture.

Three days later, Brandon was among the jurors selected to try George Boleyn and his sister, the queen.[22] The trial was held in the King's Hall at the Tower of London in light of fears regarding the transportation of two high-profile prisoners in public view. Hundreds came to the Tower to see Anne Boleyn's trial. So great were the crowds that a platform had to be constructed in the middle of the hall for Anne to sit on. At the other end of the hall sat her uncle, the Duke of Norfolk, who was to preside over the events. Official documents of the trial have been lost over time, but word of mouth, letters and reports all confirm that Anne entered the King's Hall with the poise and dignity befitting a queen. Presenting herself to the jury, Anne showed no sign of fear or nerves. She gave a small curtsey before taking the seat which had been prepared for her upon the platform.

The charges were read to Anne, and it was reported that throughout this indignity she sat serene and beautiful, showing no sign of disgust or guilt. Asked how she pleaded, the queen replied that she was not guilty of any of the charges.[23]

Those trying Anne for her crimes argued for her guilt, giving the 'evidence' presented at the Westminster and Kent indictments as examples of the horrendous crimes Anne had committed against her husband. Anne adamantly denied all the charges against her and argued that 'she had maintained her honour and her chastity all her life long'.[24] She put up a challenging defence, and it is said that some of those in the audience were even starting to doubt the charges laid against her. However, it was to no avail. One by one, each member of the jury stood and gave their verdict – every man said guilty, including Brandon. Anne Boleyn, Queen of England, had been found guilty of all the charges presented before her: adultery, incest and treason.[25] The Duke of Norfolk then read out her sentence:

> Because thou hast offended against our sovereign the King's Grace in committing treason against his person, the law of the realm is this, that though hast deserved death, and thy judgement is this: that thou shalt be burnt here within the Tower of London on the Green, else to have thy head smitten off, as the king's pleasure shall be further known of the same.[26]

In reply to this fateful sentence, Anne is said to have replied:

> My lords, I will not say your sentence is unjust, nor presume that my reasons can prevail against your convictions. I am willing to believe that you have sufficient reasons for what you have done; but then they must be other than those which have been produced in court, for I am clear of all the offences which you then laid to my charge. I have ever been a faithful wife to the king, though I do not say I have always shown him that humility which his goodness to me, and the honours to which he raised me, merited. I confess I have had jealous fancies and suspicions of him, which I had not discretion enough, and wisdom, to conceal at all times. But God knows, and is my witness, that I have not sinned against him in any other way. Think not I say this in the hope to prolong my life, for He who saveth from death hath taught me how to die, and He will strengthen my faith. Think not, however, that I am so bewildered in my mind as not to lay the honour of my chastity to heart now in mine extremity, when I have maintained it all my life long, much as ever queen did. I know these, my last words, will avail me nothing but for the justification of my chastity and honour. As for my brother and those others who are unjustly condemned, I would willingly suffer many deaths to deliver them, but since I see it so pleases the king, I shall willingly accompany them in death, with this assurance, that I shall lead an endless life with them in peace and joy, where I will pray to God for the king and for you, my lords.

One can only ponder what Brandon thought of the whole affair, sitting there listening to the crimes read out against the queen followed by her staunch defence. Now, for the first time during the legal wrangling, Brandon was sitting face to face with Anne rather than distantly removed as he had been when the indictment was first written.

After her speech, Anne curtsied again to those who had just sentenced her to death and was led out of the King's Hall back to the queen's lodgings. The gaoler accompanying her turned his axe inwards to show those present that Anne had been sentenced to death.[27]

After Anne's trial, her brother George Boleyn, Lord Rochford, was led into the King's Hall and his trial commenced. As with the previous trial, Brandon was part of the jury to judge George Boleyn on his alleged crimes. Now that Norris, Weston, Brereton, Smeaton and his sister had been found guilty and sentenced to death, there was no hope for George. He pleaded not guilty to all the charges presented, and although he put up a brave fight and is said to have challenged the charges with great wit, he was found guilty of incest and treason and sentenced to death. He was led out of the King's Hall and back to his lodgings to await his execution.[28]

It has been proposed that the charge of incest against Anne Boleyn was brought forward by Brandon. Previously Anne had declared that Brandon had slept with his daughter; was the suggestion of incest with her brother Brandon's way of getting back at Anne? Or was it merely a means to rid the court of George Boleyn, a powerful man in his own right? Either way, Brandon was no fool. He had learnt his lesson about standing up to the king and knew that his title, his lands, his very position at court were reliant upon the king's favour. As so many times previously, Brandon simply did his duty.

On the morning of 17 May, the five men were led from their lodgings within the Tower to a scaffold on Tower Hill. Cromwell sent word to Sir William Kingston, the Tower gaoler, that they were to be spared the horror of hanging, drawing and quartering, instead being dispatched at the headsman's block.[29] The men were executed in order of rank, and therefore George Boleyn was the first to meet his end. Next was Sir Henry Norris, Henry's groom of the stool for ten years. Norris commented that no one owed more to the king than he did, nor had anyone been as ungrateful to the king as he. He then went on to proclaim that the queen was innocent of all charges against her, and knelt at the block. After Norris' head fell, Sir Francis Weston was next to face the block. Fourth to meet his end was Sir William Brereton. With the block and scaffold now bloodied and holding the bodies of three men, Brereton knelt and accepted his fate. With a stroke of the axe, he was dead. Lastly, Mark Smeaton was led up the scaffold to the block. He had most likely been tortured and humiliated, and had watched four men beheaded in front of his eyes. Kneeling at the blood-soaked block, Smeaton met his end as the axe cut his head from his neck.[30]

On the same day, at Lambeth Palace, Archbishop Cranmer declared the annulment of the marriage between Anne Boleyn and Henry Tudor. Those present to hear this declaration were Sir Thomas. Audley, John, Earl of Oxford – and, of course, Charles Brandon.[31]

On 19 May, Anne chose to wear a dress of grey damask which had a crimson kirtle underneath and a mantle that was trimmed with ermine. She wore an English hood, a necklace and earrings. At 8 a.m., Sir Kingston came to tell her that the hour was approaching and that she should ready herself. She replied, 'Acquit yourself of your charge for I have long been prepared.'[32] An hour later, Anne left her chambers. She walked down the stairs from the queen's lodgings to the courtyard between the Jewel House and the King's Hall. Two hundred Yeomen were there to lead Anne to the scaffold, along with her ladies-in-waiting, Sir William Kingston and several others. She walked through the courtyard and then through the twin towers of the Coldharbour Gate to the scaffold. Reports state that approximately a thousand people surrounded the scaffold upon Tower Green to watch the execution. Those watching included Thomas Cromwell, Anne's stepson the Duke of Richmond and Charles Brandon.[33]

The scaffold was draped in black cloth and had straw scattered across it. Upon the scaffold, a French executioner, brought in especially for Anne, was dressed like all the other men to conceal his identity. His sword was hidden under the straw to spare Anne sight of the tool that would soon end her life. Slowly Anne took the steps that led up to the scaffold and took her place in the centre. She turned and 'begged leave to speak to the people, promising she would not speak a word that was not good'.[34] She then asked Kingston 'not to hasten the signal for her death till she had spoken that which she had mind to say'. Turning back to the crowd that was staring so intently at her, Anne took a deep breath and, with a voice that wavered at first but grew stronger as she continued, spoke out:

Good Christian people, I am come hither to die, according to the law, for by the law I am judged to die, and therefore I will speak nothing against it. I come here only to die, and thus to yield myself humbly to the will of the king, my lord. And if, in my life, I did ever offend the king's Grace, surely with my death I do now atone. I come hither to accuse no man, nor to speak anything of that whereof I am accused, as I know full well that aught I say in my defence doth not appertain to you. I pray and beseech you all, good friends, to pray for the life of the king, my sovereign lord and yours, who is one of the best princes on the face of the earth, who has always treated me so well that better could not be, wherefore I submit to death with good will, humbly asking pardon of all the world. If any person will meddle with my cause, I require them to judge the best. Thus I take my leave of the world, and of you, and I heartily desire you all to pray for me. Oh Lord, have mercy on me! To God I commend my soul.

After her speech, Anne's ladies helped her remove her mantle, earrings, necklace and hood. Kneeling, she was blindfolded and as she knelt upon the straw those around her knelt as well. Only Brandon and the Duke of Richmond continued to stand. As a thousand pairs of eyes looked on, Anne repeated over and over the prayer, 'Jesu, have pity on my soul! My God, have pity on my soul, To Jesus Christ I commend my soul.'[35] In the last few minutes of her life, Anne's resolve began to falter. It is said that she kept looking nervously over her shoulder, waiting for the executioner's blow to come. The executioner, seeing this, turned to his assistant and called, 'Bring me the sword.'[36] Anne turned her head in the direction of the assistant. At this moment, the executioner pulled his sword from beneath the straw. Lifting it high above his head, he swung and with one swift blow severed Anne Boleyn's neck.

Anne Boleyn was dead. Brandon had personally witnessed the terrible outcome of this day, which he had helped to bring about.

He had never seen eye to eye with Anne, and they had spoken unfavourably of each other over the years. Furthermore, Brandon benefited from Anne's death as three manors formally belonging to the Poles but in Anne's possession were granted to Brandon, adding around £100 (£32,210)[37] to his yearly income.[38]

Less than twenty-four hours after Anne Boleyn's death, Henry proposed to Jane Seymour. The king had wasted little time in taking a second wife, and on 30 May, only eleven days after she was executed, he married Jane at Whitehall Palace.[39]

The king was looking to move on and to have legitimate male heirs with his third wife. On 1 July, Parliament proposed the Second Act of Succession, which declared that young Elizabeth was as illegitimate as her half-sister Mary.[40] Now forty-five years old, Henry had three illegitimate children and no heir to succeed him on the English throne. His hopes lay in Jane Seymour providing him with a son. Before that happened, though, things would go from bad to worse.

Tragically, on 23 July, the king's illegitimate son Henry Fitzroy died at St James's Palace. The cause of death is unclear, but tuberculosis or some other lung condition has been put forward as a probable cause. He was buried at Framlingham Church in Suffolk.[41] His death came as a great shock to the king, and once more Henry was forced to think about the line of succession. With Jane Seymour not yet pregnant, the king had no living male heir; Brandon would probably have sympathised with the king. Only two years previously he had lost his son and heir Henry at the tender age of eleven. One cannot help but wonder during this time if the pair turned their conversations to lost sons and thoughts of what might have been.

The two men had little time to reflect, for rebellion was looming. The Pilgrimage of Grace was to take up a great deal of Brandon's time and effort over the closing months of 1536. The rebellion initially formed as a series of revolts in Lincolnshire. The people were unhappy with the dissolution of their abbey in Louth, and upset by many of the government commissions in the area looking at the resources of the smaller monasteries and the conduct of the clergy. There was also a widespread rumour that the government would confiscate the jewels, plate and wealth of the monasteries and even impose new taxes upon the people.[42]

On 1 October 1536, Thomas Kendall, vicar of St James' Church, Louth, preached a sermon warning the people of his congregation that the church was in danger. The following day, Nicholas Melton and a group of locals captured John Heneage, the Bishop of Lincoln's registrar, as he tried to deliver the assessment of the clergy as ordered by Thomas Cromwell. Melton ripped the papers from Heneage's hand and burned them. Melton and his followers took Heneage to Legbourne Nunnery, where several more of the king's commissioners were captured. On 3 October, approximately 3,000 men reportedly marched to Caister in an attempt to capture the commissioners working there. The commissioners managed to escape, but the people of Caister and nearby Horncastle now joined the rebellion.

The next day, Dr John Raynes, chancellor of the Bishop of Lincoln, and Thomas Wulcey, who worked for Thomas Cromwell, were captured and beaten to death by the rebels. On the same day, the rebels drew up a list of articles which contained five complaints for the king concerning the suppression of the monasteries, various taxes being imposed (or rumours thereof) and the people who were working for the king, including Thomas Cromwell. The rebels felt that these men of low birth were only supporting the Dissolution of the Monasteries to line their own pockets with the wealth of the churches. Over the next three days, more support came from Towes, Hambleton Hill and Dunholm, and significantly, on 8 October, another rising began in Beverley, Yorkshire, under one Robert Aske.[43] When the rebels met at Lincoln Cathedral, they supposedly had somewhere between 10,000 and 20,000 men. Their petition was sent on 9 October, by which time Henry was already reacting to the threat.

On 11 October, there came a formal reply to the Lincoln rebels from the king:

Concerning choosing of counsellors, I never have read, heard nor known, that princes' counsellors and prelates should be appointed by rude and ignorant common people; nor that they were persons meet or of ability to discern and choose meet and sufficient counsellors for a prince. How presumptuous then are ye, the rude commons of one shire, and that one of the most brute and beastly of the whole realm and of least experience, to find fault with your prince for the electing of his counsellors and prelates, and to take upon you, contrary to God's law and man's law, to rule your prince whom ye are bound to obey and serve with both your lives, lands, and goods, and for no worldly cause to withstand. As to the suppression of houses and monasteries, they were granted to us by the parliament, and not set forth by any counsellor or counsellors upon their mere will and fantasy, as you, full falsely, would persuade our realm to believe. And where ye alledge that the service of God is much thereby diminished, the truth thereof is contrary; for there are no houses suppressed where God was well served, but where most vice, mischief, and abomination of living was used: and that doth well appear by their own confessions, subscribed with their own hands, in the time of our visitations. And yet were suffered a great many of them, more than we by the act needed, to stand; wherein if they amend not their living, we fear we have more to answer for than for the suppression of all the rest. And as for their hospitality, for the relief of poor people, we wonder ye be not ashamed to affirm, that they have been a great relief to our people, when a great many, or the most part, hath not past 4 or 5 religious persons in them and divers but one, which spent the substance of the goods of their house in nourishing vice and abominable living. Now, what unkindness and unnaturality may we impute to you and all our subjects that be of that mind that had rather such an unthrifty sort of vicious persons should enjoy such possessions, profits and emoluments as grow of the said houses to the maintenance of their unthrifty life than we, your natural prince, sovereign lord and king, who doth and hath spent more in your defences of his own than six times they be worth.[44]

The king was not impressed that the people of his realm would dare stand up in rebellion against him. He had already sent Brandon as his lieutenant to keep an eye on them, and the duke had arrived in Huntingdon on the morning of 9 October only to find that he had been provided with no men, artillery or resources. He hurriedly wrote to the king:

Arrived this Monday, 9th inst., at 6 a.m. at Huntington, leaving his company to follow, and intended with the men he should find there to proceed to Standfforde for staying the traitors, according to the king's command. Found there neither ordnance nor artillery nor men enough to do anything; such men as are gathered there have neither harness nor weapons. Begs that ordnance, and artillery, and a thousand or two of harness may be sent with speed; also a sufficient number of horsemen [as well out of Wales as out of the north parts]. Ordnance and horsemen must do the feat; and, considering that the traitors are well horsed and harnessed and so numerous, the success of a battle would be doubtful. Has just seen the king's gracious letters to Sir Robt. Tirwhit and others now amongst the rebels, and has himself sent Tirwhit and the rest a letter, (copy enclosed). Begs to know what to do if they submit according to the king's letters; if they do not he will at first refuse to make any more suit to the king for them unless they stay themselves without approaching nearer the king's army. Thus he intends to gain time to put the king's people in readiness and have the ordnance. Begs for money, without which the men are unwilling to set forth; many captains are unable to relieve their company, though in the meantime Suffolk does what he can to help them. Reminds the king of the sending down of horsemen and ordnance. In his late letters, considering his sudden departure out of Suffolk, he desired that his cousin Sir Ant. Wingffeld, Sir Arthur Hopton, and Sir Francis Lovell might levy his servants and tenants in Suffolk for him. Now he hears the king has commanded them to remain in the country, so he lacks a great part of his servants. Begs the king to send them command to repair to him with their companies, assuring his Grace he has not taken out of Suffolk and Norfolk any gentlemen except his cousin Sir Ant. Wingfield, Sir Arthur Hopton, and Sir Thomas Tyrrell, 'and out of Norfolk' Sir Francis Lovell. Has just received a letter from Sir Francis Bryan, who is at Kimbolton with 300 horse, and trusts to have his foot with him tomorrow night. It is said the rebels will be at Standfforde 'this night,' where Sir William Aparr and others are. Has written to Aparr that if he thinks his force and Suffolk's sufficient to stop the rebels there, he (Suffolk) will repair thither; if not, then Sir Wm. Aparr and the rest, and also Sir Francis Bryan, must join forces with those of the writer at Huntingdon, where they will make a determined stay.[45]

To Suffolk's relief, within days the men who had gathered at Lincoln Cathedral had begun to melt away, suitably cowed by Henry's fighting words, many of them before the formal reply had arrived. From Huntingdon, Brandon moved to Stamford where he arrived on 11 October. On the same day, Henry VIII wrote to Gardiner:

> To repress the rising, as the duke of Suffolk has married the daughter of lord Willoughby, and is thereby become a great inheritor in those parts, the king has sent him thither as his lieutenant, and joined with him the earls of Shrewsbury, Rutland, and Huntingdon, the lord Admiral, lord Talbot, lord Borough, lord Clinton, Sir John Russell, Sir Fras. Brian, Ric. Cromwell, and all who have lands or rule thereabouts. Doubts not they will soon chastise the rebels.[46]

On 12 October, Brandon wrote to the king asking for orders. Should he pardon the Lincolnshire rebels who had dispersed and round up their leaders, or should he ride north to deal with the growing uprising led by Robert Aske in Yorkshire? Brandon worried that if he pardoned the Lincolnshire rebels and rode north they might revolt once more at his back, leaving him sandwiched between rebel armies.[47] Indeed, Aske's rebellion was spreading. It was reported that all the people of Yorkshire were now up in arms, and men were coming from East Riding and Marshland. It was around this time that Aske began to frame the rebellion as a pilgrimage that sought the king's support in preserving the Church and enacting the punishment of those subverting the law.

On 15 October, Henry wrote to Brandon that he should instruct the rebels to surrender their weapons and give all the information they could about how the rebellion started; if they did so, they could be dismissed. Henry also demanded that Brandon and the Earl of Shrewsbury, who was supporting the duke, gather the leaders of the rebellion and question them. Furthermore, the king stated that he was sending Brandon foot soldiers and cavalry for support.[48] By 15 October, the gentry among the rebels had already begun to come forward and surrender to the duke.[49]

From Stamford, Brandon and his men moved forward to Lincoln, arriving there on 17 October.[50] Meanwhile, the Yorkshire rebels marched to Pontefract Castle, where Lord Darcy and several other leading men had gathered for safety. The castle fell on the 21st, and those within, including Lord Darcy, joined the rebellion as part of its leadership.[51] On the same day, a herald from Henry VIII was sent to Pontefract Castle to read a proclamation from the king. Robert Aske refused to let the proclamation be read.[52] He wanted to take his petition straight to the king.

By now, the two sides were vastly different in numbers. Brandon's force numbered approximately 3,200 soldiers, with the combined forces of Shrewsbury and the Duke of Norfolk only adding a further 6,000, while the rebels, according a letter from Sir Brian Hastyngs to the Earl of Shrewsbury, were reported to number 'above 40,000'.[53]

On 18 October, Henry VIII wrote again to Brandon:

Though the gentlemen pretend 'this truth and fidelity towards us,' you shall try out, by examining the ringleaders of the multitude, how they really used themselves; 'which you shall not well do if you shall be over hasty in the execution of such of the mean sort' as shall best know the same. Meanwhile you may execute as many of the common traitors in Lincoln, Horncastle, Lowth, &c. as shall seem requisite 'for the terrible example of like offenders,' and not execute one alone, as by your letters you intended. If any gentlemen have notably offended, you shall spare the execution of them, and either send them to us or detain them in ward.[54]

The next day Henry VIII wrote another letter to Brandon, advising him on what to do if he could not subdue the rebels through conversation:

Then you shall, with your forces run upon them and with all extremity destroy, burn, and kill man, woman, and child the terrible example of all others, and specially the town of Louth because to this rebellion took his beginning in the same.[55]

Brandon's job was clear: stop the rebellion, whether by words or force of arms. Whatever Brandon's private thoughts, and regardless of his loyalty to the king, it must have been difficult to hear that he might have to kill women and children.

14

Lord of Lincolnshire

On 26 October, the rebels of the Pilgrimage of Grace paused at Scawsby Leys, near Doncaster, where they met the Duke of Norfolk and his army. Norfolk was not a foolish man, and he knew that fighting the rebels was not an option. He offered to negotiate. Despite vastly outnumbering Norfolk and his men, Robert Aske agreed to negotiate with the duke. It was decided that two representatives of the Pilgrimage, Sir Robert Bowes and Sir Ralph Ellerker, would take the rebels' petition to the king. A general truce was proclaimed, and Robert Aske ordered the disbanding of the Pilgrimage.[1]

The king's initial response to the demands of the rebels was not positive. He wrote a harsh letter rebutting the five articles written up by the rebels:

'First we begin and make answer to the 4th and 6th articles, because upon them dependeth much of the rest.' Never heard that princes' counsellors and prelates should be appointed by ignorant common people nor that they were meet persons to choose them. 'How presumptuous then are ye, the rude commons of one shire, and that one of the most brute and beastly of the whole realm and of least experience, to find fault with your prince for the electing of his counsellors and prelates?' Thus you take upon yourself to rule your prince. As to the suppression of religious houses, we would have you know it is granted to us by Parliament and not set forth by the mere will of any counsellor. It has not diminished the service of God, for none were suppressed but where most abominable living was used, as appears by their own confessions signed by their own hands in the time of our visitations. Yet many were allowed to stand, more than we by the act needed; and if they amend not their living we fear we have much to answer for. As to the relief of poor people, we wonder you are not ashamed to affirm that they have been a great relief when many or most have not more than four or five religious persons in them and divers but one; who spent the goods of their house in nourishing vice. As to the Act of Uses we wonder at your madness in trying to make us break the laws agreed to by the nobles, knights, and gentlemen of this realm, whom the same chiefly toucheth. Also the grounds of those uses were false and usurped upon the prince. As to the fifteenth, do you think us so faint hearted that ye of one shire, were ye a great many more, could compel us to remit the same, when the payments yet to come will not meet a tenth of the charges we must sustain for your protection? As to First Fruits, it is a thing granted by Parliament also. We know also that ye our commons have much complained in time past that most of the goods and lands of the realm were in the spiritual men's hands; yet, now pretending to be loyal subjects, you cannot endure that your prince should have part thereof. We charge you to withdraw to your houses and make no more assemblies, but deliver up the provokers of this mischief to our lieutenant's hands and submit yourselves to condign punishment, else we will not suffer this injury unavenged. We pray God give you grace to do your duties and rather deliver to our lieutenant 100 persons than by your obstinacy endanger yourselves, your wives, children, lands, goods, and chattels, besides the indignation of God.[2]

Brandon was to remain in Lincolnshire to keep the peace and watch out for further signs of rebellion.[3] He and his 3,600 men were spread throughout Lincolnshire, with Brandon based in Lincoln with a large store of weapons and corn. He could at a moment's notice sink every boat on the Trent and set his men to action.[4] He was also charged with seeking out agitators and getting information from them; if necessary, he was permitted to summarily execute rebels. In the furtherance of this task, Brandon set up a spy network to gather as much information as possible.[5]

In November, the rebel representatives Ellerker and Bowes met with the Duke of Norfolk and other members of the council. After a great deal of discussion, the council agreed that a general pardon would be given to all the rebels and that their complaints would be taken to a council meeting at York. The rebels appeared to be happy with this decision, and on 3 December 1536 a general pardon was read out. Those remaining peacefully dispersed and went back to their homes.

> Proclamation of the king's pardon to the rebels of the different districts, viz.: That those of Yorkshire, with the city of York, Kingston upon Hull, Marshland, Holdenshire, Hexham, Beverley, Holderness, &c., on their submission to Charles duke of Suffolk, president of the Council and lieutenant general in Lincolnshire, at Lincoln or elsewhere that he may appoint, shall have free pardons granted to them under the Great Seal without further bill or warrant or paying anything for the Great Seal. Richmond, 3 Dec., 28 Henry VIII.[6]

It was fortunate for Henry VIII that the rebels decided to stop their march and negotiate with the Duke of Norfolk. Their numbers dwarfed the king's, and if they marched on London they might well have taken the city. Once more, Henry VIII wrote to Brandon instructing him to keep the peace in Lincoln, with force if necessary.[7]

The king took an unnaturally friendly manner with Robert Aske, addressing him in a most pleasant way. It is thought that Henry decided to take a warm tone with him in the hopes of gaining more information about the leaders of the rebellion.[8] Despite all the king's talk, however, there was no meeting or parliament held to discuss the rebel complaints. This lack of action caused frustration and anger among some of the rebels, and in January 1537 a fresh rebellion broke out in East Riding, West Riding, Lancashire, Cumberland and Westmorland. Although these revolts were smaller, the rebels had broken their promise not to riot against the king.[9] The king now acted swiftly, ordering that those responsible for the rebellions be tried and punished. Over the next few months, between 144 and 153 people involved in the Pilgrimage of Grace were tried and sentenced to the traitor's death of being hanged, drawn and quartered.[10]

Rebel leaders Robert Aske and Lord Darcy were captured and taken to the Tower of London. Darcy was convicted of treason on 15 May, and on 30 June he was executed upon Tower Hill.[11] Aske was also found guilty, and was sentenced to be hung in chains outside Clifford's Tower, the keep of York Castle, where he would die a slow, painful death from exposure and starvation.[12]

Brandon's exact role in the trials and executions of the rebels remains unknown. It is likely that, as the king's lieutenant, he would have overseen many trials and that if those men were found guilty he would have ordered their executions. There was a report in February 1537 that Brandon had promised a pardon for seven men in Lincolnshire and yet reneged on this promise and saw that the men were hanged.[13] This information was spread by John Hogon, a kind of bard who went about the country with a fiddle telling tales and singing songs, so it is not necessarily true.

Despite being posted in Lincoln to ensure that there was no further rebellion or uprising, Brandon sought to return to London. In a letter to Thomas Cromwell, Rich Crumwell writes of Brandon's desire to return to court and to be with the king:

After the dispatch of my soldiers from Newark towards London, I came this morning to Lincoln to my lord of Suffolk who has commanded me to abide with him till his coming to London and to write to your Lordship that though he is commanded to abide here with 1,000 men, he desires to see the king at "his high feast," to do his duty and declare what he knows of the late rebellion. His Grace desires your Lordship to obtain the king's letters to him to repair to his Highness; and meanwhile he will leave here sufficient men to keep the prisoners and country, and will return when the king commands.[14]

On 12 December, Brandon wrote again to the king:

Please it your Grace, Learning the order taken by the lords of your Council at Doncaster, I discharged your army here, all but 500, which I retain till I know your pleasure touching ordnance and prisoners; after which I will wait on your Highness at Christmas.[15]

On the same day, Henry VIII wrote to Brandon expressing his thanks for Brandon's service and loyalty:

Right trusty and entirely well beloved cousin, we greet you well, and have received your sundry letters... Declaring your most entire and fervent love and zeal towards us and the advancement of our affairs, with the great desire you have not only to serve us in the same with the force of your body and person, but also with the employment of your whole substance, if the case should so require. The overtune whereof, albeit we trust we shall not need to accept, for that we have certain affiance [trust] in God that the matter shall shortly take end... yet we do no less thankfully receive the good will thereof, declaring your noble and most loyal and assured heart towards us, than if we should therewith also take presently all the whole benefit and commodity of that which is offered if the same were ten times so much. Surely. Cousin, you have in no part deceived our expectation of you, but in this (and your faithful service otherwise given us as much cause to rejoice of our favour and goodness theretofore extend unto you as of any like thing that we have done since our reign [began]. And doubt you not but, God granting us life, we shall so remember this time towards you that you shall have good cause to say you serve a master that will not put the faithful service and gratuity [gratitude] of his servant in oblivion.[16]

On 4 April 1537, almost certainly in recognition of his recent service, Brandon received a number of grants, noticeably several of them in Lincolnshire:

Charles, duke of Suffolk. Grant, in tail male, of the castle, lordship, and manor of Tatishall alias Tatyrishall, Linc., with all lands, &c., in Tatishall, Conysby, Kyrkeley super Bayteyn alias Bayne, Thorp, Stratton, Langton, Marton, Roughton, Tomby, and Toftnewton, Linc.; with court leets, views of frankpledge, &c., and a ferry on the water of Withom in Tatishall.[17]

Three days later, there came another glut of grants:

Charles, duke of Suffolk. Grant in tail of the site, &c., of the dissolved abbey of St. Mary, Leyston, Suff., the church messuages, &c., the manors of Leyston, Glernnyng, Culpho, Pethaugh, Darsham, and Laxfeld; and all lands, tenements, rents, &c., in Leyston, Theberton, Dersham, Middelton, Thorpe, Sisewell, Kelsall, Knottshall, Buxlowe, Billesforde, Aldryngham, Brusyard, Glarving, Colpho, Graundesburgh, Playford, Tuddenham, Witlesham, Laxfeld, Willoweby, and Corton, Suff.; the churches and rectories of Leyston, Alderyngham, Middelton, and Corton, Suff.; and all chantries, lands, glebes, &c., belonging to the premises, in as full manner as George late abbot held the same on 4 Feb., 27 Hen. VIII., in right of the monastery. Also the site, &c., of the dissolved monastery of St. Peter, Eye, Suff., the church, houses, &c., and the manors of Eye, Stoke, Laxfeld, Bedfeld, Occolt, and Fresyngfeld, with all lands, tenements, rents, &c., in Eye, Yaxley, Melles, Okeley, Stoke Thorneham, Pilcote, Thornham Magna, and Thornham Parva, Gislyngham, Laxfelde, Badyngham, Bedfeld, Occolte, Snape, Fresyngfeld, Waybrede, Stradbroke, Brome, Brisworth, Thrandeston, Thorndon, Pesenall, Dunwiche, Hollesley, Rikyngale, West Cretynge, Wynerston, Snape, Playforth, and Butley, Suff.; Colneqwynche alias Colnewake, Essex; Shelfanger and Reydon, Norf.; Sechebroke, Welbourne, and Barbeby, Linc.; also the churches and rectories of All Saints in Downewiche, and of Playford, Laxfeld, Yaxley, and Eye, Suff.; and the advowsons of the vicarages of the said churches of All Saints in Downewiche, Playford, Laxfeld, Yaxley, Eye, and Segebroke; and the chantries, lands, glebes, &c., belonging, &c., to hold at 136l. 8s. 10d. rent.[18]

Notably, Brandon was given Tattershall Castle, an imposing red-brick castle that had been fortified over the years to create a secure base. Brandon would use Tattershall Castle as a headquarters from which to oversee the protection of Lincolnshire. Sometime before 26 May the King ordered that Brandon permanently position himself within the county to make the king's presence known. We know this because Brandon wrote to Thomas Cromwell on this date that 'the king, at his departure, allowed him six weeks to despatch his business and remove his household into Lincolnshire. Would, nevertheless, have been in Lincolnshire ere this, as the king expected, but his son fell sick of the small-pox and his wife of the ague. Will make what speed thither he can.'[19]

Brandon does not make clear which of his two sons fell sick with smallpox. It is most likely to be Henry, his son born on 18 September 1535; Katherine gave birth to a second son, named Charles, sometime in 1537, but he may not have been born yet.[20] In regards to Katherine's health, 'ague' is a sickness which involves fever and shivering.[21] It can sometimes be related to malaria, although there are no reports that Katherine had suffered from malaria in the preceding years.

After receiving his orders, Brandon moved his family to Grimsthorpe Castle. Grimsthorpe had been given to Katherine's father William Willoughby, 11th Baron Willoughby de Eresby, in 1516 to commemorate his marriage to Maria de Salinas. Brandon would set the castle up as his primary residence in Lincolnshire, creating a magnificent quadrangle building with a centre courtyard over the next few years. Handily, the castle boasted a large park that was perfect for hunting – one of Brandon's favourite pastimes. In 1541, the king honoured Brandon with a royal visit to Grimsthorpe; the duke had spent the previous eighteen months frantically upgrading and extending the castle, using much of the materials of the nearby Vaudey Abbey, which had been dissolved.

As well as Grimsthorpe, Brandon worked hard to purchase land throughout Lincolnshire and built up a strong presence in the area. He successfully obtained the lands held by Katherine's late father, and added these to his land base.[22] Meanwhile, he was bargaining with the king and Cromwell for the sale of his lands in East Anglia. Ever the opportunist, the duke was trying to drive up the value of his lands, parks and other properties so that he would be able to gain a decent exchange with which to continue his pursuit of lands in Lincolnshire.

Ultimately Brandon had to pass his estates at Henham and Westhrope Hall to the king, as well as lands at Butley and Leiston, receiving in return £3,000 (£966,300)[23] over twenty years.[24] He also received a large grant of lands in September and December 1538 and March 1539, many of them former monastic lands, which saw his estates in Lincolnshire increase significantly.[25] By the end of 1538, Brandon had either handed over or sold all of his East Anglian properties; the only exceptions were the Willoughby manors, Gapton Hall and a manor at Tasburgh.[26]

With the Dissolution of the Monasteries well underway, Brandon also received estates worth £200[27] (£64,420).[28] Altogether, Brandon's estates in Lincolnshire were now worth around one and a half times more than the Pole, Percy and Willoughby estates and lands he had previously held. Towards the end of his life, Brandon's estates in Lincolnshire would bring him more than £1,650 (£507,474)[29] a year.[30] In addition to this, on 1 March 1537, Brandon and his heirs were named chief stewards of the lands of Revesby Abbey for the entirety of their lives.[31]

Brandon, ever the king's loyal man, set to work protecting and overseeing the county, dedicating himself to his work. Naturally, with responsibilities and duties at court, Brandon was not able to supervise the government of Lincolnshire at all times and so he introduced trusted men who had previously worked for him in East Anglia to oversee the affairs of the county. However, he still took a deep interest in Lincolnshire affairs. For instance, on 29 July he wrote to Henry VIII stating that he would 'use diligence in pursuance of the king's letters to put in execution the commission of sewers and the statute of vagabonds in Lincolnshire. Cannot perceive but that the whole country is sorry for their offences against his Highness in times past and anxious to recover favour.'[32]

Despite working together to suppress the Pilgrimage of Grace, it would appear that old tensions still simmered between the servants of Brandon and the Duke of Norfolk. While Norfolk was away from court, several of Brandon's followers – particularly one Richard Cavendish – stirred up trouble in an attempt to discredit the duke. On 2 February 1537, Norfolk wrote to Cromwell, stating, 'I never knew till my first going to Doncaster he [Brandon] bare me any grudge; but, as you write, the better we agree the better the king shall be served.'[33] Brandon for his part seems to have done little to punish Cavendish for his actions, as the man was still causing Norfolk trouble in August 1538.[34] How much actual resentment Brandon held towards Norfolk remains unclear. Perhaps he was too busy with other business at court and in Lincolnshire to see Cavendish properly punished; perhaps he simply believed that Norfolk was trying to seek sympathy from Cromwell.

While Brandon was busy trying to secure his status within Lincolnshire, he also organised the wedding of his second daughter, Eleanor. In 1533, a wedding contract between Eleanor and

Henry Clifford, heir to the earldom of Cumberland, had been arranged. The wedding did not take place until the summer of 1537.[35] Eleanor and Henry Clifford were married at Brandon's home in London, and it is reported that the king attended the wedding.[36] In honour of the wedding and his son marrying such a high-born woman, Henry Clifford's father built a magnificent gallery at his castle in Skipton.[37]

With the threat of rebellion finally suppressed, Henry VIII was to receive perhaps the greatest news of his life. Queen Jane became pregnant, and on 12 October, after a long and difficult labour, she gave birth to a son, Edward, at Hampton Court.[38] At the age of forty-seven, Henry finally had a legitimate son and heir. Planning began for a magnificent christening overseen by the king, and Brandon was recalled to court for the celebrations.

On 15 October, a grand procession took place at Hampton Court, with the newborn prince brought to the Chapel Royal, where he would be christened. Henry designed the procession to be the greatest that had ever taken place. High-ranking members of the court and clergy were required to take their place, as well as foreign diplomats and ambassadors who were expected to report back to their own kings what an extraordinary event the new prince's christening had been. Brandon had the honour of participating in the royal progress: 'Then the Prince borne under the canopy by the lady marquis of Exeter, assisted by the duke of Suffolk and the marquis her husband.'[39] Brandon also had the great honour of being appointed godfather at the confirmation. Edward's christening would go down in the record books as one of the most prestigious and magnificent events to take place at Hampton Court.

Tragically, Jane Seymour would have a minimal role in her son's life. She died just twelve days after Edward's birth of what was most likely puerperal fever, an infection of the vaginal passage or womb.[40] In a sad reflection of the christening, the queen's body was taken on a similar procession through Hampton Court to the Chapel Royal, where she lay in state for two weeks before she was taken to St George's Chapel in Windsor Castle for burial.

The last two years had been a time of great upheaval and change for Brandon and his king, and it had become clear just how highly the king valued his friend, and how deeply he trusted him to carry out his will and protect his kingdom. The Pilgrimage of Grace alone could have turned England on its head, yet Brandon had rushed to Lincolnshire to represent his king and help suppress the rebellion. If nothing else, these two years would show that Brandon was true to his motto: 'Loyaulte me oblige.'[41]

By now, Charles Brandon was in his early fifties.[42] It would not be unrealistic to think that he would start to wind down his busy military and political life. In 1538, he was described as 'a good man and captain, sickly and half lame'.[43] However, there was no truth in this description of Brandon's health. In fact, in his final seven years of life, Brandon attended more council meetings than he had ever done previously. Less than a year before his death, he would go to war against France.

Between 1538 and 1540, Brandon continued to purchase as much land as possible throughout Lincolnshire, some of which he then resold for a great deal of cash. Brandon appeared to be an astute salesman, and in five months he made five sales worth a staggering £3,327[44] (roughly £1 million).[45] On 24 May 1539, Brandon also sold several manors to Edward, Earl of Hertford, brother of the late Queen Jane.[46] In March 1539, Brandon was also able to lease, for a period of twenty-one years, lands in Somerset which had previously belonged to the king's grandmother, Lady Margaret Beaufort.[47] Brandon felt this was a huge honour, and so commissioned Hans Holbein the Younger to create for him a special seal to use within these lands. The design is of a lion's head, crowned, with the motto of the Order of the Garter surrounding it – 'HONI SOIT QUI MAL Y PENSE (shame on him who thinks evil of it)' – which was then surrounded by a circular band inscribed, 'CAROLVS DXS SVFFYCIE PRO HONORE SVO RICHEMOND.'[48] By this time, Brandon was the greatest landowner and magnate in Lincolnshire, far outdoing his previous presence in East Anglia.

In 1539, Brandon was to be honoured with promotion to one of the most important offices in the king's household. During that year, Thomas Cromwell had sought to reform the court and council. In December, those reforms came to fruition in the form of the Greenwich Ordinances.[49] As part of these ordinances, Brandon was appointed 'the Graunde Maister or Lorde Stewarde of the kings most honorable housholde'.[50] In a bill presented to Parliament that month, Brandon was officially acknowledged as 'Grande Maistre d'Hostel du Roy'.[51]

This appointment was granted to Brandon by the king. It declared that he was the first dignitary of court, responsible for the household of the court below stairs, including such things as the running of the kitchens, the provision of fuel for the household, drinks and other domestic responsibilities, as well as overseeing the maintenance of the grounds and gardens of the household. Brandon was also responsible for felonies or offences committed by the king's servants, including treason, murder or the shedding of blood. The Lord Grand Master or Lord Steward was also the head of the Board of Green Cloth, so named for the deep green cloth that covered the table at which its members sat. Among those members were the Treasurer, the Comptroller and the Master of the Coffer. The Board of the Green Cloth was responsible for the daily expenditure of the household and to ensure payments were made to servants and other members of the household. The board met twice a week, and as head of the board it was Brandon's responsibility to attend the meetings,[52] although how regularly he attended is unknown as from 1542 he would often be busy in the north on the king's business.[53]

On 10 March 1539, Brandon also received a grant of 'the little park or conygre on the north side of Tuttershall Castle' from Lord Edward Clinton, valued at £100.[54] Although not a great deal of money, it did help to expand Brandon's lands and position within Lincolnshire.

By 1540, Henry VIII had been a single man for a little over two years.[55] With only one son and heir, it was vital for the kingdom that the king remarried and hopefully provided a 'spare heir'. Marriage negotiations had begun long before, with Thomas Cromwell taking up the responsibility of finding the king a new wife and England a new queen. He initially sought a French bride for his king as Henry did not want another Spanish bride. There were several eligible young women in the French court and Henry asked the French ambassador, Castillon, if he could see the young women. At this Castillon is reported to have replied, 'Perhaps, Sire, you would like to try them one after the other, and keep the one you found the most agreeable.'[56]

Christina of Denmark, Duchess of Milan, was another possible bride for the king. She was reported to be very beautiful and is said to have resembled Lady Shelton, cousin to Anne Boleyn.

Despite Henry's initial desire to take Christina as his fourth wife, the young woman is alleged to have quipped that 'if she had two heads, she would happily put one of them at Henry's disposal'.[57] She is also reported to have stated that 'the King's Majesty was in so little space rid of the queens that she dare not trust his Council, though she durst trust his Majesty: for her council suspected that her great-aunt was poisoned, that the second was innocently put to death, and that the third lost for lack of keeping in her childbed'.[58]

With no great marriage prospects and an alliance having recently been signed between France and Spain, Thomas Cromwell urged his king to look to the Protestant States of Germany. William, Duke of Cleves had two sisters: Anne, born in 1515, and Amelia, born in 1517.[59] Cromwell sent court painter Hans Holbein to paint a portrait of the Duke of Cleves' sisters, and upon seeing Anne's portrait Henry made his choice. Anne of Cleves was beautiful, yet she did not know French, Latin or English. Nor could she play any musical instruments or follow any of the common English pastimes. Despite this, the king still wished to have her as his fourth wife. There was the issue of existing negotiations for a marriage between Anne of Cleves and the Duke of Lorraine's son, but as no pre-contract had been signed Cromwell felt that Anne was eligible to marry.[60]

The Duke of Cleves signed his sister's marriage treaty on 4 September 1539, and representatives then took the treaty to England where it was officially ratified on 4 October.[61] All that was left now was for Anne to come to England. It was decided that Anne should travel overland to Calais; however, her travel was slow and she did not arrive at Calais until 11 December 1539.[62]

On 26 December, Anne set sail for England. She arrived the next day and was met at Dover Castle by Brandon and his wife. On the 29th, Brandon wrote to Cromwell:

> it was xj of clok before we oonl[aded] them at Dover, and notwithstanding the ... commyng of them, and also that the day w[as] foule and wyndye with mooch hayle and ... contynuelly in her face, her Grace was so ... and desirous to make hast to the King['s Highness] that her Grace forced for no nother, which [we] perceyvyng were very gladde to set her G[race] furthwarde, considering if we should h[ave] lost this day, we should have had

to tarry at Sittingbourne on New Year's eve and New Year's Day, which we did not think a meet place for so long, or else to have remained here Tuesday night, Wednesday, and Thursday, too many days to lose.[63]

When Anne arrived, the mayor of Dover and the citizens were happy to receive the future queen, and they greeted her with torchlight and a display of guns. In her chambers she was greeted by around forty to fifty gentlewomen wearing velvet bonnets, and it was said that she was so joyful at the warm welcome that she completely forgot all about the horrible weather and was very merry at supper.[64]

Excited to meet his future bride, the king could not wait for their planned meeting on 1 January. Instead, he rode ahead to meet her at Rochester the next day. Certain it would be love at first sight, the king and his men disguised themselves in hooded cloaks and entered Anne's chambers while she was watching bull-baiting through a window, with the king confident that a besotted Anne would recognise him immediately. Things did not go to plan. When the king attempted to kiss Anne, the young woman was utterly shocked and turned away from the unknown interloper. Unaccustomed to English traditions and masquerades, Anne was heavily reliant upon her interpreters, who could not help her with the situation.

Realising his mistake, Henry left, removed his disguise and came back. Anne now recognised the king and bowed. The pair talked a while before Henry VIII withdrew. However, the king's grand romantic gesture had been rejected. Leaving Rochester, he returned to Greenwich and informed Cromwell that he did not like Anne and did not wish to marry her.[65] Brandon, still with Anne and unaware of the king's thoughts, could only lead the new bride to London.

15

The Right Honourable Lord Duke of Suffolk

Despite his reservations, Henry VIII went through with the marriage. He and Anne of Cleves were wed in the Queen's Closet at Greenwich on Tuesday 6 January.[1] On their wedding night, Henry was unable to consummate the marriage, and soon he was desperate to escape from a woman he neither loved nor desired. He ordered his council to look into the alleged pre-contract between Anne and the Duke of Lorraine's son, but the ambassadors from Cleves assured the council that the pre-contract had never gone further than simple discussions.[2] Frustrated, Henry was determined to remedy the situation. Since Cromwell had got him into it, the king felt that Cromwell must get him out.

Ultimately, the failure of the Cleves marriage was laid upon Cromwell, and the king's right-hand man was arrested on 10 June 1540 during a council meeting.[3] There are no records of Brandon's thoughts or actions in regards to Cromwell's downfall and arrest. The duke and Cromwell had always enjoyed an amicable working relationship, and Brandon had even sought Cromwell to be godfather to his son.[4] Besides, Brandon would have gained very little from Cromwell's fall – indeed, it would most likely have been detrimental to his interests, as he had often worked with Cromwell to achieve his land acquisitions and to further suits put to him by his clients.[5]

On 24 June, Anne of Cleves was sent to Richmond under the pretext of avoiding an outbreak of the plague.[6] Shortly afterwards she was visited by a number of the king's commissioners, led by Brandon himself. It was Brandon's responsibility to inform Anne that the king wished to submit their marriage to the judgement of convocation and to have the marriage annulled. On 6 July, Brandon wrote to the king:

We have declared your Grace's commission to the queen by an interpreter. Without alteration of countenance she answered that she was content always with your Majest ... The whole circumstance we shall decl[are at our] coming to-morrow; and this night [according to] your Highness' appointment, we tarry a ... saving the bishop of Winchester, who r[eturns to] London this night to the intent he may t[omorrow] be at the Convocation. In our opinion ... all thing shall proceed well to th[accomplishment of] your Highness' virtuous desire.[7]

On 7 July, Brandon was at Westminster to attend the commission that oversaw the annulment of the king's marriage. Brandon gave evidence against the union:

In the beginning of the treaty he noted specially that the king constantly affirmed that he would do nothing in the matter of the marriage unless the precontract between the lady Anne of Cleves and the marquis of Lorraine were first cleared. Whereupon the commissioners of the dukes of Saxe and Cleves promised on her coming to England to bring the full and evident clearing thereof, which they did not. The king, not content to be so handled, and as earnest as before to have that matter cleared, deferred the solemnization from Sunday until Tuesday 'to compass the end; wherein, the earl of Essex travailed with the King's Highness apart, and so that matter passed over.' He saw that the king liked not the queen's person, and thought that the king 'would have been glad if the solemnization might then to the world have been disappointed, without note of breach of his Highness's behalf.'[8]

By 9 July 1540, Anne of Cleves' marriage to Henry VIII had been annulled. Two days later, in the queen's inner chamber at Richmond, Brandon supervised as Anne signed her divorce papers.[9] Brandon, Southampton and Wriothesley of the King's Council also advised Anne on how she should write to her brother informing him of her annulment and her new position as the king's 'beloved sister'.[10]

Brandon also placed men in Anne's residence to report back to him on the movements of the former queen and to intercept any letters that she received from her brother.[11] It may very well be that the king himself had some involvement in this, wishing to know what passed between Anne and the Duke of Cleves, or simply that Brandon wanted to keep himself informed of what was happening in Anne's residence so that he could tell his king of any hostile reaction on the part of the Duke of Cleves. In any case, Brandon need not have been alarmed as Anne readily came to accept her new position. Henry would refer to Anne warmly as his 'sister' and allotted her an allowance of £4,000 a year as well as several residences, including Richmond Palace and Hever Castle.[12]

While the annulment drama had been progressing, the king had fallen in love. The woman in question was Catherine Howard, niece of the Duke of Norfolk and cousin to the late Anne Boleyn. Young, English, beautiful and small of stature, Catherine Howard was everything that Anne of Cleves was not, and Henry VIII was immediately smitten.[13]

If Henry VIII wished it to be, then it must be made possible; even such a loyal servant as Thomas Cromwell would be thrown to the wolves for failing him. This was not the chivalric Henry of high ideals with whom Charles Brandon had reached maturity; this was a bitter, ageing king wracked with pain from old injuries, obese in body and paranoid in his suspicion of those around him. He now seized on an even slighter chance of fathering a male heir, with tragic consequences. It is not difficult to imagine the late Tudor court as a fearful and treacherous place, with a king who now inspired terror rather than love and admiration. Only Charles Brandon seemed to sail imperturbably on, calmly carrying out his monarch's orders even as they became ever harsher and more irrational.

At around ten or twelve, Catherine Howard had been sent to live in the home of her step-grandmother, the Dowager Duchess of Norfolk. The duchess kept a large household, which included several young women who would, it was hoped, learn the skills required to secure good marriages. Catherine had learned quickly, but unfortunately it was soon discovered that her music teacher, Henry Manox, who was hired to teach her the virginals, was madly in love with the young woman. Catherine kept him at bay, but her heart had quickly turned to another. Francis Dereham was a gentleman server and a distant Howard cousin. He was handsome and had some money behind him, which he spent on small gifts for Catherine. Soon the young lady had fallen for Dereham.[14] The girls under the Dowager Duchess of Norfolk's care slept together in a large room, usually two to a bed, and it was well known that Dereham would sneak into the dorm and share Catherine's bed with her. Witnesses reported that Catherine and Dereham would hang together by their bellies like sparrows, which left little doubt that they were sexually active.[15]

When Catherine came to the king's attention, he assumed she was a virgin. Her past was kept from him – with tragic consequences for the young woman and her lovers. Henry and Catherine were married on 28 July 1540 at Oatlands Palace in Surrey, and the king wasted little time lavishing expensive gifts and presents upon his new queen.[16] On the same day that Henry VIII and Catherine married, Thomas Cromwell was executed upon Tower Hill. His head was then taken and placed on a spike on London Bridge,[17] a clear sign that he was considered a traitor.

The following year, on 11 March, the king granted Brandon the 'manor or grange of Hundleby, parcel of Stixwold, with various separate messuages and rent charges [the] manor of Legsby, parcel of Sixhills, [the] rectory and advowson of Billinghay, parcel of Catley, [the] the Greyfriars in Stamford, with the belfry, church and cemetery there, [and] the Blackfriars in Boston, with the belfry, church and cemetery there'.[18] These additional properties and lands allowed Brandon to strengthen his position within the north. He became an influential magnate with the resources to quench any possible uprisings against the king.

On 1 July 1541, Henry VIII set off on his yearly summer progress with his new wife. Despite his initial desire for Catherine, there were already strains in their marriage. During the early months that year, the king was often ill and avoiding his wife, perhaps because he was embarrassed that he could not keep up with her youthful vigour. Perhaps he was even disappointed that after a year of being married Catherine was not yet pregnant. Whatever the reasons, Henry and his court set off on progress throughout the north with the deliberate intent of displaying the royal power and supremacy to the northerners who had rebelled several years earlier.[19]

On 7 August, Brandon had the honour of hosting the king and new queen at his home at Grimsthorpe.[20] He no doubt made preparations, with a surviving letter to the Earl of Shrewsbury asking for 'a fat stag by the 5th Aug., at which time the king intends to visit him at Grymsthorpe'.[21] Before Henry and Catherine arrived, Brandon had ordered a renovation of the residence, seeing a new courtyard built in addition to a new, lavishly fitted hall. The duke intended to display as much wealth as possible, and this included having a vast number of tapestries, plate and carpets on display.[22] Brandon was not only trying to impress his king and display his wealth as an extension of the king's majesty, but was also trying to impress the other members of the council. While a royal visit from the king was a great honour, it was also costly. Brandon had to lay out a great deal of money to pay for additional food and entertainment in addition to the expenses he had already paid to have Grimsthorpe extended.[23]

Henry VIII only stayed for two nights before moving on with the rest of his royal summer progress. The king and queen returned to Hampton Court on 29 October; the next day, the king would find out about his supposedly innocent wife's past.

Mary Hall (*née* Lascelles) took it upon herself (obviously with the noblest of motives) to inform her brother, John, of Queen Catherine's past with her music teacher, Henry Manox, and of her sexual liaisons with Francis Dereham. John Lascelles went to Archbishop Thomas Cranmer, who informed the king by leaving a letter on his seat during Mass.[24] After this, the rest of Queen Catherine's past quickly unravelled as reports arrived detailing a more recent affair she had supposedly conducted right under the king's nose. Henry Manox was questioned and admitted to his past desire for Catherine. Francis Derham was also called in, and he admitted to having had a sexual relationship with Catherine while she was living with the dowager duchess. Devastated at this news, the king left Hampton Court for Whitehall on 6 November. He would never see his wife again.[25]

It was Dereham who implicated Thomas Culpeper, a handsome gentleman of the Privy Chamber who attended the king's most personal needs. There has been a great deal of debate over the centuries as to the exact nature of the relationship between Catherine and Culpeper; some suggest that it was sexual, while others propose that it was nothing more than flirtation. Whatever the precise nature of the relationship, there was no denying that Catherine had spent time alone with Culpeper behind the king's back. Their interactions continued while the king and queen were on their summer progress, although it is reported that Grimsthorpe was one of the only places where the queen had not misbehaved.[26]

Brandon played a leading role in the examination of Catherine Howard, Francis Dereham, Thomas Culpeper and the Dowager Duchess of Norfolk.[27] Catherine admitted indiscretions in her past and to having met with Culpeper at Lincoln, Pontefract and York but denied having a sexual affair with Culpeper. For her part, she laid the blame for the intimacy of the meetings on Jane Parker, Lady Rochford, sister-in-law to the late Anne Boleyn, who organised the pair's meetings. On 1 December 1541, Dereham and Culpeper were tried at Guildhall. Both were found guilty of treason. On 10 December, at Tyburn, Dereham was hanged, drawn and quartered, while Culpeper was beheaded. Both of their heads were placed on spikes on London Bridge.[28]

On 10 February, Catherine was taken via barge down the Thames to the Tower of London. Responsibility for escorting Catherine to the Tower fell to Brandon, and he organised three barges to escort the queen. Members of the Privy Council and guards were in the first barge; Catherine followed in a second barge with four ladies-in-waiting; behind, in the third, came Brandon and several soldiers.[29] As the barges passed under London Bridge, Catherine would have seen the spiked heads of her alleged former lovers Francis Dereham and Thomas Culpeper.[30]

Catherine Howard was beheaded within the Tower of London on 13 February 1542. Eustace Chapuys wrote to Charles V of Catherine's death that at 'about 7, those of the Council except Suffolk, who was ill, and Norfolk, were at the Tower, accompanied by various lords and gentlemen, such as Surrey (Norfolk's son and the queen's cousin), and she was beheaded in the same spot where Anne Boleyn had been executed'.[31] The reason behind Brandon's illness is never stated. It may have been that Brandon was genuinely sick; on the other hand, it is possible that Brandon, unable to dim the memory of Anne Boleyn's execution, could not bear to see another queen, and one barely out of her girlhood, sent to her death. The extravagant and terrible revenge taken by Henry may have tested Charles Brandon to the very limit.

As well as dealing with the king's marital problems and securing his own position in Lincolnshire, Brandon would now suffer the loss of his second-oldest daughter. By 1544, he had lost three of his eight children. Both of his sons by his third wife, Mary Tudor, had died, and sometime between 1540 and 1544 his daughter Mary by his first wife, Anne, also died.[32] Mary sat with Hans Holbein for a sketch sometime in the later years of her life. The portrait is titled *The Lady Monteagle* and shows a woman with big eyes, jewels around her neck and a French hood. Since it is known that Holbein was in England between 1526 and his death in 1543, we can assume that the sketch of Mary was done sometime in this period.

Holbein also painted miniatures of Henry and Charles, Brandon's two sons with his fourth wife, Katherine Willoughby.[33] The miniature of Henry Brandon is incredible in its detail, showing a young boy staring off into the distance, wearing rich cloth and a feather in a hat to depict his status. His left arm is resting upon a ledge which is inscribed with his age – five years – and the month and date of his birth.[34] Within the other miniature, of Charles, the boy is holding a scroll which provides the date the miniature was painted – 10 March 1541 – and Charles's age at the time: three years. It shows a blond-headed boy wearing luxurious coloured clothing and a black hat. His thoughtful gaze and the manner in which he appears to be presenting the scroll, which he presumably wrote himself, suggests a studious nature.[35]

Along with Mary, the boys, and also Katherine Willoughby, Brandon himself was also painted by Holbein, or a member of his workshop. The portrait shows a distinguished but stern-looking man with a white beard and wrinkles on a face that has seen many years. Brandon's famous beard remains although now it is wispy and white, though still covering a square jaw. A black cap covers his head, probably hiding hair the same colour as the beard. Thin lips are pressed together as almond-shaped eyes stare out from the painting. Brandon is sitting in a large, richly decorated chair. He is wearing a thick, rich brown fur coat, intricately designed sleeves and his famous Knight of the Garter chain. He also wears a single leather glove, and holds what looks like a bunch of posies. Although now in the dwindling years of his life, Brandon still cuts a distinguished and imposing figure.[36]

Meanwhile, in the early 1540s, relations between England and Scotland were breaking down. There had been many forays by the English into Scottish towns just across the border in which they had burned villages and stolen livestock.[37] The king needed someone he could trust to guard the northern March against reprisals, and so once more he turned to Brandon.[38] The duke was appointed as Royal Lieutenant of the North and sent to the border in January 1543, staying to oversee defences until March 1544. The previous year, on 11 September 1542, he had been appointed warden of the Eastmarch, Middlemarch and Westmarch of Scotland.[39]

In November 1543, Henry VIII wrote to Brandon regarding his current position stating that he 'intended to revoke him home before Christmas, as he desired; but the state of affairs in Scotland is now suddenly driven into such terms that a personage of reputation must be in those parts to comfort the king's friends and keep enemies in awe. Desires him, as he has already travailed so much there, to take some more pain therein, until it appears what this variety of things in Scotland will grow to; and his service will both please the king and turn to his honour.'[40] Brandon's duties at this time encompassed more than just protecting the border from Scottish invasion, piracy and insurrection; he was also entrusted with overseeing trials and administering punishments accordingly.[41]

During his sojourn in the north people sought out Brandon for patronage. An example of this was in July 1543 when not just one person but multiple fishermen on the Yorkshire coast turned to Brandon for help as they were being harassed by French ships.[42] Previously, on 22 August 1524, the Countess of Oxford had written to Brandon seeking his support in ejecting people out of the Castle of Campys. She wrote:

> The writ she had from Wolsey for Cambridgeshire does not serve her, for the persons at the castle of Campys answered the justices that they would not depart till their master ordered them. The justices did not think they could remove them by their own power, or by raising the country, without greatly disturbing the King's peace. They have proceeded no further in executing the said writ. Cannot obtain her possessions without his help and her brother's (Norfolk).[43]

In November 1534 Brandon had written to Lord Lisle, Deputy of Calais, requesting assistance for his kinsman Henry Cavendish: 'I beg you to be good lord to my kinsman Henry Caundishe, the bearer, living in Calais, for a soldier's room of 12d. or 8d. a day, or, if none be void, to take him into your retinue till you can advance him otherwise.'[44]

In February 1540, Brandon also wrote to Thomas Cromwell seeking the reappointment of Ralph Delaha who had been bailiff and receiver of the manor of Breerly for the last eighteen years but was recently dismissed by Lord Monteagle.[45] The following month, on 26 March 1540, Brandon wrote to the mayor and aldermen of London wanting to know why a John Dyon, whom he had recommended as a justice of the peace, had not been accepted in the position. In the same month, Brandon also wrote to Cromwell asking him to intercede with the king in favour of his servant Edmond Hall, who wished to purchase land that the king was selling in Lincolnshire.[46]

After our hearty commendations; where you have been long suitors for the discharge of £80 yearly, ye shall understand that at this present the King's majesty's affairs be so weighty and of such importance, s yet no conclusion can be had therein to your expectation. But think not the contrary, when convenient opportunity may thereunto serve us, we will, according to our former letters, take so good an end as it shall be to your contentation, as well in that matter as also in all your reasonable requests hereafter to be made unto us.

Yet we no a little marvel that you will say us nay in a request made unto you for John Dyon to be one of your justices of peace, who is a man of good learning, judgement and right meet [very suitable] for the same. Wherefor these shall be eftsoons [once again] to require you forthwith [immediately] to proceed to the election of him thereunto, or else to certify us in writing why you make denial thereof, by this bearer William Alynson, who hath honestly and diligently applied your matter here very painfully. Thus fare you well, from the Court the 26th March, Your friend, Charles Suffolk.[47]

Brandon was also known to have strong connections with George Brooke, 9th Baron Cobham and Governor of Calais (virtually all that remained to the English on the mainland of France and not much to show for generations of warfare). He wrote to the baron in 1544 thanking him for the quails and venison he sent. He also asks for Brooke's favour and goodwill toward a servant.

After my right hartie comendacoons to yo good Lordshipp w like thanks aswell for yo gentell lite dyrected to me from Callays of the xvii of this instant as also for yo qwailes which this p sent mornyng I have receyved by yo servant And where you desier to knowe in what pot in Kent I shall remayn to th entent you wold from tyme to tyme signifye to me of such newes as be currant ther for yo soo doing I geve unto you most harty thanks For aunswere wherunto you shall understand that as far as I knowe yet I shall demure in this town but whersoev I shall be you shall have knowlege therof from tyme to tyme I fynde myself moch beholding to my Lady yo bedfellow who hath sent me venison and made me good chere Also as tuching Lightmaker for a complaynt that he shuld make By my trouth my Lord beleve me he nev complayned to me of any suche mattr but indede he told me that the displeashur that was was for that another of his countrey wold have taken away his men and as long as he shall behave hymself honestly I hartley desier you to beare and owe unto hym yo good wyll and favor for my sake and yf he doo otherwyse then to be unto hym no woorse thenne you wold be to another Thus fare yo Lordshipp right hartely well From Rochester the xix of June Yo Lordshipp's assured freend CHARLYs SUFFolke.[48]

By 1544, letters written to Brandon were referring to him as 'ye myghty grace the ducke of Sothfolke' and 'the right honorable lord duke of Solffolk'.[49]

On 21 April 1544, Brandon was granted the office of Supervision of the Ceremonies on the forthcoming St George's Day (23 April).[50] It is unclear why Henry VIII could not attend the celebrations, but to replace the king in such a ceremony was an honour for Brandon and showed he was almost at the pinnacle of power at the court.

Brandon was also one of the men responsible for brokering a treaty between England and Scotland. Throughout the early months of 1543, he was one of several men who wrote directly to Sir George Douglas and the Earl of Angus in the hopes of organising a peace treaty which would see the infant Mary, Queen of Scots married to Henry VIII's young son, Prince Edward.[51] A tentative peace treaty with Scotland was signed on 1 July 1543 at Greenwich[52] and on 7 July Brandon was ordered by the Privy Council to 'to take hostages and agree with prisoners of Scotland for their ransoms'.[53]

Brandon was also responsible for proclaiming the truce in the North.[54] However, he had little time for dealing with prisoners and ransoms as only seven days later the Scots broke the peace treaty.[55] Brandon was furious at the breakdown of the treaty that he had worked so hard to broker, perhaps even insulted that those with whom he had corresponded and negotiated should turn against him and break his trust. The angry duke was now eager for war with Scotland, and on 21 September 1543 he wrote to the Privy Council:

I dowt not to sustaigne not oonly that jomaye, but I trust many worse then that, as well as they that arr more yonger then I.

Wherefore I most humble beseche the Kinges Mghnes that his majeste woll graunt me that I may not only serve his majestie in that jorney, but in all other suche lyke; trustinge to do his highnes suche service as shalbe to his majeste contentacione. For I ensewer you, that and I shuld be lefte behynde in suche jornaye, it shuld not be a lytle to my discomeforthe for the lacke that shold be reputide in me; whiche men wold thinke either my taryeenge was for lacke of good will to serve in suche jorneys, or ells for lacke of harte, whiche I wold be very sorye shuld be reputide in me.[56]

While an invasion of Scotland was indeed being planned, Brandon would not be the one to lead it. On 29 January 1544, Henry VIII replied to Brandon's letter:

Fynally, albeit we have determined to revoque youe shortly from thens, to thintent youe might prepare yourself to passe over with us to Fraunce, and to send our right trusty and right wel- biloved cousin thErle of Hertford down thither to supplie your place, yet for asmuche as youe have ben there nowe a greate while, and taken moche payn in our service, if youe s hall thinke this entreprise, faisible, and that there is honour to be gotten by the same, we wold be loth but that youe shuld have thonour thereof recompense of your former travail, being nethertheles contented.[57]

Seeking distraction from his pain and frustration in action, Henry VIII was again turning his sights on his old enemy, France, and he wanted his trusted military advisor and old friend by his side. English forces did indeed invade Scotland, but under the command of the Earl of Hertford, who was given strong orders by the Privy Council:

burn Edinburgh town, and so deface it as to leave a memory for ever of the vengeance of God upon "their falsehood and disloyalty," do his best without long tarrying to beat down the castle, sack Holyrood House, and sack, burn and subvert Lythe and all the towns and villages round, putting man, woman and child to fire and sword where resistance is made; then pass over to Fifeland and extend like destruction there, not forgetting to turn upside down the Cardinal's town of St. Andrews, so 'as th'upper stone may be the nether and not one stick stand by another,' sparing no creature alive, especially such as be allied to the Cardinal, and, if the castle can be won destroying it piecemeal.[58]

Hertford followed his orders. On 4 May, the English forces landed near the port of Leith. After forcing the gates of Edinburgh, they entered the city three days later, successfully burning much of the city to the ground.[59]

With Scotland subdued, the king turned his attention to this new war against France – but not before appointing Brandon as Steward of the Duchy of Lancaster as well as chief steward of all castles, manors and other possessions formerly belonging to the monasteries and priories north of the Trent. This latter position came with an annuity of £100.[60]

The war with France would be Henry VIII's last campaign against his old enemy, and he sought to align with Charles V once more in an attempt to capture Paris. (A peace treaty between the Holy Roman Emperor and England had been signed back in February 1543.)[61] As ever, Charles Brandon was called to action, and at the considerable age of fifty-nine or sixty he went to war again. While Henry's initial strategy was to take Paris, he abandoned this idea and acknowledged that a more realistic (and presumably much less costly) target was Boulogne, which could be used as ransom.[62] Brandon was appointed lieutenant and captain-general of the army[63] and tasked with taking the city. He appears to have been excited about what lay ahead, as he made jokes with the other members of the council about the upcoming war.[64] To aid him in dividing the French forces, the Duke of Norfolk was ordered to besiege Montreuil.[65]

Before going to war, on 20 June 1544, Brandon wrote his will. It would not do to have contesting or arguments regarding the disposition of his wealth should he die on campaign. The will is a fascinating read. It begins:

I CHARLES DUKE OF SUFFOLK, being of hole and perfite memory, considering the greate ambiguities, doubts, and questions that dayly do ryse and growe in last willes, the twentie day of June, in the yere of oure Lord God a thousande five hundredth xliiij., make this my last testament of all my goodes, catalles, and my will of my lands, teements, and hereditaments, according to the lawes of the realme.

Brandon first and foremost bequeaths his soul to God and requests that his body be buried 'without any pompe or outward pryde of the worlde'. He also requests that Masses and dirges be said for his soul according to the rites of the Church of England and that no black gowns or black coats be worn by those who mourn his death – save for the servants and torchbearers who attend his burial.

The next thing that Brandon requests is that the executors of his will – Katherine Willoughby, Lord Chancellor Thomas Wriothesley, Sir Anthony Browne and Lord Chamberlain William St John – pay off all his outstanding debts. Brandon also asks that his executors immediately give one hundred pounds to the poorest households in Tattershall, Gresham, Ellowe and Grimsthorpe.[66] Brandon was evidently concerned for his soul and wished to do all that he could to see his time in purgatory shortened.

The first person to whom Brandon grants property is his king, who is to receive a gold cup valued at £100. Interestingly, he requests that the cup be made of the gold from his Order of the Garter chain. Brandon must have attached great value to the chain and the honour it represented, and wished to pass it to his king and long-time friend. He also asks that a gold cup worth one hundred marks be given to Prince Edward.[67] Brandon also begs the king to bring up his sons 'in lernyng and other vertuose educacion, and most especially of Henry my eldest sonne, wherby he might the rather atteyn to be able to so to serve his most excellent Majestie and my Lorde Prince his master'.[68] He beseeches the king to take his eldest son, Henry, into his service so that he may be educated and serve alongside Prince Edward. Brandon was very aware of the benefits of growing up with royalty, and he was hoping to set up the same situation for his son.

To his wife, Brandon bequeaths five hundred marks, plate worth the same amount, jewels and pearls to the value of five hundred marks, household goods valued at the same and all the sheep and land in Lincoln. He also instructs that all her plate to be returned to her.[69] This is with the proviso that if she marries after his death but before his son's coming of age, or refuses to follow the will, then the executors of Brandon's will have the right to keep all of the goods bequeathed until his son comes of age.[70]

To Frances and Eleanor, his daughters by his third wife, Mary Tudor, Brandon provides the value of two hundred pounds' worth of plate to each. He also bequeaths cattle to both women.[71]

To his son and heir, Henry, Brandon provides the most considerable portion of his lands, money and property. He bequeaths to his son all his horses, mares and geldings (of which there were many), all his remaining gold, silver and gilded plate, jewels, clothing and household belongings. He notes that all these belongings are to be given to Henry Brandon only when he reaches eighteen or twenty-one, depending on what the executors of the will decide. Brandon then states that if Henry should die before he reaches eighteen years of age, all the above mentioned shall go to Charles, his second son with Katherine Willoughby.

Brandon also makes provision for the sad possibility that both of his sons die before they are twenty-one years of age. If this happens, all the goods Brandon had provided for his sons should be divided between his wife Katherine and his daughters Eleanor and Frances or the heirs of Eleanor and Frances.[72] He also makes provision for his grandson William Stanley, son of Brandon's daughter Mary and her husband Thomas Stanley, Lord Monteagle. Brandon provides for the marriage of Anne Howard for William and the yearly rents, issues and profits of the manors, lands and tenements in the county of Lancaster to the annual value of one hundred pounds.[73]

Brandon did not forget his servants. To those who would not continue under the service of his wife or sons he granted two years' wages and a black coat; to those who would remain in the service of his wife or sons he gave a year's wage.[74]

To his executors (besides his wife) he gives plate to the value of forty pounds as well as fifteen years' worth of rent from a large number of houses, tenancies and lands that Brandon owned throughout England.[75] He also asks that his executors use eight thousand marks from these incomes to purchase lands for his son Charles.[76] Furthermore, he grants the custody and marriage of Agnes Woodhall, daughter and heir of Anthony Woodhull of Thenford, to his son Charles.[77] Brandon asks that the king hold Tattershall Castle and several other important manors and lands, mostly in Lincoln, for his eldest son until he comes of age.[78] Brandon ends his will merely stating:

In wytnes wherof to thiese my present will and testament I have subscribed my name and putto my seal the day and year abovesaied.[79]

16

The Final Battle

With his will written, Brandon could leave for Calais in the knowledge that his property and possessions would be disposed of according to his wishes. By the end of June 1544, he and his men were in France. Shortly afterwards, they began the great siege of Boulogne.[1] Brandon was firmly in control of his men and the campaign, working with his council to ensure that not only the soldiers but also the horses that had been brought across had enough food and water.[2] He determined that no concessions should be made to the city and its civilian population, and over six weeks he oversaw around 100,000 gun stones fired into the town. Tunnels and trenches were meanwhile dug to undermine the outer walls of the city.[3]

Brandon took an active, front-line role in the fighting. Lord Lisle wrote that the duke 'has been as far as any gunner in the field. Yesternight after supper I went with him to the trenches, in one of which three pioneers were killed a little before. He passeth so little upon shot of artillery that he enforceth others to be hardy whether they will or not.'[4] Even when Henry VIII arrived at the battlefront, albeit at a safe distance, much of the organisation and operation of the siege was still left to Brandon.[5] Boulogne finally surrendered on 14 September, and a treaty was organised between Brandon and the captain of Boulogne, Messire Jacques de Coucy, Seigneur de Vervins.[6] The duke had the honour of riding into the city to signal its surrender.

Satisfied with this victory, the king returned home after issuing Brandon with orders to provide aid to the Duke of Norfolk at Montreuil. Before he could do so, however, on 18 September, France signed a peace treaty with Charles V, leaving England alone in the war.[7] Poor weather and lack of supplies saw Brandon, Norfolk and their soldiers retreat to Calais.[8] On 7 October, a distressed Brandon wrote to the king:

> As the king showed him special favour and credit, he had rather spend his life than be driven to make any excuse why he did not as commanded. Nothing has grieved him more than this departure from Boleyne and he saw none here but were ready to tarry at Boleyne if the case would have suffered it. Begs Henry to accept the doings here, and not to show displeasure to the rest, whereby people and captains might be discouraged hereafter.[9]

The king did not take offence at Brandon's retreat, but he did ask him to stay at Calais so that he and his men could provide support to the garrison of Boulogne if needed. On 26 October, Henry wrote to Brandon with favour:

> For his acceptable service in winning Bulloyn, and for a special confidence in him, has resolved to have him remain on that side (as the Council's letters to him and others will show) until affairs there are more perfectly established. Requires him to have a good respect to his own health, and, if the danger of infection at Calais be such as is reported, to remain with his attendants at Guisnes or some other place within the marches.[10]

By 22 November, Brandon was back in England.[11] Despite being forced to retreat, the war had brought Brandon several interesting rewards. He was able to purchase Tattershall College for only £2,666 (£819,954.96),[12] less than eight times its annual worth.[13] In May 1545, Brandon was granted the ability to retain one hundred men as part of his guard.[14] This was a massive reward considering how suspicious the king had grown in his final years.

The previous year, on 12 July, Henry VIII had married his sixth and final wife, Katherine Parr, in the Queen's Closet at Hampton Court. Katherine was the daughter of Sir Thomas Parr, a favourite of the king during the early years of his reign, and Maud Parr, who had served as a lady-in-waiting to Henry's first wife, Katherine of Aragon.[15] While Brandon did not attend the wedding as he was then busy in his duties as Royal Lieutenant of the North, his wife did. She was also appointed as a lady-in-waiting to the new queen and would become close friends with her, the two women sharing a love of the new learning that was spreading across Europe.[16]

One historian has speculated that Henry VIII had romantic feelings for Katherine Willoughby and sought to make her his wife after Brandon's death. Katherine was regularly at court, by her husband's side when he was attending the king or in service to Anne of Cleves and Catherine Howard before she moved on to become a lady-in-waiting to Katherine Parr.[17] In 1538, Chapuys had written to the Queen of Hungary explaining that 'the painter returned with the duchess' likeness, which has pleased the king much, and put him in much better humour. He has been masking and visiting the duchess of Suffolk.'[18]

The fact that the king visited and entertained with Katherine Willoughby has been used to suggest that he was romantically interested in her from as early as 1538. However, it should be pointed out that the 'duchess' referred to in the letter was Christina of Denmark, Duchess of Milan, not Katherine Willoughby. Henry was investigating Christina as a potential fourth wife at the time, so it makes little sense that he would then romantically pursue Katherine Willoughby. However, Imperial ambassador Francois van der Delft wrote to Charles V telling him of rumours he had heard about the king and Katherine Willoughby:

> Sire, I am confused and apprehensive to have to inform your Majesty that there are rumours here of a new Queen, although I do not know why, or how true it may be. Some people attribute to it the sterility of the present queen, whilst others say there will be no change whilst the present war lasts. Madame Suffolk is much talked about, and is in great favour; but the king shows no alteration in his demeanour towards the queen, though the latter, as I am informed, is somewhat annoyed at the rumours.[19]

It must be noted that this letter was written on 27 September 1546, over a year after Brandon's death. The letter also states that the king is annoyed by the rumours, which perhaps suggests that he was not romantically interested in Katherine Willoughby, or at least that he was not seeking to cast off his sixth wife and replace her with a seventh.

There are few records of Brandon's health over the last few years of his life. In January 1542, Brandon was allowed to sit during the opening of Parliament, and in October of the same year he wrote to Thomas Wriothesley, Earl of Southampton, of a sore leg which immobilised him for a short time. We do not know whether the two incidents were related, but a leg injury is a valid reason not to stand in Parliament.[20]

In March 1545, Brandon suffered another bout of ill health. We know this because, later on, in 1547, Lord Nevell wrote to Sir William Paget that he had been tricked by a man named Wisdom into purchasing a ring which would bring him money and fortune. Lord Nevell caught the man and brought him to Brandon's home at Barbican in hopes to declare the matter to the duke, but he was unable to see the duke as he had been ill the night before and had only just fallen asleep.[21] Another source states that Brandon was indeed sick at the time, but not so much that he could not receive visitors.[22]

During August that year, the Privy Council, which included Brandon, moved from Petworth to Guildford in Surrey. The Privy Council met daily from the 15th to the 21st, discussing issues such as the licence of a shipment of woad and the general granting of licences and warrants.[23] However, on the 19th Cornelius Scepperus, an ambassador to Charles V, arrived at Guildford to see the king. Scepperus wrote to his master stating that Brandon was ill and unable to take him to the king; instead he was escorted by Winchester and Paget.[24] Brandon is recorded as having attended the council meeting on that day,[25] but Scepperus' letter indicates that Brandon's health must have been in serious decline by this time.

On 21 August, Henry VIII moved to Woking, and a Privy Council meeting was held there on the same day. Brandon did not attend.[26] It is most likely that he was seriously ill at this time, and so remained at Guildford. Perhaps he hoped to join the king later, after some much-needed rest. Whatever his thoughts, Brandon would in fact never see his king again. Charles Brandon, Duke of Suffolk, died on 22 August 1545 at four o'clock in the afternoon.[27]

Despite wishing to be buried in the college church of Tattershall in Lincoln without any pomp or display, Brandon was buried at St George's Chapel in Windsor near the south door of the choir at the king's expense. Charles Wriothesley recorded the sad news:

This moneth also died at Gilford the excelent Prince Charles Brandon, Duke of Suffolke, and Lord Great Master of the Kinges Household, whose death all true Englishment maie greatlie lament, which had been so valiant a captaine in the Kinges warres, booth in Scotland, Fraunce, and Irelande, to the great damage and losse of the Kinges enemies, whose bodie was honorably buried at Windsor at the Kinges costes.[28]

In his *Chronicle of the History of England*, Hall wrote his own tribute:

In thys moneth died Chalres, the noble and valiaunt duke of Suffolke a hardye gentleman, and yet not so hardy, as almoste of all estates and degrees of menne high and lowe, rych and poore, hartely beloued and hys death of theme muche lamented, he was buryed at Wyndsore.[29]

During the afternoon of 8 September 1545, Brandon's body was taken to the Great Chamber at Guildford where it was laid upon a trestle. It was then covered in a rich pall of gold cloth of issue bearing his coat of arms. A cross was laid over his body, and two lit candles were placed on the trestle. The Great Chamber was hung with black cloth and Brandon's arms, and the floor was also laid with black cloth. At the end of the trestle was a stool covered in black cloth on which mourners could kneel. The Lord Marquis of Dorset was present, and dirges were said for Brandon's soul. The room is reported to have been full of gentlemen and lords who mourned the loss of the duke.[30]

The next day, at roughly seven o'clock, Charles Brandon was removed from Guildford and taken to Windsor Castle. Brandon's body was laid upon a chariot painted black and drawn by five horses. He was covered in a pall of cloth of gold, and the chariot was covered in black cloth with white crosses. Upon the black cloth were images representing Bandon's family history. One represented Brandon alone, one his grandparent's marriage, one his parents' marriage, and there was one for each of his betrothals to Anne Browne, Mary Tudor and Katherine Willoughby. At either end of the chariot sat a hooded gentleman usher.[31]

Brandon's long funeral procession was led by John Osborne and Thomas Tooby, dressed in black and carrying black staves as they rode. Next came the cross of St Mary Church of Guildford. Then followed the priests and clerks and a large number of other men including William Clifton, John Parker, John Swaynsland, Thomas Darcy, John Rousse, Henry Neuell, Anthony Seckford, Nicholas Bayly, John Dyon, John Drewry, John Gedge and George St Poll, to name a few.[32] Following these men rode three officers of Brandon's household:

treasurer Sir William Naunton, steward Mr Wingfield and comptroller Mr John Mowbray. After them came Francis Seckford, who carried Brandon's banner of arms, and then there were men wearing Brandon's coat of arms, his helm and crest and his sword.[33] On the right side of the chariot rode Sir Christopher Beynham, who distributed alms to the poor along the journey, accompanied by men bearing the banner of St George and the banner of the Holy Trinity. On the left rode men carrying the banner of St Barbara, the Banner of our Lady.[34]

At three in the afternoon, the procession rode into the town of Windsor where it was met by the mayor of Windsor along with poor men dressed in hooded black gowns and holding torches. The procession then entered Windsor Castle, and Brandon was taken out of the chariot and carried by John and Anthony Seckford, Thomas Darcy (who had been with Brandon when he commanded in the north), and Tattershall bailiff John Porter. A rich canopy of cloth of gold covered Brandon's body while it was carried into St George's Chapel.[35] The interior of the chapel was hung with black cloth and covered with images of Brandon's arms. Brandon's body was once more placed upon a trestle covered in cloth of gold. Once this was done, the gentlemen and lords departed to put on their gowns for the funeral. They returned at four o'clock, when the funeral service began with the announcement: 'For the sol of the Right Noble high and mighty Prince Chalres Duke of Suff Lord Presidente of the Kinges Ma[jesties] most honourable Counnsell & great M[aster] of his household k[night] nad Companyon of the Noble Order of the Gartier.' The funeral service was conducted jointly by Stephen Gardiner, Bishop of Winchester, and Henry Holbeach, Bishop of Rochester.[36]

After the service, Charles Brandon, Duke of Suffolk, was buried close to the Quire near the south door of the choir. After a handful of dirt was thrown into the grave, the officers of Brandon's household – Sir William Naunton, Mr Wingfield, Mr John Mowbray and Mr Thomas Seckford – broke their staves and threw them into the grave as a mark of respect.[37]

The next morning, 10 September, another Mass was held and a sermon conducted by Stephen Gardiner and Henry Holbeach before the Requiem Mass was sung. After this, mourners approached. One of these was William Parr, Earl of Essex, younger brother of the late Jane Seymour and a close friend.[38] The pair had raced hounds together in May 1543[39] and communicated regularly while Brandon guarded the northern border.[40] The Earl of Essex, along with the Earl of Arundel, brought up Brandon's coat of arms while the Earl of Huntington and Lord William Howard brought the targe. Sir Anthony Browne and Sir Anthony Wingfield brought Brandon's helm and crest. Once the service was finished, banners were set up around Brandon's burial plot. It is reported that there was great weeping at the funeral, with many lamenting his death.[41]

The king was said to have been struck with grief at the loss of his oldest and most loyal friend. Upon hearing the news of Brandon's death, he declared the duke had been one of his best friends. He went on to say that Brandon had always been loyal and generous and that he had never taken unfair advantage of a friend or enemy, being fair towards everybody.[42]

In 1749, Joseph Pote, in his book *The History and Antiquities of Windsor Castle*, wrote:

> In this Arch, close to the Choire lyes buried, the most noble Prince Charles Brandon, Duke of Suffolk, He married Mary Queen Dowager of France, and Sister to K. Henry VIII. His Grace died Anno 1545 and was buried at the Royal Expence, and probably with some honourable Memorial, tho' now nothing remains to distinguish the Grave of this noble Duke, but a rude brick pavement, and the remainder of his Atcheivements affixed to the Pillar above.

It appears that there must have been a memorial or monument to commemorate Brandon's burial which had fallen into ruin over the years. An entry in the *1787 Chapter Acts* suggests this: 'Ordered that leave be given to lay a stone above the grave of Charles Brandon Duke of Suffolk, according to His Majesties directions.'[43]

When Henry Emlyn began his repaving work of the Quire aisle and nave, he oversaw the laying of a black marble stone over Brandon's grave. Upon the stone is written: 'Charles Brandon Duke of Suffolk KG Died 24 August 1545 Married Mary Daughter of Henry VII Widow of Louis XII King of France.' Frustratingly, this date is inaccurate, stating Brandon died on 24 August rather than the 22nd. Still, it is almost poetic that Henry VIII chose to see his long-time friend buried at St George's Chapel, as he would be buried there nearly eighteen months later, alongside his third wife, Jane Seymour.

Charles Brandon, Duke of Suffolk, was extremely loyal to his king and worked hard to maintain their friendship. His father had died defending Henry VII at the Battle of Bosworth, and Brandon continued this family loyalty with his heir. He became Henry's friend and remained so throughout his life. Brandon did not influence Henry VIII's decisions in religious or state matters; instead, he followed his king's lead and rarely stepped out of line. He was a loyal servant and courtier, and this was a quality that Henry VIII seemed to value within his friend.

In 1840, Charles Knight wrote of Brandon:

> It was proof of is sagacity to have adopted by choice the character of mere courtier; but he moved in it with rare dignity; and envy, malice, and duplicity seemed to have been unknown to him. Possessing a fine person, an agreeable address, and a sparkling wit, which he knew well how to temper with discretion – skilled at all courtly exercises of the day, and honoured with the confidence of the king, Charles Brandon rapidly rose to distinction; and by avoiding all interference with religion and politics; the rocks on which so many so many in that hazardous reign ruined their fortunes, he contrived to maintain his place in the king's friendship to the last.[44]

Most of all, more than his skills at jousting or his ability to lead men into battle, the greatest quality that held Brandon in good stead throughout his life was that he knew his king. James Granger wrote of Brandon in 1824:

> Charles Brandon was remarkable for the dignity and gracefulness of his person, and his robust and athletic constitution. He distinguished himself in the tilts and tournaments, the favourite exercises of Henry. He was brought up with that Prince, studied his disposition, and exactly conformed to it. The conformity gradually brought on a stricter intimacy; and the king, to bring him nearer to himself, raised him from a private person to a duke.[45]

Brandon 'studied his disposition, and exactly conformed to it'. This ability to read his king and friend, and conform to his wishes and desires, is ultimately what made Charles Brandon the success that he was. He knew his king perhaps better than anyone else. He knew what angered the king and what gave him cheer. Even when Henry VIII was continually changing his religious views, Brandon was able to understand the king's beliefs and adapt his own. This did not mean that Brandon was devoid of beliefs and opinions separate from those of the king; indeed, he showed in his life that he did not always privately agree with Henry. He did not agree with the king's treatment of his wife Katherine of Aragon when he banished her from the court, and he did not agree with Henry's romantic interest in Anne Boleyn. Despite speaking out about these things, Brandon knew when he had to conform to the king's wishes.

Brandon was also careful not to speak publicly about his religious beliefs. While a reasonably conservative Catholic, he knew the king wanted to reform the Church in England, and he went along with these changes. He was careful to keep his views to himself and only moved against others, such as the Boleyn faction, when he believed that it was necessary for his standing with the king. Despite all the religious and political upheaval in England at this time, Brandon always managed to walk the fine line of keeping those around him happy while being loyal to his king.

After Brandon's death, John Dymock wrote to Wriothesley that '[m]y lord's Grace owes a good deal of money'.[46] However, this was not quite the case. Upon his death, Brandon's estates combined with the Willoughby estates brought in around £3,400 (£1 million) a year, minus £413 (£127,000) that was part of Norfolk's pension. In 1553, Brandon's debts to the king were estimated to be around £3,059, of which he had left £620 (£190,000)[47] a year in his will to pay off.[48] All in all, by the time of his death Brandon had paid off a great deal of his debt and through shrewd purchases, clever haggling and an advantageous marriage had managed to increase his yearly income. He had also become the largest magnate in Lincolnshire, leaving much of his lands, manors and wealth to his sons. Furthermore, he had impressively extended his castles at Grimsthorpe and Tattershall.

Brandon was survived by his fourth wife, Katherine Willoughby, and five surviving children, three daughters and two sons. His surviving daughters were Anne, thirty-eight, born from his first marriage to Anne Browne; and Frances, twenty-eight, and Eleanor, somewhere between twenty-four and twenty-seven, from his marriage to Mary Tudor. Brandon's surviving sons were Henry and Charles Brandon, aged ten and eight years respectively, from his marriage to Katherine Willoughby.

17

The Last of the Brandon Men

Upon Charles Brandon's death, his oldest surviving son, Henry, inherited the greater part of his estates and wealth, although he could not access them until he reached his majority. Young Henry's wardship and the right to organise his marriage was granted to his mother, Katherine Willoughby, in May 1546 for the sum of £1,500[1] (£461,000),[2] to be paid in seven instalments.[3]

Frustratingly, we know very little of either Henry or Charles Brandon's young lives. There are few mentions of them, and tragically both would die just six years after their father.

What we do know is that the Brandon boys were educated with Prince Edward, Henry VIII's son and heir. They were taught by Richard Coxe, John Cheke and Roger Ascham, and then from February 1550 by John Cheke and Sir Anthony Crooke. Presumably, it was hoped that Henry and Edward would recreate the friendship their fathers had forged when they were teenagers.

Edward, as the future king, would have been given the best education possible at the time, and the Brandons would have shared in this. They would have been schooled in Latin, French and Greek, Renaissance humanism, the Classics, calligraphy, music, tennis, hunting and archery, as well as learning about war and military strategy. Amusingly, the usual childish reaction to schoolwork can be inferred from doodles in the pages of Edward's work,[4] although one hopes that their writing was neater and more legible than their father's!

Edward would have received religious instruction according to the precepts of his father's faith, which was predominantly

Catholic in nature and little touched by the new Protestantism. By association, it can be surmised that Henry and Charles Brandon were also brought up attending Mass and listening to sermons. However, this was to change dramatically.

On 28 January 1547, Henry VIII died, and Edward was crowned King Edward VI at just nine years of age. His father had decreed that a regency council should rule England until the boy king reached maturity – which, tragically, never happened. Under regency rule, the English Reformation gathered pace. Church life changed quickly. Rosary beads were condemned, the ringing of bells during services was abolished, and even the stunning paintings that covered church walls and the magnificent stained-glass windows were to be painted over and removed.[5]

Both Brandon boys would have experienced these reforms and been encouraged to learn the new Protestant religion and take on board its teachings. Their father Charles was still a relatively conservative Catholic upon his death, although their mother was a staunch supporter of the new faith. Despite this, we know nothing of how Henry and Charles Brandon personally felt. Considering their young age, it is likely that religious matters simply didn't trouble them very much.

During Edward VI's coronation, both Henry and Charles Brandon were knighted, and Henry Brandon had the honour of carrying the king's orb.[6] In addition to this, Sir Charles Brandon, the illegitimate older brother of Charles and Henry, participated in the jousts to celebrate the new king.[7] After the coronation, Henry Brandon remained in the new king's household. He participated in various courtly events, including revelling with the king in March 1547 and 'running at the ring' in 1550. He also participated in formal events at court including witnessing the induction of John Russell, Keeper of the Privy Seal, as Earl of Bedford.[8]

Before his death, Charles Brandon, Duke of Suffolk, had been a party to the negotiations for the Treaty of Greenwich, which would see Edward married to the young Mary, Queen of Scots and consequently the unification of England and Scotland. The treaty, signed on 1 July 1543, only lasted seven days before the Scots broke it. This was to have ramifications for Charles Brandon's son, Henry, six years later.

On 10 September 1547, Scotland and England went to war. Edward Seymour, Duke of Somerset, now regent of Edward VI's council, hoped to capture the child Mary and convey her to England. The war was to be short and brutal, and it would achieve absolutely nothing of political importance. It would also reopen hostilities with France at a time when the English treasury was severely depleted due to the resumption of war in the last years of Henry VIII's reign. In an engagement that became known as the Battle of Pinkie, a formidable professional English army backed by a strong naval detachment routed the larger but less well-armed and trained Scottish forces. It was one of the most disastrous defeats in Scottish history, with thousands of Scotsmen killed. However, Mary had been safely hidden away, and despite the victory, Somerset (who had personally led the English army) did not have the young queen.

In desperation, Mary of Guise, the Queen of Scots' mother, reached out to France for help.[9] In June 1548, a French army landed at Leith to aid the Scots. They went on to besiege Haddington, and soon a betrothal was organised between Mary, Queen of Scots and Francis, Dauphin of France. Mary was then taken from Scotland to be brought up in France.[10] Unable to gain custody of Mary, and with no real reason to continue the war, Somerset signed the Treaty of Boulogne with France on 24 March 1550 and formally declared peace in England on Saturday 29 March. The treaty provided for the return of the city of Boulogne to the French, and in return France had to pay 400,000 crowns and withdraw their troops from Scotland.[11] Also, six Englishmen would go to France as hostages and six Frenchmen to England. One of the English hostages was Henry Brandon, 2nd Duke of Suffolk.[12]

Although he was a hostage, Brandon was to be treated in a manner according to his status. On 28 March, word was sent to Katherine Willoughby that she should give her son Henry as a hostage to the French. He was to come accompanied with all the furnishings he would need, and his time in France would be funded out of the king's coffers.[13] In addition, Brandon also took with him twenty-two horses.[14] In France, young Henry impressed the French nobility with his good Latin and his ability to ride while wearing armour. It was also rumoured that the French king wished for Henry Brandon to marry Monsieur de Vendôme's sister.[15] Brandon did not live at the French court for long, in any case, as it is recorded that on 17 June 1550 he was at a lavish masque in London, where he dressed up as a nun.[16]

Katherine Willoughby had already decided that both of her children should attend St John's College, Cambridge, as it had a reputation as a centre of reform for the Protestant religion.[17] Perhaps she also wished to protect her young sons from the extravagance of court, and to breed in them a more serious outlook. At St John's, Henry and Charles were educated by many leading tutors including Thomas Wilson, who later would write fondly of both boys.[18] At St John's, both boys were subjected to a strict and gruelling regime of education which began with them rising at around four or five in the morning to attend church. Afterwards, their studies lasted twelve hours, with little time for leisure or entertainment. In the evening they had a simple dinner and went to bed.[19] This must have been quite a shock to the boys, who had spent several years in luxury at court.

In March 1551 it was recorded that both Warwick and Somerset had been attempting to have their daughters married to Henry Brandon, Duke of Suffolk, then aged fifteen. Katherine refused the matches, stating that her son was too young.[20]

In the summer, another case of the dreaded sweating sickness broke out in England.[21] This illness had first struck in the fifteenth century and appeared on and off between 1485 and 1551; the outbreak of 1551 was particularly severe. The symptoms seemed to be something like influenza or pneumonia, with the patient suffering great thirst, pains and aches all over the body, and also the titular sweating. Many people who caught the sweat were dead within twenty-four hours. Dr John Caius, writing in 1551 in his book *A Boke or Counseill Against the Disease Commonly Called the Sweate, or Sweatyng Sicknesse*, claimed that the disease was caused by 'infection, impure spirits in corrupt bodies and evil qualities in the air, and by the nature and site of the soil in the region'.[22]

Hearing of the outbreak, Katherine ordered that her sons and their cousin George Stanley move to Kingston, several miles from St John's. However, George Stanley soon died, and both Brandon boys were moved to Buckden Towers, Cambridgeshire. Tragically, on 14 July 1551, both Henry and Charles died of the sickness within a half an hour of one another.[23] Thomas Wilson, who had been a tutor to both boys, described their deaths:

They both were together in one house, lodged in two separate chambers, and almost at one time both sickened, and both departed. They died both dukes, both well learned, both wise, and both right Godly. They both gave strange tokens of death to come. The elder, sitting at supper and very merry, said suddenly to that right honest matron and godly gentlewoman [probably Mrs Margaret Blakborn, who had acted as their governess and who would later share Katherine's exile], 'O Lord, where shall we sup tomorrow at night?' Whereupon, she being troubled, and yet saying comfortably, 'I trust, my Lord, either here, or elsewhere at some of your friends' houses.' 'Nay,' said he, 'we shall never sup together again in this world, be you well assured,' and with that, seeing the gentlewoman discomfited, turned it unto mirth, and passed the rest of his supper with much joy, and the same night after twelve of the clock, being the fourteenth of July, sickened, and so was taken the next morning, about seven of the clock, to the mercy of God. When the eldest was gone, the younger would not tarry, but told before (having no knowledge thereof by anybody living) of his brother's death, to the great wondering of all that were there, declaring what it was to lose so dear a friend, but comforting himself in that passion, said, 'Well, my brother is gone, but it makes no matter for I will go straight after him,' and so did within the space of half an hour.[24]

It is reported that Katherine Willoughby was at Kingston when she heard that her sons had fallen ill. Despite being sick herself, Katherine hurried to Buckden to be with her boys, but tragically Henry died before his mother arrived. It is unclear if she was there to comfort her youngest, Charles, before he too passed, but one could only hope she provided him with some solace in his final hour. Henry and Charles Brandon were buried at St Mary's Church, next to Buckden Towers.[25]

Thomas Wilson further praised the boys, describing a little of their personalities and their love of learning in his book *Art of Rhetoric*:

The elder, waiting on the King's Majesty that now is, was generally well esteemed, and such hope was conceived of his towardness, both for learning and all other things, that few were like unto him in all the court. The other, keeping his book among the Cambridge men, profited (as they well know) both in virtue and learning, to their great admiration. For the Greek, the Latin, and the Italian, I know he could do more than would be thought true by my report. I leave to speak of his skill in pleasant instruments, neither will I utter his aptness in music, and his toward nature to all exercises of the body. But his elder brother in this time – besides the other gifts of the mind, which passed all others and were almost incredible, – following his father's nature was so delighted with riding and running in armor upon horseback, and was so comely for that feat, and could do so well in charging his staff, being but fourteen years of age, that men-of-war even at this hour moan much the want of such a worthy gentleman. Yeah, the Frenchman that first wondered at his learning when he was there among them and made a noteable oration in Latin were much more astonied when they saw his comely riding, and little thought to find these two ornaments joined both in one, his years especially being so tender and his practice of so small time.

Afteward, coming from the court, as one that was desirious to be among the learned, he lay in Cambridge together with his brother, they were both so profited and so gently used themselves, that all Cambridge did reverence both him and his brother as two jewles sent from God. The elder's nature was such that he thought himself best when he was among the wisest, and yet contemned none, but thankfully used all, gentle in behaviour without childishness, stout of stomach without all pride, bold without all wariness and friendly with good advisement. The younger, being not so ripe in years, was not so grave in look, rather cheerful than sad, rather quick than ancient; but yet if his brother were set aside, not one that went beyond him. A child that by his own inclination that so much yielded to his ruler as few by chastement have done the like, pleasant of speech, prompt of wit, sitting by nature, haught without hate, kind without craft, liberal of heart, gentle in behaviour, forward in all things, greedy of learning, and loath to take a foil in any open assembly. They both in all attempts sought to have the victory, and in excersise of wit not only the one with the other did oft stand in contention, but also they both would match with the best, and thought themselves most happy when they might have any occasion to put their wits to trail.[26]

Even putting any boasting aside, it is clear that both boys were very bright and showed a great deal of promise. They seem to have had a great love of learning, and enjoyed sharing their knowledge and having their thoughts and ideas challenged. It also seems that Henry shared his father's skill and ability in horse riding and jousting. Losing her two sons at such a tender age must have been devastating for Katherine Willoughby. In September, she wrote to William Cecil, who would become one of Elizabeth I's closest advisors, stating that she was 'thankful to God for all his benefits. Her resignation under this last sharp and bitter trial (the death of her two sons, ob. 14 July).'[27]

In August 1551, Jehan Scheyfve wrote to the emperor to say that Edward VI 'is still at Hampton Court, where he is surrounded by seven or eight gentlemen of his chamber only. He remains almost in hiding, and the French lords saw little of him. The reason seems to be the shock and surprise he received at the news of the Duke of Suffolk's death; for the king loved him dearly.'[28]

With the legitimate male line of the Brandon family no more, it was the Brandon daughters who carried on the Brandon blood. Brandon's first-born child, Anne, who was born in 1507, would outlive her father but caused such a scandal that he excluded her from his will. Anne and her husband Edward Grey, Lord Powis, were not on good terms, and on 30 June 1537 Brandon had written to Cromwell from his residence at Grimsthorpe, interceding for his daughter. Brandon begged Cromwell 'to continue his goodwill to his daughter Powes, to whom he will be good lord and father if she will follow Cromwell's advice and live after such an honest sort as shall be to your honour and mine'.[29] Anne apparently did not take her father's advice, nor Cromwell's, for she took a lover. It is reported that one night Anne's husband Edward stormed into her chambers and removed her lover, Randle Hanworth, and while this caused quite a stir, nothing was openly done either to see husband and wife reunited or to end the marriage. Thomas Cromwell had to step in and negotiate an agreement between the couple which allowed them to separate.

In 1537, Brandon petitioned the court to make Anne's husband pay an annuity of £100 (£30,000)[30] to help support his wife. With Thomas Cromwell's help, Brandon proved successful in his petition. However, three years later Grey petitioned the Privy Council, of which Brandon was a member, asking the council to punish Anne for adultery and also stating that Anne and her lover were trying to kill him. Unsurprisingly, nothing came of this.[31] Anne continued to enjoy court life, although she had to borrow money from both Cromwell and her father, and was left out of Brandon's will, most probably for the great scandal that she had caused by openly taking a lover while a married woman.[32] (Clearly, Anne had considerable charm and powers of persuasion not only to escape punishment but also to be financed in her pursuit of pleasure.) For his part, Edward Grey was never faithful to his wife and had at least three illegitimate children with his mistress Jane Owell.[33]

Sometime between 1545 and 1551, Anne used forged documents (supposedly written by her late father) to obtain lands which she then sold to John Beaumont, a judge in Chancery. This action defrauded her brother-in-law Henry Grey, Marquis of Dorset (husband of Frances, Brandon's eldest daughter with his third wife, Mary Tudor). The illegal actions came to light in 1552, and John Beaumont was arrested; however, Anne does not seem to have faced any punishment.[34]

After the death of her husband on 2 July 1551, Anne married her lover Randle Hanworth. In 1556, the indefatigable and newly respectable Anne, with the aid of her husband, brought suit against Frances and her then husband Adrian Stokes regarding lands in Warwickshire which had previously belonged to their father. This does not seem to have come to anything, as Anne died in early January 1557 or 1558. She was buried on 13 January in St Margaret's, Westminster.[35]

Mary Brandon, Charles's second daughter by his first wife Anne Bowne, predeceased her father. She had six children with her husband, Thomas Stanley, 2nd Baron Monteagle, of whom three daughters and one son survived to adulthood. Mary's son was named William and became William Stanley, 3rd Baron Monteagle, upon his father's death. William married twice; however, upon his death he only left a single daughter.

Eleanor Brandon, Charles's second daughter with his wife Mary Tudor, would only survive her father by a little over two years. Despite being eighth in line for the English throne, just as the exact date of her birth is not recorded, there do not seem to be any records of any significant events in her life. She seems to have lived quietly with her husband Henry Clifford, 2nd Earl of Cumberland, after their marriage in 1537. Clifford was a busy courtier, acting as Sheriff of Westmorland, Constable and Steward of the Castle and Honour of Knaresborough in 1542 as well as Councillor of the North in the same year. He was also Captain of the West Marches in 1544.[36] Eleanor's residence during this time remains unknown, but she likely spent some of her time at her husband's castle in Skipton, where lavish extensions were added for the celebration of her marriage. Eleanor had three children with her husband: a daughter named Margaret, born in 1540; and two sons, Henry and Charles, who both died in infancy.[37] Eleanor died on 27 September 1547 at Brougham Castle, Westmorland, and was buried at Skipton in Yorkshire.[38]

Of all Brandon's children, it is probably his daughter Frances, also by his wife Mary Tudor, who is most remembered. Born on 16 July 1517, Frances was just sixteen years of age when she married Henry Grey, Marquis of Dorset.[39] Frances had three surviving daughters: Jane, born in October 1537; Katherine, born in August 1540; and Mary, born in 1545. Frances would be a regular member at court, attending the funeral of Henry VIII's third wife, Jane Seymour, and participating in the festivities to celebrate the arrival of his fourth wife, Anne of Cleves. It has been suggested that Frances was with her father at Guildford when he died on 22 August; however, there does not seem to be any firm evidence to support this.[40]

Brandon left Frances £200 (£60,000)[41] worth of plate in his will, and if both her half-brothers died before her she would inherit the lands and property that Brandon left to them. As it would happen, both boys died in 1551, and therefore Frances inherited much of her late father's possessions and property.[42] In addition to this, after the death of her half-brothers the title of Duke of Suffolk passed to her husband, Henry Grey, on 11 October 1551.[43]

Frances' eldest daughter, Jane, would become the famous Lady Jane Grey, the Nine Day Queen. Whole books have been dedicated to Jane and her tragic journey to the throne and then the executioner's block, so a simple summary shall be suffice to outline Frances' role in her daughter's rise and fall. In 1553, Jane married Guildford Dudley, son of John Dudley, Duke of Northumberland and Protector of the Realm while King Edward VI was underage.

It was soon apparent that Edward was sick and would not live long; the king died on 6 July 1553. Before his death, the boy king wrote his 'Device for the Succession', in which he overlooked his half-sisters Mary and Elizabeth in favour of Lady Jane Grey, his cousin. Edward was a staunch Protestant and wished for England to continue to follow the Protestant faith. Mary, Edward's half-sister, was a devout Catholic and had been her whole life; therefore, he did not wish for her to succeed the throne and return England to Rome. But if the boy king overlooked Mary, then he would also have to overlook his other half-sister Elizabeth, which he did on the grounds of bastardy.[44]

Lady Jane Grey was a firm Protestant, and in her Edward saw a way to keep England in his faith. What he did not anticipate was the support that Mary Tudor would receive. Upon Jane's coronation, Frances, now mother to the Queen of England, carried her daughter's train. However, things would not go as Edward VI hoped. While Jane was proclaimed queen in London, Mary was proclaimed queen in Norfolk and parts of Suffolk.[45] Mary soon gained the support of vast numbers of the commons, gentry and nobility who supported her claim to be queen. Whatever the popular sentiment regarding Jane, followers of the 'old religion' were seizing their chance. Many of the gentry in the rural shires had remained staunchly Catholic and happily rallied to the cause to see a Catholic queen installed on the throne of England.

One by one, the members of the council turned their back upon Jane. On 19 July 1553, soldiers arrived at the Tower to inform Jane that she was no longer queen.[46] As well as Jane, Frances and her husband Henry Grey were arrested for their roles in putting Jane upon the throne. After a personal plea from Frances to the new queen, Frances and her husband were released from the Tower. Henry Grey, Duke of Suffolk, returned to his house in Richmond while Frances attended court.[47] It is interesting to note that Frances became a regular member of the court after her role in attempting to put her daughter on the throne.

In early 1554, Thomas Wyatt, son of the famous poet and courtier who had been romantically linked to Anne Boleyn, led a rebellion against Mary I. The rebels wished to stop Mary's marriage to the Spanish Phillip and the legalisation of Catholic Masses. Frances' husband, Henry Grey, attempted to raise men in the

Midlands while Wyatt raised rebels in Kent.[48] Ultimately the revolt was a failure, and while there had never been any intention to return Jane Grey to the throne, the attempted rebellion was fatal for the young woman. She was unwittingly caught up in the revolt, and many saw her as a figurehead. Jane would continue to be dangerous to Mary I while she lived, so she was executed within the Tower of London on 12 February 1554.[49] On 23 February, Henry Grey was also executed for his role in the rebellion.[50]

On 1 March 1554/55, Frances married Adrian Stokes, a firm Protestant and her master of horse.[51] Stokes was far beneath her station, but there may have been a good reason for this; perhaps Frances simply married for love, but it would not have hurt that, at such a sensitive time, such a match put Frances out of contention for the throne.

For the short remainder of her life, and despite the loss of her first husband and her daughter, Frances remained on good terms with Queen Mary. After the queen's death in 1558, Frances' cousin Elizabeth came to the throne. Frances spent little time at court after her remarriage, and in the last years of her life she suffered from poor health. Frances died in London on 21 November 1559 with her two surviving daughters by her side. She was buried in St Edmund's Chapel in Westminster Abbey; her funeral was paid for by Queen Elizabeth.[52]

Frances' two other children, Lady Katherine Grey and Lady Eleanor Grey, would also cause some scandal at court. On 25 May 1553, at Durham House, Lady Katherine was married to Henry, Lord Herbert, son of William Herbert, 1st Earl of Pembroke. Afterwards, Katherine went to live with her husband at Baynard's Castle. After the debacle with Lady Jane Grey, Henry's father William sought to have the marriage annulled. He was successful.

Katherine's second marriage would see her sent to the Tower of London. In December 1560, she married Edward Seymour, 1st Earl of Hertford, in a secret ceremony. Queen Elizabeth was furious at this unapproved, high-power match, and sent the pair to the Tower of London. Despite this, Katherine gave birth to two sons: Edward Seymour, Lord Beauchamp and Thomas Seymour. Unfortunately, due to the death of a witness and the loss of documents, Katherine could not prove her marriage, and her sons were declared illegitimate.

Frustrated, Queen Elizabeth ordered that Katherine be removed from the Tower of London. She was sent with her second son to live with Lord John Grey at Pirgo. From there they were sent to live with Sir William Petre. In 1566, she was moved again to Ingatestone and finally to Cockfield. By this time she was ill, and she died on 26 January 1568 aged just twenty-seven. Her two sons survived her.

Katherine's younger sister Mary did not fare much better. On 16 July 1565, Mary married Thomas Keyes, Esquire, Queen Elizabeth's serjeant porter. Technically Mary was in line for the throne, and she too had married far beneath her station. However, the marriage had been kept a secret, and Elizabeth was furious. Thomas Keyes was sent to Fleet Prison and Mary into house arrest under the care of William Hawtrey. In August 1567, Mary was sent to live with her step-grandmother, Katherine, Duchess of Suffolk. She brought with her very few personal belongings. Thomas Keyes was finally released from Fleet Prison in 1569. He died two years later, having never seen his wife again.

In May 1572, Elizabeth finally released Mary from house arrest. Mary had no one to take her in and very few belongings; however, by 1573 she had established herself in London. By February 1577 she was back at court as one of Elizabeth's maids of honour. Mary's rehabilitation would not last long, for she fell sick and died in April 1578. She was buried in her mother's tomb at Westminster Abbey.

*

The lives of the Brandon men epitomise the *Rota Fortunae* or Wheel of Fortune. This is the medieval concept that one rides upon a wheel spun by the goddess Fortune. A person's life would go from highs to lows: upon one spin a man might soar to great heights, achieving wealth, status, land, position and power, and yet upon another spin all that had been gained could just as easily be lost. If there were ever a family that illustrated such a concept, it would be the men of the Brandon line.

In his lifetime, each man rose to great heights, earning a knighthood, achieving wealth, property, status, land and much more. And yet they also faced many losses. Sir William Brandon I had everything taken from him when his sons were declared traitors to Richard III, yet another spin of the wheel saw it all returned when Henry Tudor claimed the English throne. In the prime of his life, Sir William Brandon II fell at the Battle of Bosworth, and at that moment Charles Brandon lost his father. Upon his brother's death, Robert Brandon became the head of the family, and yet it was his younger brother Thomas who rose to greater heights. Thomas became Henry VII's master of horse, achieving much and having many riches lavished upon him, yet for all this he died without heirs.

It was on Charles Brandon that the family's hopes rested, and for a time it would seem he could achieve anything and win the greatest prizes. He rose in favour with the new king, Henry VIII, became one of the greatest men in the kingdom, wielded much power and yet tragically lost two sons before his death in 1545. Two young boys, Henry and Charles Brandon, carried on the family line, both friends of the new king, and both appeared to have bright and prosperous futures. Yet in 1551 the Wheel of Fortune turned once more, and both boys died in their teens.

One can suggest that the fate of the Brandon men ended with the Wheel of Fortune pointed downward, but I would argue otherwise. Within the pages of this book, the lives of the Brandon men are remembered. Five hundred years after their deaths, you, the reader, are learning about them. Their lives and their legacies are not forgotten.

The Brandons lived and prospered during one of the most tumultuous and compelling periods in English history, weaving their way through various tribulations with astonishing dexterity, often to emerge more influential than before. Despite the obstacles placed in their paths, the house of Brandon persevered, reaching dizzying heights under the successive reigns of some of England's greatest monarchs. The Brandon men served in the shadow of England's kings, and now they live on in history.

Notes

1 Setting the Scene

1. Royle 2009, p. 24.
2. Weir 2008, p. 72-73.
3. Jones 2015, p. 31-33.
4. Jones 2015, p. 46.
5. Jones 2015 p. 6.
6. Royle 2009, p. 175.
7. National Archives, Little Doomsday.
8. National Archives, DL 25/736.
9. Woodger 2017.
10. Calendar of Patent Rolls Henry VI, Vol 2, p. 404.
11. Calendar of Patent Rolls Henry VI, Vol 2, p. 533.
12. National Archives E 122/96/30.
13. Richardson 2011, p. 368.
14. De Commines 1877, p. 201.
15. Hardying 1812, p. 410.
16. Jones 2015, p. 77–79.
17. Jones 2015, p. 83–87.
18. Jones 2015, p. 95–97.
19. Jones 2015, p. 102–104.
20. Jones 2015, p. 108–111
21. Castor 2000, p. 114–115.
22. Calendar of Patent Rolls Henry VI, Vol 5, p. 236.
23. Mackman and Stevens CP 40/753, rot. 106d.
24. Mackman and Stevens CP 40/753, rot. 106d.
25. Mackman and Stevens CP 40/759, rot. 271.
26. Jones 2015, p. 128.
27. Jones 2015, p. 132–133.
28. Lewis 2017, p. 31
29. Jones 2015, p. 139.

2 The Wars of the Roses

1. Gillingham 1981, p. 28.
2. Jones 2015, p. 143.
3. Jones 2015, p. 144–155.
4. Calendar of Patent Rolls Henry VI, Vol. 5, p. 178.
5. Calendar of Patent Rolls Henry VI, Vol. 5, p. 240.
6. Castor 2000, p. 180
7. Calendar of Patent Rolls Henry VI, Vol. 5, p. 395.
8. Calendar of Patent Rolls Henry VI, Vol. 6, p. 300.
9. Calendar of Patent Rolls Henry VI, Vol. 5, p. 491.
10. Calendar of Patent Rolls Henry VI, Vol. 5, p. 493.
11. Calendar of Patent Rolls Henry VI, Vol. 5, p. 518.
12. Lewis 2015 p. 82–91.
13. Davies 1838, p. 79.
14. Lewis 2015 p. 96–105.
15. Lewis 2015, p. 114.
16. Lewis 2015 p. 117–119.
17. Lewis 2015 p. 120–129.
18. Lewis 2017 p. 89–90.
19. Warkworth 1839, p. 29.
20. National Archives C 241/244/8.
21. National Archives Currency Converter.
22. Bicheno, 2016 p. 60.
23. Paston p. 31.
24. Calendar of Patent Rolls Edward IV p. 75.
25. Mackman and Stevens CP 40/808, rot. 144.
26. Richardson 2011, p. 368.
27. Crouse 1781, p. 10, Harris Nicolas 1826, p. 433.
28. Brennan 2017.
29. Gunn 2015, p. 62–63.
30. Mackman and Stevens CP 40/816, rot. 315.
31. Mackman and Stevens CP 40/814, rot. 129d.
32. National Archives BCM/D/1/1/20.
33. Calendar of Patent Rolls Henry VII Vol. 1, p. 162.
34. Calendar of Patent Rolls Edward IV & Henry VI, p. 85.
35. Calendar of Patent Rolls Edward IV & Henry VI, p. 560.
36. Calendar of Close Rolls Edward IV Vol. 1, May 29.
37. Porter 2016, p. 15–16.
38. Gunn 2016, p. 257.
39. Calendar of Close Rolls Edward IV Vol. 2, 791.
40. Calendar of Patent Rolls Edward IV & Henry VI, p. 167.
41. The Wars of the Roses.

3 My Greatest Enemies

1. Grose 1849, p. 13.
2. Smith 2018.

3. Smith 2018.
4. Turner 1842, p. 103.
5. Turner 1842, p. 110.
6. Grose 1849, p. 13.
7. Paston p. 228–229.
8. Paston p. 229.
9. Bloomfield and Parkin 1810, p. 210.
10. Archer-Hind, L., Fenn, J. 1924, p. 108.
11. Paston p. 512.
12. Bicheno 2016.
13. Bruce 1836, p. 18–20.
14. Clark 2007
15. Bruce 1836, p. 28–31.
16. Shaw 1906, p. 14.
17. Breverton 2014, p. 187.
18. Bruce 1836, p. 38.
19. Bicheno 2016, p. 201.
20. De Commines 1855, p. 393–394.
21. Calendar of Patent Rolls Edward IV & Henry VI, p. 352.
22. Calendar of Patent Rolls Edward IV & Henry VI, p. 353.
23. Calendar of Close Rolls Edward IV, Vol. 2, 822.
24. Calendar of Close Rolls Edward IV Vol. 2, 846.
25. Calendar of Close Rolls Edward IV Vol. 2, 858.
26. Richardson 2011 p. 369.
27. Inquisitions Post Mortem, Henry VII, 885, Gunn 2015, p. 55.
28. Gunn 2015, p. 55.
29. Richardson 2011, p. 369.
30. Inquisitions Post Mortem, Henry VII, 36.
31. Calendar of Patent Rolls Edward IV & Henry VI, p. 556.
32. Barnard 1854, p. 118.
33. Royle 2009, p. 355–358.
34. Calendar of Patent Rolls Edward IV, Edward V & Richard III, p. 22.
35. Mackman and Stevens CP 40/874, rot. 383d.
36. Breverton 2014, p. 203.
37. Grafton 1809, p. 114.
38. Clowes 1848, p. 3.
39. Calendar of Patent Rolls Edward IV, Edward V & Richard III, p. 397.
40. Clowes 1848, p. 23.
41. Clowes 1848, p. 46.

4 Hedging Bets

1. Penn 2011, p. 2.
2. Breverton 2014, p. 42.
3. Bradley 2019, p. 42..
4. Royle 2009, p.398-401.
5. Calendar of Patent Rolls Edward IV, Edward V & Richard III, p. 423.
6. Seward 2007, p. 318, 392.

7. Ross 2015, p. 84.
8. Hall 1809, p. 408.
9. Calendar of Patent Rolls Edward IV, Edward V & Richard III, p. 526.
10. Calendar of Patent Rolls Edward IV, Edward V & Richard III, p. 530.
11. Calendar of Patent Rolls Edward IV, Edward V & Richard III, p. 533.
12. Clowes 1848, p. 128.
13. Clowes 1848, p. 144.
14. Gairdner 1898 p. 242.
15. Medieval Lives: Birth, Marriage and Death 2013.
16. Breverton 2014, p. 220.
17. Doran 2008, p. 13.
18. Skidmore, 2013, p. 259.
19. Ellis 1884, p. 221.
20. Skidmore 2013, p. 285.
21. Skidmore 2013, p. 274.
22. Breverton 2014, p. 242.
23. Langley & Jones 2013.
24. Skidmore 2013, p. 291.
25. Breverton 2014, p. 246.
26. Breverton 2014, p. 246.
27. Ellis 1884, p. 225.
28. Hutton 1813, p. 218.
29. Ellis 1884, p. 224.
30. Meyer 2010, p. 12.
31. Skidmore 2013, p. 322.
32. Skidmore 2013, p. 320.

5 The Rise of the Next Generation

1. Rendle 1878, p. 100.
2. Campbell 1873, p. 124–125.
3. Oxford Dictionary of National Biography – Charles Brandon.
4. Doran 2009, p. 84.
5. Wilson 2009, p. 9.
6. Breverton 2014, Chapter 22.
7. Wilson 2009, p. 48.
8. Breverton 2014, Chapter 28.
9. Royle 2009, p. 421.
10. Campbell 1873, p. 104.
11. Calendar of Patent Rolls Henry VII Vol. 1, p. 164.
12. Campbell 1873, p. 143.
13. Campbell 1873, p. 135.
14. Lysons and Lysons 1814.
15. National Archives Currency Converter.
16. Gunn 2016, p.159.
17. Leland and Hearne 1770, p. 205, Gunn 2016, p. 24.
18. Oxford Dictionary of National Biography – Thomas Brandon.
19. National Archives Currency Converter.

20. Gunn 2016, p. 269.
21. Ellis 1884.
22. Lewis 2017, p. 182–183.
23. Burke 1834, p. 685.
24. Calendar of Patent Rolls Henry VII Vol. 1, p. 179.
25. Calendar of Patent Rolls Henry VII Vol. 1, p. 349.
26. Calendar of Patent Rolls Henry VII Vol. 1, p. 239.
27. Calendar of Patent Rolls Henry VII Vol. 1, p. 347.
28. Calendar of Patent Rolls Henry VII Vol. 1, p. 318.
29. Calendar of Patent Rolls Henry VII Vol. 1, p. 276.
30. Gunn 2016, p. 98.
31. Campbell 1837, p. 479.
32. Campbell 1837, p. 495.
33. Calendar of Patent Rolls Henry VII Vol. 1, p. 319.
34. Calendar of Patent Rolls Henry VII Vol. 1, p. 345.
35. Gunn 2016, p. 186.
36. Loades 2012, p. 118.
37. Middleton-Stewart 2001.
38. Gunn 2016, p. 181.
39. Gunn 2016, p. 60.
40. Calendar of Patent Rolls Henry VII Vol. 1, p. 439.
41. Calendar of Patent Rolls Henry VII Vol 1, p. 453.
42. Inquisitions Post Mortem, Henry VII, 1098, 1099.
43. National Archives C 1/696/20.
44. Hutchinson 2011, p.19–23.
45. Gairdner 1861, p. 397.
46. Gairdner 1861, p. 397.
47. Gairdner 1861, p. 398.
48. The Chamber Books E101/414/6 folio 24r.
49. The Chamber Books E101/414/6 folio 70r.
50. The Chamber Books BL Add MS 7099 folio 14.
51. The Chamber Books E101/414/16 folio 44r.
52. The Chamber Books E101/414/16 folio 61v.
53. The Chamber Books E101/414/16 folio 63v.
54. The Chamber Books E101/415/3 folio 62r.
55. The Chamber Books BL Add MS 59899 folio 41v.
56. National Archives E 210/819.
57. Smyth 1567–1641, p. 144.
58. Gibbs 1912, p. 135.
59. Harris Nicolas 1826, p. 432–433.
60. Burke 1834, p. 686.
61. Oxford Dictionary of National Biography – Thomas Brandon.
62. Gunn 2016, p. 204.
63. Calendar of Patent Rolls Henry VII Vol. 1, p 368–369.
64. National Archives C 241/273/55.
65. Oxford Dictionary of National Biography – Charles Brandon.
66. Loades 2012, p. 119.
67. Richardson 1970, p. 34.

68. Loades 2012, p. 46
69. Harris Nicolas, 1842, Appendix G.
70. Gairdner 1861, p. 189.
71. Calendar of State Papers Venice, Vol. 1, 830.
72. The Chamber Books BL Add MS 59899 folio 3r.
73. Gunn 2016, p. 94.
74. Oxford Dictionary of National Biography – Thomas Brandon.
75. Calendar of Patent Rolls Henry VII Vol 2, p. 332.
76. Loades 2012, p. 119.
77. Calendar of Patent Rolls Henry VII Vol. 2, p. 107.
78. Calendar of Patent Rolls Henry VII Vol. 2, p. 217.
79. Calendar of Patent Rolls Henry VII Vol. 2, p. 412.
80. Calendar of Patent Rolls Henry VII Vol. 2, p. 180.
81. Calendar of Patent Rolls Henry VII Vol. 2, p. 294.
82. Calendar of Patent Rolls Henry VII Vol. 2, p. 298.

6 The Fairest Man at Arms

1. Penn 2011, p. 171.
2. Hutchinson 2011, p. 95.
3. Levitt 2014.
4. Oxford Dictionary of National Biography – Charles Brandon.
5. The Chamber Books BL Add MS 21480 folio 22r.
6. Wilson 2009, p. 85.
7. Christie & Masson 1838, p. 18.
8. Davey 1911, p.43–44.
9. Davey 1911, p. 44.
10. Letter and Papers Vol. 1, 2171.
11. Benger 1822, p. 53.
12. Hume 1889, p. 134.
13. Weir 2008, p. 98.
14. Letters and Papers Vol. 3, 402
15. Letters and Papers Vol 1. Preference
16. Starkey 1990, p. 40.
17. Starkey 1990, p. 40.
18. The National Archives Currency Converter.
19. Letters and Papers Vol. 4, 5859.
20. Sadlack 2011, 396.
21. Oxford Dictionary of National Biography – Charles Brandon.
22. Oxford Dictionary of National Biography – Charles Brandon.
23. Shaw 1906, p.56.
24. Taylor.
25. Hannay, Brennan and Lamb 2015, p. 204.
26. Loades 2012, p. 47.
27. Sadlack 2011, p. 109.
28. Gunn 2016, p. 97.
29. Hannay, Brennan and Lamb 2015, p. 204, Ashmole 1672, p. 440.
30. Oxford Dictionary of National Biography – Thomas Brandon.

31. Burke 1846.
32. Calendar of Patent Rolls Henry VII Vol. 2, p. 302.
33. Penn 2011, p. 341.
34. Penn 2011, p. 341–345.
35. Letters and Papers Vol. 1 20.
36. Gunn, 2016, p. 46.
37. Oxford Dictionary of National Biography – Thomas Brandon.
38. Hall 1809, p. 41.
39. Weir 2008, p. 11.
40. Penn 2011.
41. Walford 1878.
42. Hutchinson 2011, p. 135.
43. Wilson 2009, p. 47.
44. Letters and Papers Vol. 1, 888, 1144.
45. Letters and Papers Vol. 1, 1123 (65).
46. Baldwin 2015, p. 29.
47. Letters and Papers Vol. 1, 353.
48. Gunn 2015, p. 17.
49. Hannay, Brennan and Lamb 2015.
50. Gunn 2016, p. 281.
51. Gunn 2016, p. 195, Nicolas 1826, p. 497.
52. Harris Nicolas 1826, p. 497.
53. The National Archives Currency Converter.
54. Gunn 2016, p. 216, 308.
55. Gunn 2016, p. 256.
56. Brigden 2012.
57. Suffolk Place and the Mint.
58. National Archives Currency Converter.
59. Letters and Papers, Vol. 1, 447, 23.
60. Letters and Papers Vol. 1, 681, 40.
61. Hutchinson 2011, p. 153.
62. Hall 1809, p. 24.
63. Hall 1809, p. 25.
64. Hall 1809, p. 25.
65. Johnson 1969, p. 70.
66. Letters and Papers Vol. 1, 682.
67. Loades 2012, p. 122.
68. Swales 2017.
69. The Chamber Books BL Add MS 21481 folio 114r.
70. The National Archives Currency Converter.
71. Block 2016.
72. Letters and Papers Vol. 1, 1601, 35.
73. The National Archives Currency Converter.
74. The National Archives Currency Converter.
75. Gunn 2015, p. 30.
76. The Chamber Books BL Add MS 21481 folio 124r.
77. Loades 2012, p. 122.

78. Letters and Papers Vol. 13, 642.
79. Heritage Gateway.

7 The King's Favourite

1. Wilson 2009, p. 62.
2. Wilson 2009, p. 63.
3. Wilson 2009, p. 668.
4. Loades 2012, p. 120.
5. Hutchinson 2011, p. 160.
6. Wilson 2009, p. 69.
7. Wilson 2009, p. 69.
8. Doran 2008, p. 94.
9. Gunn 2015, p. 28.
10. Shaw 1906, p. 35.
11. Oxford Dictionary of National Biography – Charles Brandon.
12. Letters and Papers Vol. 1, 2941.
13. Letters and Papers Vol. 1, 2941.
14. Hutchinson 2011, p. 181.
15. Hutchinson 2011, p. 181.
16. Calendar of State Papers Venice Vol. 2, 464.
17. Wilson 2009, p. 85.
18. Letters and Papers Vol. 1, 2701.
19. Wilson 2009, p. 85.
20. Velde 2014.
21. Royal Collection Trust 2015.
22. The Royal Household 2015.
23. A copy of Brandon's plate can be seen at the Royal Collection online. <http://www.royalcollection.org.uk/microsites/knightsofthegarter/MicroObject.asp?row=8&themeid=456&item=9>.
24. Oxford Dictionary of National Biography – Charles Brandon.
25. Perry 2002, p. 122.
26. Gunn 2015, p. 31.
27. The National Archives Currency Converter.
28. The National Archives Currency Converter.
29. Letters and Papers Vol. 1, 2537.
30. Letters and Papers Vol. 1, 1947.
31. Nicholas 1846, p. 71.
32. Letters and Papers Vol. 1, 2171.
33. Letters and Papers Vol. 1, Preference.
34. Letters and Papers Vol. 1, Preference.
35. Lodge 1823, p. 2.
36. Benger 1822 p. 53.
37. History of Jousting.
38. Medieval Jousting Tournaments.
39. Medieval Rules for Jousting.
40. Hall 1809, p. 674.

41. Perry 2002, p. 150.
42. Knapton 2014.
43. Wilson 2009, p. 49.
44. Levitt 2014.
45. Hutchinson 2009, p. 13.
46. Weir 2008, p. 103.
47. Loades 2012, p. 128 and 200.
48. Letters and Papers Vol. 2, 367.
49. Letters and Papers Vol. 1, 2620.
50. Knight 1840, p. 232.
51. Letters and Papers Vol. 9, 386.
52. Letters and Papers Vol. 5, 431.
53. Letters and papers Vol. 5, 521.
54. Letters and Papers Vol. 5, 576.
55. Letters and Papers Vol. 5, 1403.
56. Borman 2015, p. 218
57. Letters and Papers Vol. 9, 178, 301.
58. Letters and papers Vol. 14, 71.
59. Weir 2008, p. 485.
60. Hutchinson 2006, p. 119.
61. Letters and Papers Vol. 1 2620.
62. Hutchinson 2009, p. 2.
63. Hutchinson 2009 p. 6.
64. Hutchinson 2009, p. 7.
65. Hutchinson 2009, p. 13.
66. The National Archives Currency Converter.
67. Weir 2008, p. 103.
68. Letters and Papers Vol. 1, 2617.
69. The National Archives Currency Converter.
70. Harding 2017.
71. The National Archives Currency Converter.
72. Letters and Papers Vol. 1, 2679.

8 Journey to France

1. Perry 2002, p. 70.
2. Wilson 2009, p. 62.
3. Loades 2012, p. 64.
4. Hutchinson 2011, p. 186.
5. Perry 2002, p. 123.
6. Letters and Papers Vol. 1, 3101.
7. Perry 2002, p 126.
8. Letters and Papers Vol. 1, 3146.
9. Hutchinson 2011, p. 187–189.
10. The National Archives Currency Converter.
11. Loades 2012, p. 76.
12. Loades 2012, p. 77.
13. Loades 2012, p 111.

14. Bunbury 1844, p. 16.
15. Loades 2012, p. 78.
16. Sadlack 2011, p. 208–209.
17. Loades 2012, p. 81–82.
18. Letters and Papers Vol. 1, 3376.
19. Letters and Papers Vol. 1, 3376.
20. Hutchinson 2011, p. 190.
21. Hutchinson 2011, p. 191.
22. Letters and Papers Vol. 1, 3387.
23. Letters and Papers Vol. 1, 3477.
24. Loades 2012, p. 85.
25. Loades 2002, p. 95.
26. Letters and Papers Vol. 1, 3580.
27. Loades 2012, p. 95.
28. Letters and Papers Vol. 1, 3387.
29. Norton 2013, p. 124.
30. Wilson 2009, p. 47.
31. Perry 2002, p. 147.
32. Letters and Papers Vol. 1, 3429.
33. Perry 2002, p. 149.
34. Letters and Papers Vol. 1, 3461.
35. Loades 2012, p. 92.
36. Loades 2012, p. 93.
37. Perry 2002, p. 149.
38. Perry 2002, p. 150.
39. Sadlack 2011, p. 245.
40. Sadlack 2011, p. 245.
41. Ellis 1827, p. 255–258.
42. Loades 2012, p. 96.
43. Hutchinson 2011, p. 192.
44. Perry 2002, p. 152.
45. Loades 2012, p. 101.
46. Licence 2014, p. 115.
47. Loades 2012, p. 102.
48. Loades 2012, p. 111.
49. Sadlack 2011, p. 237–238.
50. Loades 2012, p. 103.
51. Sadlack 2011, p. 263.
52. Calendar of State Papers Venice, Vol. 2, 583.
53. Loades 2012, p. 103–104.
54. Perry 2002, p. 155.

9 A Marriage of Unequals

1. Letters and Papers Vol. 2, 15.
2. Perry 2002, p. 155–156.
3. Letters and Papers Vol 2, 80.
4. Richardson 1970, p. 172.

5. Everett Green 1857, p. 81–82.
6. Letters and Papers Vol. 2, 113.
7. Letters and Papers Vol. 2, 134.
8. Letters and Papers Vol. 2, 134.
9. Letters and Papers Vol. 2, 134.
10. Letters and Papers Vol 2, 135.
11. Letters and Papers Vol. 2, 80.
12. Letters and Papers Vol 2, 145.
13. Letters and Papers Vol 2, 146.
14. Letters and Papers Vol 2, 203.
15. Mumby 1913, p. 324
16. Letters and Papers Vol 2, 223.
17. Letters and Papers Vol 2, 343.
18. Letters and Papers Vol 2. 827.
19. Bryan
20. Spears 2012
21. Loades 2012, p. 114.
22. Mumby 1913, p. 325–327.
23. Letters and Papers Vol. 2, 225.
24. Letters and Papers Vol. 2, 227.
25. Letters and Papers Vol. 2, 226.
26. Letters and Papers Vol. 2 256.
27. De Savoie. Duchesse d'Angoulême, Louise p. 397.
28. De Savoie. Duchesse d'Angoulême, Louise p, 388.
29. Letters and Papers Vol. 2, 240.
30. Letters and Papers Vol 2, 281.
31. Calendar of State Papers Vol. 3, 1486.
32. Letters and Papers Vol. 2, 283.
33. Mumby 1913, p. 333–334.
34. Gunn 2015, p. 44.
35. Richardson 1970, p. 185.
36. Loades 2012, p. 117.
37. The National Archives Currency Converter.
38. The National Archives Currency Converter.
39. Letters and Papers Vol. 2, 237.
40. Letters and Papers Vol. 2, 436.
41. Loades 2012, p. 117.
42. The National Archives Currency Converter.
43. Loades 2012, p. 117.
44. Calendar of State Papers Venice Vol. 2, 618.
45. Carroll 2010.
46. Bloomfield 1810.

10 Return to Favour

1. Sadlack 2011, p. 353.
2. Letters and Papers Vol. 2, 1652.
3. Loades 2012, p. 157.

4. Letters and Papers Vol 4, 5859
5. Loades 2012, p. 158.
6. Letters and Papers Vol. 2, 1935.
7. Letters and Papers Vol. 2, 2170.
8. Letters and Papers Vol. 2, 2347.
9. Loades 2012, p. 135.
10. Calendar of State Papers Venice Vol. 2, 878.
11. Letters and Papers Vol. 2, 2733.
12. Letters and Papers Vol. 2, 4334.
13. Oxford Dictionary of National Biography – Charles Brandon.
14. Letters and Papers Vol. 2, 3462.
15. Calendar of State Papers Venice, Vol. 2, 918.
16. Calendar of State Papers Venice, Vol. 2, 919.
17. Sadlack 2011, p. 355.
18. Letters and Papers Vol. 2, 3489.
19. Everett Green 1857, p. 1521.
20. Letters and Papers Vol. 2, 4134.
21. Everett Green 1857, p. 121–122.
22. Sadlack 2011, p. 356.
23. The National Archives Currency Converter.
24. The National Archives Currency Converter.
25. The National Archives Currency Converter.
26. Calendar of State Papers Spain Vol. 2, 270, 273, 277, 331, 251.
27. The National Archives Currency Converter.
28. The National Archives Currency Converter.
29. Loades 2012, p. 132.
30. The National Archives Currency Converter.
31. Letters and Papers Vol. 3, 2856.
32. National Archives 2ANC3/B/2.
33. Loades 2012, p. 137.
34. The National Archives Currency Converter.
35. The National Archives Currency Converter.
36. Loades 2012, p. 131–132.
37. Gunn 2015, p. 90.
38. Letters and Papers Vol. 4, 2744.
39. The National Archives Currency Converter.
40. Gunn 2015, p. 68.
41. The National Archives Currency Converter.
42. Loades 2012, p. 138–139.
43. Wodderspoon 1839, p. 61.
44. The National Archives Currency Converter.
45. Oxford Dictionary of National Biography – Charles Brandon.
46. Hopper 2004, p. 94.
47. Wodderspoon 1839, p. 61–62.
48. Wilson 2009, p.117.
49. Wilson 2009, p. 120.
50. Wilson 2009, p. 121.
51. Wilson 2009, p.108.

52. Doran 2008, p. 114.
53. Loades 2011, p. 112.
54. Wilson 2009, p. 122.
55. Sadlack 2011 P. 344.
56. Sadlack 2011, p. 344.
57. Calendar of State Papers Venice Vol. 3, 41.
58. Letters and Papers Vol. 3, 869.
59. Wilson 2009, p. 123.
60. Barber and Barker 1989, p. 134.
61. Sadlack 2011, p. 350.
62. Starkey 2009, p. 94.
63. Loades 2011, p. 113.
64. Gunn 2015, p. 60.
65. Wilson 2009, p. 122.
66. Letters and Papers Vol. 3, 906.
67. Wilson 2009, p. 124.
68. National Archives 2ANC3/B/3.
69. Wilson 2009, p. 124.
70. The National Archives Currency Converter.
71. Loades 2012, p. 132.
72. Letters and Papers Vol. 3429.
73. Gunn 2015, p. 67.
74. Letter and Papers Vol. 3, 3197.
75. Letters and Papers Vol. 3 3281.
76. Wilson 2009, p. 141.
77. Letters and Papers Vol. 3, 3288.
78. Loades 2011, p. 172.
79. Oxford Dictionary of National Biography – Charles Brandon.
80. Loades 2012, p. 150.
81. Oxford Dictionary of National Biography – Charles Brandon.
82. Wilson 2009, p. 141.
83. Calendar of State Papers Venice, Vol. 3, 782.
84. Loades 2011, p. 172.
85. Loades 2011, p. 172–173.
86. Loades 2011, p. 173.
87. Wooding 2015 p. 121.
88. MacCulloch 1995, p. 45.
89. The National Archives Currency Converter.
90. All Kinds of History 2014.
91. Kadouchkine 2014.
92. The National Archives Currency Converter.
93. Wooding 2015, p. 122.
94. The National Archives Currency Converter.
95. The National Archives Currency Converter.
96. MacCulloch 1995, p. 45.
97. The National Archives Currency Converter.
98. All Kinds of History 2014.
99. Wilson 2009, p 144.

100. MacCulloch 1995, p. 45.
101. Wilson 2009, p. 144.
102. All Kinds of History 2014.
103. Staging the Henrician Court 2015.
104. Betteridge & Freeman 2012.
105. Kadouchkine 2014.

11 Family Matters

1. Full name: The Ninety-Five Theses on the Power and Efficacy of Indulgences or Disputatio pro declaratione virtutis indulgentiarum.
2. Wilson 2009, p. 112.
3. Weir 2008, p. 103.
4. Hall 1809, p. 263–264.
5. Wriothesley 1875, p. 13.
6. Loades 2012, p. 164.
7. Loades 2012, p. 164.
8. Oxford Dictionary of National Biography – Charles Brandon.
9. Loades 2012, p. 164.
10. The National Archives Currency Converter.
11. Letters and Papers Vol. 2, 529.
12. Richardson 2011, p. 372.
13. Emerson 2015.
14. The National Archives Currency Converter.
15. The National Archives Currency Converter.
16. Gunn 2015, p. 126.
17. National Archives 2ANC3/B/6.
18. Harris 2002, p. 78.
19. Letters and Papers Vol. 7, 1187.
20. Oxford Dictionary of National Biography – Charles Brandon.
21. The National Archives Currency Converter.
22. Hart 2009, p. 45.
23. Letters and Papers Vol. 4 1431.
24. National Archives 2ANC3/B/4.
25. National Archives 2ANC3/B/4.
26. Gunn 2015, p. 85.
27. The National Archives Currency Converter.
28. Gunn 2015, p. 47.
29. Loades 2012, p. 128.
30. Loades 2012, p. 171.
31. Letters and Papers Vol 4, 3760.
32. Hall 1809, p. 674.
33. Loades 2012, p. 168.
34. Loades 2012, p. 168–169.
35. Loades 2011, p. 192.
36. Ives 2005, p. 96.
37. Fraser 2002, p. 181.
38. Letters and Papers Vol. 4, 4851, 4857.

39. Ives 2005, p. 96.
40. Weir 1991, p. 204.
41. Weir 1991, p. 204.
42. Ives 2005, p. 114.
43. Calendar of State Papers Spain Vol 3 Part 2, 1527–1529, 621.
44. Letters and Papers Vol. 4, 5535, 5547.
45. Letters and Papers Vol. 4, 5597, 5598.
46. Letters and Papers Vol. 4, 5635.
47. Letters and Papers Vol. 4, 5733.
48. Fraser 2002, p. 204.
49. Fraser 2002, p. 204.
50. Du Bellay, i. 115.
51. Calendar of State Papers, Venice Vol. 4, 694.
52. The National Archives Currency Converter.
53. Haigh 1993, p. 108

12 The Tempestuous Years

1. Letters and Papers Vol. 12, Part 2 998.
2. World Heritage Encyclopaedia – Arthur Bulkeley.
3. Letters and Papers Vol 8, 894.
4. Oxford Dictionary of National Biography – Charles Brandon.
5. Baldwin 2015, p. 67.
6. Weir 2008, p. 467.
7. Baldwin 2015, p. 57.
8. Baldwin 2015, p. 72.
9. Howell 1809, p. 564.
10. Loades 2012, p. 178.
11. Hume 1905 p. 137.
12. Letters and Papers, Vol. 5 340.
13. Letters and Papers, Vol. 5 287.
14. Calendar of State Papers Venice Vol. 4 761.
15. Letters and Papers Vol 5, 1183.
16. Letters and Papers Vol. 7, 1498, 37.
17. Letters and Papers Vol. 6 415.
18. Loades 2012, p. 182.
19. Loades 2012, p. 179–181.
20. De Worde 1884, p. 15.
21. Velde, F 2014.
22. Chapman 1974, p. 122.
23. Letters and Papers Vol 6. 324.
24. Letters and Papers Vol 6. 759.
25. Letters and Papers Vol 6. 780.
26. Calendar of State Papers Spain Vol. 4, 1161.
27. Weir 1991, p. 262–263
28. Letters and Papers Vol. 6 1541.
29. Weir 1991, p. 262–263.
30. Weir 1991, p. 263.

31. Calendar of State Papers Spain Vol. 4, 1164.
32. Perry 2002, p. 267.
33. Letters and Papers Vol. 6 548.
34. Letters and Papers Vol. 6. 601.
35. Letters and Papers Vol. 7, 9.
36. Letters and Papers Vol. 5, 686.
37. Letters and Papers Vol. 7 391.
38. Sadlack 2011, p. 403.
39. Loades 2012, p. 187.
40. Letters and Papers Vol. 6 693.
41. Loades 2012, p. 188.
42. Sadlack 2011, p. 406.
43. Loades 2012, p. 189.
44. Loades 2012, p. 190.
45. Sadlack 2011, p. 407–408.
46. Loades 2012, p. 191.
47. Loades 2012, p. 191–192.
48. The National Archives Currency Converter.
49. The National Archives Currency Converter.
50. Loades 2012, p. 192.
51. The National Archives Currency Converter.
52. Baldwin 2015, p. 23.
53. Letters and Papers Vol. 4, 5336.
54. Ives 2005, p. 18.
55. Letters and Papers Vol. 2 529.
56. Wilkinson 2010, p. 115.
57. Baldwin 2015, p. 40.
58. Baldwin 2015, p. 40.
59. Letters and Papers Vol. 6 1069.
60. Letters and Papers Vol 6, 1069.
61. Calendar of State Papers Spain Vol. 2, 1123.
62. Letters and Papers Vol. 6 1111.
63. Baldwin 2015, p. 28–29.
64. Baldwin 2015, p. 45.
65. The National Archives Currency Converter
66. Letters and Papers Vol. 15, 942, 52.
67. Letters and Papers Vol. 9 1063.
68. The National Archives Currency Converter.
69. The National Archives Currency Converter.
70. The National Archives Currency Converter.
71. The National Archives Currency Converter.
72. Loades 2012, p. 193.
73. Letters and Papers Vol. 9, 437.
74. The National Archives Currency Converter.
75. Loades 2012, p. 194.
76. Letters and Papers Vol. 7 281.
77. Weir 2008, p. 349.
78. Letters and Papers Vol. 9 386.

79. Baldwin 2015, p. 42.
80. Baldwin 2015, p. 42.
81. The National Archives Currency Converter.
82. Letters and Papers Vol. 9 217.
83. National Archives 2ANC3/B/8.

13 The King's Man

1. Fraser 2002, p. 281.
2. Mackay 2014, p. 153.
3. Mackay 2014, p. 156.
4. Letters and Papers Vol. 10 200.
5. *Inside the Body of Henry VIII.*
6. Lipscomb 2009, p. 61.
7. Norton 2013, p. 184.
8. Letters and Papers Vol. 10 282.
9. Baldwin 2015, p. 46.
10. Letters & Papers Vol. 10 243.
11. Chilvers 2010, p. 16.
12. Suffolk Place and The Mint.
13. York House.
14. Ives 2005, p. 308–309.
15. Fraser 2002, p. 287–291.
16. Weir 2009, p. 89–92.
17. Weir 2009, p. 132–137.
18. Letters and Papers Vol. 10, 876.
19. Letters and Papers Vol. 10, 848.
20. Weir 2009, p. 196.
21. Weir 2009, p. 196–197.
22. Letters and Papers Vol. 10, 876.
23. Weir 2009, p. 213.
24. Weir 2009, pg. 215.
25. Weir 2009, pg. 218.
26. Weir 2009 pg. 218.
27. Weir 2009, pg. 220.
28. Fraser 2002, p. 309–311.
29. Weir 2009, pg. 241.
30. Weir 2009, pg. 241–245.
31. Letters & Papers Vol. 10 896.
32. Weir 2009, pg. 261.
33. Weir 2009, pg. 264.
34. Weir 2009, pg. 266.
35. Weir 2009, pg. 270.
36. Weir 2009, pg. 271.
37. The National Archives Currency Converter.
38. Gunn 2015, p. 135.
39. Fraser 2002 p. 317.
40. Fraser 2002, p. 329.

41. Oxford Dictionary of National Biography – Henry Fitzroy.
42. Lipscomb 2009, p. 150.
43. Lipscomb 2009, p. 151.
44. Gasquet 1889, p. 68–69.
45. Letters and Papers Vol. 11 615.
46. Letters and Papers Vol. 11 656.
47. Letters and Papers Vol. 11 672.
48. Letters and Papers Vol. 11 717.
49. Letters and Papers Vol. 11 721.
50. Letters and Papers Vol. 11 939.
51. Lipscomb 2009, p. 152.
52. Lipscomb 2009, p. 153.
53. Letters and Papers Vol. 11 759.
54. Letters and Papers Vol. 11 764.
55. Letters and Papers Vol. 11 780.

14 Lord of Lincolnshire

1. Lipscomb 2009, p. 153.
2. Letters and Papers Vol. 11 780.
3. Letters and Papers Vol. 11 765.
4. Letters and Papers Vol 11, 1155
5. Letters and Papers Vol. 11, 764, 1103.
6. Letters and Papers Vol 11. 1235.
7. Letters and Papers Vol. 11 1236.
8. Lipscomb 2009, p. 164.
9. Lipscomb 2009, p. 165.
10. Kesselring 2002, p. 601.
11. Bernard 2007, p. 402.
12. Surdhar 2013.
13. Letters and Papers Vol. 12. Part 1, 424.
14. Letters and Papers Vol. 11 1238.
15. Letters and papers Vol. 11, 1283.
16. Starkey 1990, p. 81.
17. Letters and Papers Vol. 14 1103.
18. Letters and Papers Vol. 14 1103.
19. Letters and Papers Vol. 12. 1284.
20. Baldwin 2015, p. 52.
21. Baldwin 2015, p. 204.
22. Chilvers 2010 p. 35.
23. The National Archives Currency Converter.
24. Letters and Papers Vol. 13, I, 1349, 1329.
25. Letters and Papers Vol. 13, ii, 1182, 18, Vol 14, I, 651, 45.
26. Gunn 2015, p. 159.
27. Gunn 2015, p. 157.
28. The National Archives Currency Converter.
29. The National Archives Currency Converter.
30. Gunn 2015, p. 159.

31. Gunn 2015, p. 145.
32. Letters and Papers Vol. 12 364.
33. Letters and Papers Vol. 12 I, 318.
34. Letters and Papers Vol. 13, ii, 6, 57.
35. Richardson 2011, p. 372.
36. Urban 1803, p. 528.
37. Burke 1833, p. 36.
38. Licence 2014, p. 288.
39. Letters and Papers Vol. 12 911.
40. Licence 2014, p. 288–289.
41. Brigden 2001.
42. Brimacombe 2004, p. 81.
43. Brady 1876, p. 493.
44. Letters and Papers Vol 13, I, 642, ii, 1118, 1119, 1182, 20, 21, 27, Vol 14, I, 191, 27, 28, 359, 651, 48, 1018.
45. The National Archives Currency Converter.
46. Letters and Papers Vol. 14, I, 1018.
47. Letters and Papers Vol. 14, I, 651, 38.
48. Binyon 1900, p. 335–336.
49. Chilvers 2010, p. 19.
50. House of Lords Precedence Act 1539.
51. Lehmberg 1977, p. 102.
52. Records of the Lord Steward, the Board of Green Cloth and other officers of the Royal Household.
53. Gunn 2015, p. 167.
54. National Archives 2ANC3/B/13.
55. Weir 1991, p. 377.
56. Weir 1991, p. 381.
57. Licence 2014, p. 298.
58. Weir 1991, p. 384.
59. Weir 1994, p. 385.
60. Weir 1994, p. 389.
61. Weir 1994, p. 390.
62. Weir 1994, p. 392.
63. Letters and Papers Vol. 14, 754.
64. Letters and Papers Vol. 14, 754.
65. Licence 2014, p. 308.

15 The Right Honourable Lord Duke of Suffolk

1. Darsie 2019, p. 119.
2. Starkey 2004, p. 630.
3. Starkey 2004, p. 638.
4. Letters & Papers Vol. 9 386.
5. Letters & Papers Vol. 15, 860.
6. Darsie 2019, p. 167.
7. Letters and Papers Vol. 15, 845.
8. Letters and Papers Vol. 15, 850.

9. Letters and Papers Vol. 15, 872.
10. Letters and Papers Vol. 15, 898, 908.
11. Letters and Papers Vol. 15, 991.
12. Starkey 2004, p. 642.
13. Starkey 2004, p. 644.
14. Starkey 2004, p. 647.
15. Licence 2014, p. 318.
16. Licence 2014, p. 326.
17. Licence 2014, p. 327.
18. National Archives 2ANC3/B/16.
19. Licence 2014, p. 334.
20. Licence 2014, p. 335.
21. Letters and Papers Vol. 16, 961.
22. Gunn, 2015, p. 200.
23. Chilvers 2010, p. 19.
24. Licence 2014, p. 336.
25. Licence 2014, p. 337.
26. Baldwin, 2015 p. 61
27. Letters and Papers Vol. 16, 1414, 1422, 1426.
28. Licence 2014, p. 339–340.
29. Calendar of State Papers, Spain Vol. VI, 232.
30. Baldwin Smith 2008, p. 187.
31. Letters and Papers Vol. 17, 124.
32. Richardson 2011, p. 372.
33. Harbison 2014.
34. Royal Collection Trust 2018.
35. Royal Collection Trust 2018.
36. Royal Collection Trust 2018.
37. Hutchinson 2006, p. 104.
38. Letters and Papers Vol. 18, I 224.
39. National Archives 2ANC3/B/18.
40. Letters and Papers Vol. 18, 412.
41. Letters and Papers Vol. 18, i 814, 884.
42. Letters and Papers Vol. 18, I 962.
43. Letters and Papers Vol. 4, 106.
44. Letters and Papers Vol. 7, 1470.
45. Letters and Papers Vol. 15, 163.
46. Letters and Papers Vol. 15, 296.
47. Starkey 1990, p. 85.
48. Lodge 1823, p. 7.
49. Letters and Papers Vol. 19, 116.
50. National Archives 1ANC12/A/1.
51. Letters and Papers Vol. 18, I 96, 109, 152, 172 and 186.
52. Wilson 2009, p. 315.
53. Letters and Papers Vol. 18, I 836.
54. Letters and Papers Vol. 18, I 836.
55. Wilson 2009, p. 315.
56. Bain 1890, p. 64.

57. Bain 1890, p. 266.
58. Letters and Papers Vol. 19, 314.
59. Hutchinson 2006, p. 105.
60. National Archives 2ANC3/B/21.
61. Wilson 2009, p. 318.
62. Wilson 2009, p. 324.
63. Letters and Papers Vol. 19, ii 222.
64. Letters and Papers Vol. 19, I 694.
65. Hutchinson 2006, p. 110.
66. Hutchinson 2006, p. 110.
67. Nicholes and Bruce 1863, p. 29.
68. Nicholes and Bruce 1863, p. 34.
69. Nicholes and Bruce 1863, p. 29.
70. Nicholes and Bruce 1863, p. 33.
71. Nicholes and Bruce 1863, p. 29.
72. Nicholes and Bruce 1863, p. 30.
73. Nicholes and Bruce 1863, p. 31.
74. Nicholes and Bruce 1863, p. 33.
75. Nicholes and Bruce 1863, p. 34.
76. Nicholes and Bruce 1863, p. 37.
77. Nicholes and Bruce 1863, p. 38.
78. Nicholes and Bruce 1863, p. 39.
79. Nicholes and Bruce 1863, p. 41.

16 The Final Battle

1. Wilson 2009, p. 325.
2. Letters and Papers Vol. 19, I 835.
3. Hutchinson, 2006, p. 111.
4. Letters and Papers Vol. 19, I 949.
5. Gunn 2015, p. 178.
6. Letters and Papers Vol. 19, ii 222.
7. Hutchinson 2006, p. 112.
8. Letters and Papers Vol. 19, 424.
9. Letters and Papers Vol. 19, ii 378.
10. Letters and Papers Vol. 19, ii 483.
11. Gunn 2015, p. 179.
12. The National Archives Currency Converter.
13. Gunn 2015, p. 180.
14. Letters and Papers Vol. 20, I, 846, 92.
15. Oxford Dictionary of National Biography Katherine [Kateryn, Catherine; née Katherine Parr].
16. Baldwin 2015, p. 61.
17. Baldwin 2015, p. 75.
18. Letters and Papers Vol. 13, 583.
19. Calendar of State Papers, Spain Vol. 8, 204.
20. Letters and Papers Vol. 17, 957.

21. Letters and Papers Vol. 21, 417.
22. Ryrie 2008, p. 21–22.
23. Letters and Papers Vol. 20, 134, 140, 147, 156, 176.
24. Calendar of State Papers, Spain Vol. 8, 126.
25. Letters and Papers Vol. 20, 176.
26. Letters and Papers Vol. 20, 176.
27. Letters and Papers Vol. 20, 197.
28. Wriothesley 1875, p. 160.
29. Hall 1809, p. 863.
30. Bodleian Library, MS Ashmole 1109, fo. 142v, 143r.
31. Bodleian Library, MS Ashmole 1109, fo. 143r, 143v, 144r.
32. Bodleian Library, MS Ashmole 1109, fo. 143r.
33. Bodleian Library, MS Ashmole 1109, fo. 143v.
34. Bodleian Library, MS A Baldwin p. 99shmole 1109, fo. 143v, 144r.
35. Bodleian Library, MS Ashmole 1109, fo. 144v, 145r.
36. Bodleian Library, MS Ashmole 1109, fo. 145r.
37. Bodleian Library, MS Ashmole 1109, fo. 145v.
38. Gunn 2015, p. 174.
39. Letters and Papers Vol. 18, I, 536.
40. Letters and Papers Vol. 18, I, 809, 957, 964.
41. Bodleian Library, MS Ashmole 1109, fo. 145v, 146r.
42. Hutchinson 2006, p. 119 and Weir 2008, p. 485.
43. Pote and Leake 1749, p. 367–368.
44. Knight 1840, p.231.
45. Granger 1824, p. 104.
46. Letters and Papers Vol. 20, ii, 598.
47. The National Archives Currency Converter.
48. Gunn 2015, p. 191.

17 The Last of the Brandon Men

1. Oxford Dictionary of National Biography – Charles Brandon.
2. The National Archives Currency Converter.
3. Baldwin 2015, p. 63.
4. Skidmore 2017, p. 31.
5. Skidmore 2007, p. 70.
6. Oxford Dictionary of National Biography – Charles Brandon.
7. Nicholas 1857, p. 313.
8. Calendar of Patent Rolls Edward VI, Vol. 3, p. 162.
9. McCall 2016.
10. Skidmore 2007, p. 95.
11. Trueman 2008.
12. Treaty of Boulogne.
13. Nicholas 1857, p. 251.
14. Calendar of State Papers Spain Vol. 10, Vienna, Imp. Arch. E. 17.
15. Calendar of State Papers Spain Vol. 10, Vienna, Imp. Arch. E. 19.
16. Calendar of State Papers Spain Vol. 10, Vienna, Imp. Arch. E. 17.

17. Baldwin 2015, p. 97.
18. Franklin-Harkrider, 2008, p. 81.
19. Baldwin 2015, p. 37.
20. Calendar of State Papers, Spain Vol. 10, March 1.
21. Oxford Dictionary of National Biography – Charles Brandon.
22. Kohn 2007, p. 106.
23. Baldwin 2015, p. 99.
24. Wilson 2009, p. 104–105.
25. Oxford Dictionary of National Biography – Charles Brandon.
26. Wilson 2009, p. 58–59.
27. Calendar of State Papers Domestic: Edward VI, Mary and Elizabeth Vol. 3, September 1551
28. Calendar of State Papers Spain Vol. 10, Vienna, Imp. Arch. E. 19.
29. Letters and Papers Vol. 12, ii, 171.
30. The National Archives Currency Converter.
31. Richardson 2011, p. 371.
32. Gunn 2015, p. 163.
33. Burke 1846, p. 251.
34. Emerson 2015.
35. Richardson 2011, p. 371.
36. Richardson 2011, p. 372.
37. Emerson 2015.
38. Richardson 2011, p. 372.
39. Perry 2002, p. 267.
40. Oxford Dictionary of National Biography – Frances Brandon.
41. The National Archives Currency Converter.
42. Oxford Dictionary of National Biography – Frances Brandon.
43. Richardson 2011, p. 168.
44. de Lisle 2013, p. 259.
45. de Lisle 2013, p. 273.
46. de Lisle 2013, p. 276.
47. Oxford Dictionary of National Biography – Frances Brandon.
48. de Lisle 2013, p. 283–284.
49. de Lisle 2013, p. 286.
50. Oxford Dictionary of National Biography – Frances Brandon.
51. Richardson 2011, p. 168.
52. Emmerson 2015.

Bibliography

All Kinds of History, *1525: Amicable Grant* 2014, <https://tudorrebellions. wordpress.com/2014/11/23/1525-amicable-grant/>.

Archer-Hind, Laura and Fenn, John, *The Paston Letters* (London: J. M. Dent & Sons, Ltd., 1924).

Ashmole, Elias, *The Institution, Laws & Ceremonies of the Most Noble Order of the Garter* (London: J. Macock, 1672).

Bain, Joseph, *The Hamilton papers. Letters and papers illustrating the political relations of England and Scotland in the XVIth century* (Scotland: Edinburgh, H. M. General Register House, 1890).

Baldwin, David, *Henry VIII's Last Love: The Extraordinary Life of Katherine Willoughby, Lady-in-Waiting to the Tudors* (Gloucestershire: Amberley Publishing, 2015).

Baldwin Smith, Lacey, *Catherine Howard* (Gloucestershire: Amberley Publishing, 2008).

Barber, Richard and Barker Juliet, *Tournaments: Jousts, Chivalry and Pageants in the Middle Ages* (Woodbridge: The Boydell Press, 1989).

Barnard, Francis Pierrepont, *Edward IV's French expedition of 1475: the leaders and their badges, being Ms. 2. M. 16* (Dursley: College of Arms, 1854).

Benger, E, Memoirs of the Life of Anne Boleyn, Queen of Henry VIII (Available from the collections of New York Public Library, 1822).

Bernard, G.W., *The King's Reformation Henry VIII and the Remarking of the English Church* (United Kingdom: Yale University Press, 2007).

Betteridge, Thomas and Freeman, Thomas, *Henry VIII and History* (England: Ashgate Publishing Limited, 2012).

Bicheno, Hugh, *Blood Royal: The Wars of Lancaster and York, 1462–1485* (London: Head of Zeus, 2016).

Binyon, Laurence, *Catalogue of Drawings by British Artists and Artists of Foreign Origin Working in Great Britain* (London: Printed by the order of the Trustees, 1900).

Block, J.S., *Stories from the Darker Side of Love: Tales of broken families and tangled relationships in Tudor England* (BookBaby, 2016).

Bloomfield, Francis and Parkin, Charles, *An Essay Towards a Topographical History of the County of Norfolk, containing a description of the towns, villages and hamlets* (London: W. Miller, 1810).

Blomefield, Francis, *East Flegg Hundred: Great Yarmouth, chronology of particular events, An Essay Towards A Topographical History of the County of Norfolk: Volume 11*, pp. 394-399. (London: *British History Online*, 1810). <http://www. british-history.ac.uk/topographical-hist-norfolk/vol11/pp394-399>.

Borman, Tracy, *Thomas Cromwell The untold story of Henry VIII's most faithful servant* (London: Hodder & Stoughton, 2015).

Brady, Maziere, *The episcopal succession in England, Scotland and Ireland, A.D. 1400 to 1875: with appointments to monasteries and extracts from consistorial acts taken from mss. in public and private libraries in Rome, Florence, Bologna, Ravenna and Paris* (Rome: Tipografia della Pace, 1876).

Bradley, John, *John Morton: Adversary to Richard III, Power Behind the Tudors* (Gloucestershire: Amberley Publishing, 2019).

Breverton, Terry, *Jasper Tudor Dynasty Maker* (Gloucestershire: Amberley Publishing, 2014).

Brigden, Susan, The Penguin History of Britain: *New Worlds, Lost Worlds: The Rule of the Tudors 1485–1630* (United Kingdom: Penguin, 2001).

Brigden, Susan, Thomas Wyatt: *The Heart's Forest* (United Kingdom: Faber & Faber, 2012).

Brimacombe, Peter, *Tudor England* (United Kingdom: Jarrold Publishing, 2004).

Bruce, John, *Historie of the arrivall of Edward IV in England and the finall recouerye of his kingdomes from Henry VI A.D. M.CCCC.LXXI* (United Kingdom: J. B. Nichols and son, 1836).

Bryan, L, *The Mirror of Naples*, <http://under-these-restless-skies.blogspot.com. au/2013/12/the-mirror-of-naples.html>.

Burke, John, The Portrait Gallery of Distinguished Females Including Beauties of the Courts of George IV. and William IV. (London: Bull and Churton, 1833).

Burke, John, A genealogical and heraldic History of the Commoners of Great Britain and Ireland, enjoying territorial possessions or high official rank, but uninvested with heritable honours, *Volume 1*, (London: R Bently, 1834).

Burke, John, *A General and Heraldic Dictionary of the Peerages of England, Ireland & Scotland, Extinct* (London: Henry Colburn Publisher, 1846).

Calendar of the patent rolls preserved in the Public Record Office, 1429–1436 Henry VI v.2. Great Britain.

Calendar of the patent rolls preserved in the Public Record Office, 1446–1452 Henry VI v.5. Great Britain

Calendar of the patent rolls preserved in the Public Record Office, 1452–1461 Henry VI v.6. Great Britain.

Calendar of the patent rolls preserved in the Public Record Office, 1461–1467 Edward IV v. 1. Great Britain

Calendar of the patent rolls preserved in the Public Record Office, 1467–1477 Edward IV Henry VI. Great Britain.

Calendar of the patent rolls preserved in the Public Record Office, 1476–1485 Edward IV Edward V Richard III. Great Britain.

Calendar of the patent rolls preserved in the Public Record Office, 1485–1494 Henry VII v. 1. Great Britain

Calendar of the patent rolls preserved in the Public Record Office, 1494–1509 Henry VII v. 2. Great Britain.

Calendar of the patent rolls preserved in the Public Record Office, 1549–1551 Edward VI v. 3. Great Britain.

Calendar of State Papers Domestic: Edward VI, Mary and Elizabeth, 1547-80, (London: British History Online, 1856) <http://www.british-history.ac.uk/cal-state-papers/domestic/edw-eliz/1547-80>.

Calendar of State Papers Relating To English Affairs in the Archives of Venice, (London: Her Majesty's Stationery Office, 1871).

Calendar of State Papers, Spain, Volume 10, 1550–1552, (London: *British History Online*) <http://www.british-<history.ac.uk/cal-state-papers/spain/vol10/pp225-237>.

Campbell, William, *Materials for a history of the reign of Henry VII: from original documents preserved in the Public Record Office* (London: Longman & Co, 1873).

Carroll, L, Notorious Royal Marriages: *A Juicy Journey Through Nine Centuries of Dynasty, and Desire* (New York: New American Library, 2010).

Castor, Helen, The King, the Crown, and the Duchy of Lancaster: *Public Authority and Private Power, 1399–1461* (Oxford: Oxford University Press, 2000).

Chapman, H.W., *Anne Boleyn* (London: Jonathan Cape, 1974).

Chilvers, Allan, *The Berties of Grimsthorpe Castle* (Bloomington Indiana: Author House, 2010).

Chris Given-Wilson, Paul Brand, Seymour Phillips, Mark Ormrod, Geoffrey Martin, Anne Curry and Rosemary Horrox, '*Henry VI: November 1459*', *Parliament Rolls of Medieval England* (Woodbridge: *British History Online*, Boydell, 2005), <http://www.british-history.ac.uk/no-series/parliament-rolls-medieval/november-1459>.

Christie and Masson, Catalogue of the Entire Collection of Portraits of the Most Illustrious Persons of British History: *Consisting of the Drawings Made (with Permission) from the Original Pictures in the Royal Collection, the Galleries of the Nobility & Gentry, and the Public Collections Throughout the Kingdom* (United Kingdom: The Firm, *1838).*

Clarke, David, *Barnet 1471: Death of a Kingmaker* (Great Britain: Pen and Sword Books, 2007).

Clowes, William, Report of the Deputy Keeper of the Public Records, *Volume 9* (London: Clowes and Sons, 1848).

Crouse, J, The History and Antiquities of the County of Norfolk: Blofield, Brothercross and Clacklose (Norwich: J. Crouse, 1781).

Darsie, Heather R., *Anna Duchess of Cleves: The King's Beloved Sister* (Gloucestershire: Amberley Publishing, 2019).

Davey, Richard, *The sisters of Lady Jane Grey and their wicked grandfather; being the true stories of the strange lives of Charles Brandon, duke of Suffolk, and of the ladies Katherine and Mary Grey, sisters of Lady Jane Grey, "the nine-days' queen,"* (London: Chapman and Hall, 1848).

Davies, John Silvester, *An English Chronicle of the Reigns of Richard II., Henry IV., Henry V., and Henry VI.* (London: The Camden Society, 1838).

De Commines, Philippe, The Memoirs of Philippe de Commines, Lord of Argenton: Containing the Histories of Louis XI and Charles VIII Kings of

France and of Charles the Bold, Duke of Burgundy to which is Added, The Scandalous Chronicle, Or Secret History of Louis XI, (London).

De Worde, Wynkyn, *The Maner of the tryumphe of Caleys and Bulleyn and The noble tryumphaunt coronacyon of Quene Anne, wyfe unto the most noble kynge Henry VIII*, Edinburgh, 1884, <https://archive.org/stream/maneroftryumpheo00goldiala#page/n3/mode/2up>.

de Listle, Leanda, *Tudor: The Family Story* (United Kingdom: Vintage, 2013).

du Bellay, du Cardinal Jean, *Correspondance du Cardinal Jean du Bellay, Tome Premier 1529–1535* (Paris Librairie: C. Klincksieck, 1969).

Doran, Susan, *The Tudor Chronicles* (London: Quercus Publishing, 2008).

De Savoie. Duchesse d'Angoulême, Louise Journal de Louise de Savoye, duchesse d'Angoulesme, d'Anjou et de Valois <https://books.google.com.au/books?id=P7cPAAAAQAAJ&printsec=frontcover&dq=inauthor:%22Louise+(De+Savoie.+Duchesse+d%27Angoul%C3%AAme)%22&hl=en&sa=X&ved=0ahUKEwi1kf-RsdfPAhUBbSYKHa-VCfAQ6AEIHTAA#v=onepage&q&f=false>.

Ellis, Sir Henry, *Original Letters Illustrative of English History; Including Numerous Royal Letters: From Autographs in the British Museum, and One or Two Other Collection* (London: Harding and Lepard, 1827).

Ellis, Sir Henry, Three books of Polydore Vergil's English History: *Comprising the reigns of Henry VI., Edward IV., and Richard III* (London: Camden Society, 1884).

Emerson, Kathy Lynn, *A Who's Who of Tudor Women* <http://www.kateemersonhistoricals.com/TudorWomenIndex.htm>.

Everett Green, Mary Anne, *Lives of the Princesses of England, from the Norman Conquest* (London: Longman, Brown, Green, Longman, & Roberts, 1857).

Franklin-Harkrider, Melissa, *Women, Reform and Community in Early Modern England: Katherine Willoughby, Duchess of Suffolk, and Lincolnshire's Godly Aristocracy, 1519–1580* (Woodbridge: The Boydell Press, 2008).

Fraser, Antonia, *The Six Wives of Henry VIII* (London: Phoenix Press, 2002).

Gasquet, Francis Aidan, *Henry VIII. The English Monasteries. An Attempt To Illustrate The History Of Their Repression* (London: John Hodges, 1889).

Gairdner, James, Letters and Papers Illustrative of the Reigns of Richard III and Henry VII (London: London, 1861).

Gairdner, James, History of the Life and Reign of Richard the Third (Cambridge: University Press, 1898).

Gairdner, James, *Letters and Papers, Foreign and Domestic, of the Reign of Henry VIII, 1509-47* (United Kingdom: His Majesty's Stationery Office, 1862–1932).

Gibbs, Vicary, *The complete peerage of England, Scotland, Ireland, Great Britain, and the United Kingdom: extant, extinct, or dormant* (London: The St. Catherine Press, 1912).

Gillingham, John, *The Wars of the Roses Peace & Conflict in the 15th Century England* (London: Phoenix Press, 1981).

Goodman, Ruth, *How to Be a Tudor: A Dawn-to-Duke Guide to Everyday Life* (United Kingdom: Penguin Books, 2016).

Grafton, Richard, Grafton's Chronicle, Or History of England: *To which is Added His Table of the Bailiffs, Sheriffs and Mayors of the City of London from the Year 1189, to 1558, Inclusive: in Two Volumes, Volume 2* (London, 1809).

Granger, James, A Biographical History of England, from Egbert the Great to the Revolution, Volume 1 (London: W. Baynes and Son, 1824).

Grose, Francis, *The antiquities of the county of Norfolk* (London: John Grey Bell, 1849).

Gunn, Steven, *Charles Brandon* (Gloucestershire: Amberley Publishing, 2015).

Gunn, Steven, *Henry VII's New Men and The Making of Tudor England* (Oxford: Oxford University Press, 2016).

Haigh, Christopher, English Reformations: *Religion, Politics, and Society Under the Tudors* (Oxford: Clarendon Press, 1993).

Hall, Edward, *Hall's chronicle: containing the history of England, during the reign of Henry the Fourth, and the succeeding monarchs, to the end of the reign of Henry the Eighth, in which are particularly described the manners and customs of those periods. Carefully collated with the editions of 1548 and 1550* (London: J. Johnson, 1809).

Hannay, M., Brennan, M.G. and Lamb, M.E, The Ashgate Research Companion to The Sidneys, 1500–1700: *Volume 2: Literature*, (New York: Ashgate Publishing, 2015).

Harbison, Craig, *Hans Holbein the Younger*, Encyclopaedia Britannica, 2014 <http://www.britannica.com/EBchecked/topic/269121/Hans-Holbein-the-Younger>.

Harding Alan, *CORBET, Roger (1501/2-38), of Moreton Corbet, Salop; Linslade, Bucks. and London*, The History of Parliament Trust 1964-2017 <http://www.historyofparliamentonline.org/volume/1509-1558/member/corbet-roger-15012-38>.

Hardying, John, *The chronicle of Iohn Hardyng* (London, F. C. and J. Rivington, 1812)

Harris Nicolas, Sir Nicholas, Testamenta Vetusta: *Being Illustrations from Wills, of Manners, Customs, &c. as Well as of the Descents and Possessions of Many Distinguished Families. From the Reign of Henry the Second to the Accession of Queen Elizabeth*, Volume 2 (London: Nicolas and Son, 1826).

Harris Nicolas, Sir Nicholas, *Proceedings and Ordinances of the Privy Council of England Volume VL* (United Kingdom: G. Eyre and A. Spottiswoode, 1837).

Harris Nicolas, Sir Nicholas, History of the Orders of Knighthood of the British Empire; of the Order of the Guelphs of Hanover; and of the Medals, Clasps, and Crosses, Conferred for Naval and Military Services, *Volume 2* (London: John Hunter, 1842).

Harris, Barbara J., *English Aristocratic Women, 1450–1550: Marriage and Family, Property and Careers* (New York: Oxford University Press, 2002).

Hart, Kelly, *The Mistresses of Henry VIII* (Gloucestershire: The History Press, 2009).

Heritage Gateway, *Suffolk HER*, 2012 <http://www.heritagegateway.org.uk/Gateway/Results_Single.aspx?uid=MSF13436&resourceID=1017>.

History, *History of Jousting* <http://www.history.co.uk/shows/full-metal-jousting/articles/history-of-jousting>.

Hood, Dr Catherine, Hutchinson, Robert and Worlsey, Dr Lucy, *Inside The Body of Henry VIII* (National Geographic, 2009).

House of Lords Precedence Act 153, Legislation, The National Archives <http://www.legislation.gov.uk/aep/Hen8/31/10>.

House of Lords Precedence Act 153, Legislation (The National Archives) <http://www.legislation.gov.uk/aep/Hen8/31/10>.

Howell, Thomas Bayly, *Cobbett's complete collection of state trials and proceedings for high treason: and other crimes and misdemeanor from the earliest period to the present time ... from the ninth year of the reign of King Henry, the Second, A.D.1163, to ... [George IV, A.D.1820* (London: R. Bagshaw, 1809).

Hume, Martin, *The Wives of Henry the Eighth and the Parts They Played in History* (London: Eveleigh Nash, 1905).

Hutchinson Robert, *The Last Days of Henry VIII* (London: Phoenix, 2006).

Hutchinson, Robert, *Young Henry: The Rise of Henry VIII* (London: Orion Books, 2011).

Hutton, William, The Battle of Bosworth Field, Between Richard the Third and Henry Earl of Richmond, August 22, 1485 (Fleet Street: Nichols, Son, and Bentley, 1813).

Ibeji, Dr Mike, Black Death (BBC, *2011)* <https://www.bbc.co.uk/history/british/middle_ages/black_01.shtml>.

Ives, Eric, *The Life and Death of Anne Boleyn* (Oxford: Blackwell Publishing, 2005).

Johnson, David, *Southwak and the City*, (United Kingdom: Oxford UP, 1969).

Jones, Dan, *The Hollow Crown: The Wars of the Roses and the Rise of the Tudors* (London: Faber & Faber, 2015).

Kadouchkine, Oliver, *The Amicable Grant, 1525*, 2014 <http://jwsmrscott.weebly.com/tudorpedia/the-amicable-grant-1525>.

Kesselring, Krista, *Reviewed Work: The Defeat of the Pilgrimage of Grace. A Study of the Postpardon Revolts of December 1536 to March 1537 and Their Effect* by Michael Bush, David Bownes (The Sixteenth Century Journal, vol. 33, no. 2, pp. 600–602, 2002).

Kohn, George C., *Encyclopedia of Plague and Pestilence: From Ancient Times to the Present*, (New York: Infobase Publishing, 2007).

Knapton, Sarah, *Jousting secret explains how Charles Brandon rose in the court of Henry VIII*, The Telegraph, 2014 <http://www.telegraph.co.uk/history/11196723/Jousting-secret-explains-how-Charles-Brandon-rose-in-the-court-of-Henry-VIII.html>.

Knight, Charles, The Penny Magazine of the Society for the Diffusion of Useful Knowledge, *Volume 9* (London: C Knight & Company, 1840).

Langley, Philippa and Jones, Michael, The King's Grave: *The Search for Richard III* (United Kingdom: Hachette, 2013).

Licence, Amy, *In Bed with the Tudors: The sex lives of a dynasty from Elizabeth of York to Elizabeth I* (Gloucestershire: Amberley Publishing, 2012).

Licence, Amy, *Bessie Blount Mistress to Henry VIII* (Gloucestershire: Amberley Publishing, 2013).

Licence, Amy, *The Six Wives & Many Mistresses of Henry VIII* (Gloucestershire: Amberley Publishing, 2014).

*Little Doomsday (*National Archives) < http://www.nationalarchives.gov.uk/domesday/discover-domesday/little-domesday.htm>.

Levitt, Emma, *"A second king": chivalric masculinity and the meteoric rise of Charles Brandon, duke of Suffolk (c. 1484- 1545)"* (University of Winchester-Gender and Medieval Studies, 2014).

Lewis, Matthew, *The Wars of the Roses* (Gloucestershire: Amberley Publishing, 2015).

Lehmberg, Stanford E., The Later Parliaments of Henry VIII, 1536–1547 (United Kingdom: Cambridge University Press, 1977).

Leland, John and Hearne, Thomas, *Joannis Lelandi Antiquarii de rebus britannicis collectanea* (Impensis Gul. & Jo. Richardson, 1770).

Lewis, Matthew, *The Wars of the Roses in 100 Facts* (Gloucestershire: Amberley Publishing, 2017).

Lewis, Matthew, *Richard III Loyalty Binds Me* (Gloucestershire: Amberley Publishing, 2018).

Lipscomb, Suzannah, *1536 The Year that Changed Henry VIII* (Oxford: Lion Hudson plc, 2009).

Loades, David, *The Tudors History of a Dynasty* (London: Continuum International Publishing Group, 2012).

Lodge, Edmund, Portraits of Illustrious Personages of Great Britain …: *With Biographical and Historical Memoirs of Their Lives and Actions, Volumes 1-2*, (London: Harding, Mavor and Lepard, 1823).

Loades, David, *Mary Rose* (Gloucestershire: Amberley Publishing, 2012).

Lysons, Daniel and Samuel Lysons, 'Parishes: St Blazey – Bodmin', *Magna Britannia: Volume 3, Cornwall* (London: T Cadell and W Davies, 1814), 24-38. *British History Online* <http://www.british-history.ac.uk/magna-britannia/vol3/pp24-38>.

MacCulloch, Diarmaid, *The Reign of Henry VIII Politics, Policy and Piety* (New York: St Martin's Press, 1995).

Mackay, Lauren, *Inside the Tudor Court* (Gloucestershire: Amberley Publishing, 2014).

Mackman, Jonathan and Matthew Stevens, 'CP40/753: Easter term 1449', *Court of Common Pleas: the National Archives, Cp40 1399–1500, British History Online*, (London: Centre for Metropolitan History, 2010) <http://www.british-history.ac.uk/no-series/common-pleas/1399-1500/easter-term-1449>.

Mackman, Jonathan and Matthew Stevens, 'CP40/759: Michaelmas term 1450', *Court of Common Pleas: the National Archives, Cp40 1399–1500, British History Online*, (London: Centre for Metropolitan History, 2010) <http://www.british-history.ac.uk/no-series/common-pleas/1399-1500/michaelmas-term-1450>.

Mackman, Jonathan and Matthew Stevens, 'CP40/808: Easter term 1463', *Court of Common Pleas: the National Archives, Cp40 1399–1500, British History Online* (London: Centre for Metropolitan History, 2010), <http://www.british-history.ac.uk/no-series/common-pleas/1399-1500/easter-term-1463>.

Mackman, Jonathan and Matthew Stevens, 'CP40/814: Hilary term 1465', *Court of Common Pleas: the National Archives, Cp40 1399–1500, British History Online* (London: Centre for Metropolitan History, 2010) <http://www.british-history.ac.uk/no-series/common-pleas/1399-1500/hilary-term-1465>.

Mackman, Jonathan and Matthew Stevens, 'CP40/874: Michaelmas term 1480', *Court of Common Pleas: the National Archives, Cp40 1399–1500, British History Online* (London: Centre for Metropolitan History, 2010) <http://www.british-history.ac.uk/no-series/common-pleas/1399-1500/michaelmas-term-1480>.

Maskelyne, and Lyte, H. C. Maxwell, Inquisitions Post Mortem, Henry VII, Entries 1-50, *Calendar of Inquisitions Post Mortem: Series 2, Volume 2, Henry VII, pp. 1-45, British History Online* (London: His Majesty's Stationery Office, 1915) <http://www.british-history.ac.uk/inquis-post-mortem/series2-vol2/pp1-45>.

Maskelyne, and Lyte, H. C. Maxwell, 'Inquisitions Post Mortem, Henry VII, Entries 1051–1100', *Calendar of Inquisitions Post Mortem: Series 2, Volume 1, Henry VII*, pp. 452-469, *British History Online* (London: Her Majesty's Stationery Office, 1898) <http://www.british-history.ac.uk/inquis-post-mortem/series2-vol1/pp452-469>.

McCall, Chris, *The Story of England's 'Rough Wooing' of Scotland*, 2016 <https://www.scotsman.com/lifestyle-2-15039/the-story-of-england-s-rough-wooing-of-scotland-1-4093982>.

Medieval Lives: Birth, Marriage and Death (Scotland: BBC 2013)

Meyer, G.J., *The Tudors The Complete Story of England's Most Notorious Dynasty* (New York: Delacorte Press, 2010).

Medieval Jousting Tournaments, 2014 < http://www.medieval-life-and-times.info/medieval-knights/medieval-jousting-tournaments.htm>.

Medieval Rules for Jousting, Medievalist.Net, 2015 <http://www.medievalists.net/2015/01/07/medieval-rules-jousting/>.

Middleton-Steward, Judith, Inward Purity and Outward Splendour: *Death and Remembrance in the Deanery of Dunwich, Suffolk, 1370–1547* (Norwich: Boydell & Brewer, 2001).

Mumby, F., *The youth of Henry VIII; a narrative in contemporary letters* (New York: Houghton Mifflin Company, 1913).

Nicholas, John Gough (ed.), *The chronicle of Calais, in the reigns of Henry VII. and Henry VIII. to the year 1540* (London: Camden Society, 1846).

Nicholas, John Gough, *Literary Remains of King Edward the Sixth: Edited from His Autograph Manuscripts, with Historical Notes and a Biographical Memoir, Part 2* (London: J. B. Nichols and sons, 1857).

Nichols, J. G. and Bruce, J., *Wills from Doctors' Commons. A selection from the Wills of Eminent Persons Proved in the Prerogative Court of Canterbury, 1495–1695*, (United Kingdom: Camden Society, 1863).

Norton, Elizabeth, *Bessie Blount Mistress to Henry VIII* (Gloucestershire: Amberley Publishing, 2013).

Norton, Elizabeth, *The Boleyn Women The Tudor femmes fatales who changed English history* (Gloucestershire: Amberley Publishing, 2013).

Oxford Bodleian Library, *The Interment of Charles Brandon, Duke of Suffolk*, MS Ashmole 1109, ff. 142-6.

Oxford Dictionary of National Biography Brandon, Charles, first duke of Suffolk (c.1484–1545), (Oxford University Press) < http://www.oxforddnb.com/>.

Oxford Dictionary of National Biography Brandon, Sir Thomas (d. 1510), (Oxford University Press) <http://www.oxforddnb.com/>.

Oxford Dictionary of National Biography Grey [other married name Stokes], Frances [née Lady Frances Brandon], (Oxford University Press) < http://www.oxforddnb.com/>.

Oxford Dictionary of National Biography Katherine [Kateryn, Catherine; née Katherine Parr], 2015, (Oxford University Press) <http://www.oxforddnb.com/>.

Paston, *The Paston Letters A Selection in Modern Spelling* (Oxford: Oxford University Press).

Penn, Thomas, *Winter King The Dawn of Tudor England* (London: Penguin Group, 2011).

Perry, Maria, *Sisters to the King* (London: Andre Deutsh, 2002).

Porter, Stephen, *Everyday Life in Tudor London* (Gloucestershire: Amberley Publishing, 2016).

Pote, Joseph and Leake, S. Martin., The History and Antiquities of Windsor Castle, and the Royal College, and Chapel of St. George (Joseph Pote Bookfeller, 1749).

Records of the Lord Steward, the Board of Green Cloth and other officers of the Royal Household, The National Archives, <http://discovery.nationalarchives. gov.uk/details/r/C202>.

Rendle, William, *Old Southwark and its people* (Southwark: W. Drewett, 1878).

Richardson, Douglas, *Plantagenet Ancestry: A Study In Colonial And Medieval Families, 2nd Edition* (USA: CreateSpace, 2011).

Richardson, Walter C., *Mary Tudor The White Queen* (Great Britain: University of Washington Press, 1970).

Ross, James, The Foremost Man of the Kingdom: *John de Vere, Thirteenth Earl of Oxford (1442–1513)* (Woodbridge: The Boydell Press, 2015).

Royle, Trevor, *The Wars of the Roses, England's First Civil War* (United Kingdom: Abacus, 2009).

Royal Collection Trust, *The Knights of the Garter under Henry VIII*, 2015 <http:// www.royalcollection.org.uk/microsites/knightsofthegarter/MicroSectionList. asp?type=More&exid=144>.

Royal Collection Trust, *Charles Brandon, 3rd Duke of Suffolk (1537/8–1551)*, 2018 <https://www.rct.uk/collection/search#/3/collection/422295/charles-brandon-3rd-duke-of-suffolk-15378-1551>.

Royal Collection Trust, *Henry Brandon, 2nd Duke of Suffolk (1535–1551)*, 2018 <https://www.rct.uk/collection/search#/2/collection/422294/henry-brandon-2nd-duke-of-suffolk-1535-1551>.

Royal Collection Trust, *Katherine, Duchess of Suffolk (1519–1580)*, 2018 <https://www.rct.uk/collection/search#/1/collection/912194/katherine-duchess-of-suffolk-1519-1580>.

Ryrie, Alec, The Sorcerer's Tale: Faith and Fraud in Tudor England (Oxford: Oxford University Press, 2008).

Sadlack, Erin, *The French Queen's Letters* (New York: Palgrave Macmillan, 2001).

Seward, Desmond, *The Wars of the Roses: The Bloody Rivalry for the Throne of England* (London: Constable & Robinson LTD, 2007).

Shaw, William Arthur, *The Knights of England. A complete record from the earliest time to the present day of the knights of all the orders of chivalry in England, Scotland, and Ireland, and of knights bachelors, incorporating a complete list of knights bachelors dubbed in Ireland, London* (London: Sherratt and Hughes, 1906).

Skidmore, Chris, *Edward VI The Lost King of England* (London: Weidenfeld & Nicolson, 2007).

Skidmore, Chris, *The Rise of the Tudors The Family That Changed English History* (New York: St. Martin's Press, 2013).

Smith, Earnest D., *The Story of Caister Castle and Car Collection* (Caister Castle, 2018).

Smyth, John, *The Berkeley Manuscripts: The Lives of the Berkeleys, Lords of the Honour, Castle And Manor of Berkeley, In the County of Gloucester,*

From 1066 to 1618; With a Description of the Hundred of Berkeley And of Its Inhabitants (Gloucester: J. Bellows, 1567–1641).

Spears, J, *The Cheapside Hoard*, 2012 <http://onthetudortrail.com/Blog/2012/02/23/the-cheapside-hoard/>.

Staging the Henrician Court bringing early modern drama to life, *The Amicable Grant 1525* <http://stagingthehenriciancourt.brookes.ac.uk/historicalcontext/the_amicable_grant_1525.html>

Starkey, David, *Lives and Letters of The Great Tudor Dynasties: Rivals in Power* (New York: Grove Weidenfeld, 1990).

Starkey, David, *Six Wives The Queens of Henry VIII* (London: Vintage, 2004).

Starkey, David, *Man & Monarch Henry VIII* (London: The British Library, 2009).

Suffolk Place and the Mint, in Survey of London: Volume 25, St George's Fields, The Parishes of St. George the Martyr Southwark and St. Mary Newington, pp. 22-25 (London, 1955) <http://www.british-history.ac.uk/survey-london/vol25/pp22-25>.

Surdhar, Christina, *Bloody British History: York* (United Kingdom: The History Press, 2013).

Swales, R.J.W. *WINGFIELD, Sir Anthony (by 1488–1552), of Letheringham, Suff.*, The History of Parliament Trust 1964-2017 <http://www.historyofparliamentonline.org/volume/1509-1558/member/wingfield-sir-anthony-1488-1552>.

Taylor, M.J, *BRANDON, Sir Charles (by 1521-51), of Sigston, Yorks*, The History of Parliament Trust 1964-2017 < http://www.historyofparliamentonline.org/volume/1509-1558/member/brandon-sir-charles-1521-51>.

The National Archives (Kew, Richmond, Surrey) < http://www.nationalarchives.gov.uk/>.

The National Archives Currency Converter (The National Archives) <http://www.nationalarchives.gov.uk/currency/default0.asp#mid>.

The Royal Household, *Order of the Garter*, 2015 <http://www.royal.gov.uk/monarchUK/honours/Orderofthegarter/orderofthegarter.aspx>.

The Wars of the Roses, <http://www.warsoftheroses.com/timelines.php>.

Trueman, C. N., *Foreign Policy 1549 to 1553*, 2008 <http://www.historylearningsite.co.uk/tudor-england/foreign-policy-1549-to-1553/>.

Treaty of Boulogne, World Heritage Encyclopedia <http://www.self.gutenberg.org/articles/treaty_of_boulogne>

Tudor Chamber Books, Kingship, Court ad Society: The Chamber Books of Henry VII and Henry VIII, 1485–1521 (The University of Winchester) <https://www.tudorchamberbooks.org/>.

Turner, Dawson, *Sketch of the history of Caister Castle* (London: Whittaker and Co., 1842).

Urban, Sylvanus, *The Gentleman's Magazine and Historical Chronical* (London: Nichols and Son, 1803).

Velde, François, *List of the Knights of the Garter*, <http://www.heraldica.org/topics/orders/garterlist.htm>.

Walford, Edward, 'Southwark: High Street', in Old and New London: Volume 6, pp. 57-75, (London, 1878) <http://www.british-history.ac.uk/old-new-london/vol6/pp57-75>.

Walford, Edward, 'Greenwich', in Old and New London: Volume 6, pp. 164–176, *British History Online*, (London, 1878) <http://www.british-history.ac.uk/old-new-london/vol6/pp164-176>.

Warkworth, John, *A Chronicle of the First Thirteen Years of the Reign of King Edward the Forth, Volume 10* (London: The Camden Society, 1839).

Wedgewood, Josiah C, History Of Parliament (1439–1509) (London: His Majesty's Stationary Office, 1936).

Weir, Alison, *The Six Wives of Henry VIII* (New York: Grove Press, 1991).

Weir, Alison, *Lancaster and York: The Wars of the Roses* (London: Vintage, 1995).

Weir, Alison, *Henry VIII King & Court* (London: Vintage Books, 2008).

Weir, Alison, *Henry VIII King & Court* (London: Vintage Books, 2008).

W. H. B., Bird and K. H., Ledward, 'Close Rolls, Edward IV: 1471–1472', *Calendar of Close Rolls, Edward IV: Volume 1, 1468–1476, British History Online* (London, 1953) <http://www.british-history.ac.uk/cal-close-rolls/edw4/vol2/pp222-234>.

W. H. B., Bird and K. H., Ledward, 'Close Rolls, Edward IV: 1471–1472', *Calendar of Close Rolls, Edward IV: Volume 2, 1468–1476, British History Online* (London, 1953) <http://www.british-history.ac.uk/cal-close-rolls/edw4/vol2/pp222-234>.

Wilkinson, Josephine, *Mary Boleyn The True Story of Henry VIII's Favourite Mistress* (Gloucestershire: Amberley Publishing, 2010).

Wilson, Derek, *A Brief History of Henry VIII* (London: Constable and Robinson Ltd., 2009).

Wodderspoon, John, Historic Sites and Other Remarkable and Interesting Places in the County of Suffolk (Cornhill: R. Root, 1839).

Woodger, L.S., *BRANDON, Robert, of Bishop's Lynn, Norfolk* (The History of Parliament Trust 1964-2017) <http://www.historyofparliamentonline.org/volume/1386-1421/member/brandon-robert>.

Wooding, Lucy, Henry VIII (London: Routledge, 2005).

World Heritage Encyclopaedia, *Arthur Bulkeley* <http://self.gutenberg.org/articles/arthur_bulkeley>.

Wriothesley, Charles 1875, *A chronicle of England during the reigns of the Tudors, from A. D. 1485–1559* (Camden Society).

York House, in Survey of London: Volume 18, St Martin-in-The-Fields II: the Strand, pp. 51-60 (London, 1937) <http://www.british-history.ac.uk/survey-london/vol18/pt2/pp51-60>.

Acknowledgements

I would like to thank some people who have helped me along my journey from my very first ideas about researching the life of the Brandon men, right through to the final publication. First and foremost, I must thank my husband, Peter, for his never-ending love and support, and for putting up with the countless hours that I have spent lost in books or research papers. And to my beautiful daughter Ellie, for all her cuddles and kisses which were exactly what I needed while I was writing. I also must thank my mum for passing on to me her love and passion for reading, research and history. I want to thank my best friend Amanda for her love, support and constant encouragement; I don't know what I'd do without you! I also must thank the very talented and patient Roger Banks for all his advice, encouragement and literary support.

Heartfelt thanks to Professor Steven Gunn, Matthew Lewis and Nathen Amin for all their advice, support and encouragement; our many discussions on the Wars of the Roses and the Tudor period have been absolutely invaluable and will always mean a great deal to me. I also must give Matthew an extra thank you for all his hard work on creating such a beautiful map for the book. A very big thank you goes to Richard Goddard for his insightful and inspiring tour of Tewksbury battlefield and helping me to walk in the footsteps of Sir William Brandon; it was an experience that touched me deeply and I will cherish it forever. Also, a very big thank you to Patrick Barker, who kindly showed me and my family around the site of Westhorpe Hall and gave us access to some of its fascinating history and allowed me to stand where Charles Brandon stood; I will never forget it. I would also like to thank Hilary Harrison and Geoffrey Wheeler from the Barnet Museum for their support and assistance researching the Battle of Barnet.

I must also thank my amazing Tudor friends, who are far too many to mention, but you know who you are, so thank you for your never-ending encouragement and support. And of course, to everyone at Amberley Publishing, thank you for your support and for giving me this opportunity to share the story of the Brandon men with the world.

Index